A

INVESTIGATION AND RESPONSIBILITY

Public responsibility in the United States,
1865–1900

INVESTIGATION AND RESPONSIBILITY

Public responsibility in the United States, 1865–1900

WILLIAM R. BROCK

Fellow of Selwyn College, Cambridge
Professor Emeritus of Modern History, University of Glasgow

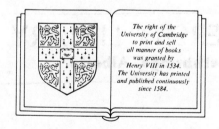

The right of the
University of Cambridge
to print and sell
all manner of books
was granted by
Henry VIII in 1534.
The University has printed
and published continuously
since 1584.

CAMBRIDGE UNIVERSITY PRESS

Cambridge

London   New York   New Rochelle

Melbourne   Sydney

Published by the Press Syndicate of the University of Cambridge
The Pitt Building, Trumpington Street, Cambridge CB2 1RP
32 East 57th Street, New York, NY 10022, USA
296 Beaconsfield Parade, Middle Park, Melbourne 3206, Australia

First published 1984

Printed in Great Britain at the University Press, Cambridge

Library of Congress catalogue card number: 83-26205

ISBN 0 521 25897 9

British Library Cataloguing in Publication Data

Brock, William R.
Investigation and responsibility.
1. Representative government and representations –
United States.
I. Title
353   JK 2443

ISBN 0 521 25897 9

SE

CONTENTS

In gratitude to friends and former colleagues
in the History Departments
of the University of Glasgow

PREFACE

This book is about the United States in the later years of the nineteenth century. I beg reviewers not to use the phrase "gilded age" except to record my rejection of a meretricious label that has done much to obscure the true character of a period to which we owe so much. For good or ill, it is not an age apart but the beginning of the epoch in which we now live.

Much scholarly energy has been expended upon "the best men," but I have tried to discover what some of the good men were doing. The men and women who worked so hard, with poor rewards and little recognition, to raise the standards of civilized life deserve some memorial. Or rather, the record which they made for themselves in the voluminous reports of state agencies merit reappraisal. Any historian will be aware of the danger of relying upon this kind of source material; men who are called upon to justify their own work are not likely to represent themselves as ignorant, idle, corrupt or untrustworthy, or to write charitably of those whom they find obstructive or wrong-headed. We are however dealing with an enormous body of evidence – the annual or biennial reports of the major agencies flourishing over many years in a great number of states – and it is therefore possible to achieve a balanced assessment of their assumptions, merits, or limitations. Believing that it is one function of a historian to allow the men of the past to speak for themselves, I have refrained from putting into their heads thoughts which do not appear in the record. It may be possible to prove that they did not mean what they said or should have meant something else; but this effort I leave to others. If the evidence tilts in one direction it reveals aspects of the period which have often been ignored and frequently misunderstood.

I have concentrated upon four major agencies set up in the states: the boards of state charities, the boards of public health, the bureaus of labor statistics, and the railroad commissions. This does not of course exhaust state activities during the period, and in particular it does not deal with ways in which the states sought to promote settlement and enterprise within their borders. There were also a large number of commissions or bureaus, mentioned in passing but not examined in detail, which dealt with single problems – dairy production, fisheries, forests, banks, and insurance – and cumulatively these enlarge considerably the picture of state intervention. In the time-honored phrase, "much research remains to be done." The four major agencies have been selected because they raise the greatest number of general questions, permit the widest possible comparison between different states, and tackle the issues which still lie at the heart of all social policy: the treatment of the unfortunate, the health of the people, the conditions of work, and the regulation of economic power. I did not include education because it deserves a big book on its own, but I am well aware of the massive investment in schools, vocational training, and universities, and of its association with the growing professionalism of the period.

Preliminary research was supported by a grant from the British Academy and its completion made possible by an Emeritus Fellowship from the Leverhulme Foundation. I must also thank the History Department at the University of Maryland, Baltimore County, for arranging my schedule as a visiting professor so that I could spend many hours in the Library of Congress.

Anyone who works in the great libraries, state historical societies, and state archives of America learns to appreciate advice and help that go far beyond the calls of duty.

Cambridge   W.R.B.
June 1983

1

PUBLIC RESPONSIBILITY

In *The American Commonwealth* James Bryce noted that Americans readily ascribed "the prosperity of the country to . . . non-interference as well as to the self-reliant spirit of the country," but that in practice "the new democracies of America are just as eager for state interference as the democracy of England, and try their experiments with even more light-hearted promptitude."[1] In the first edition of 1888 he included tables to illustrate the extent of legislation on public health, liquor, railroads, conditions of work in factories, shipping, employment of seamen, and the licensing of physicians. A table of laws and examples drawn from twenty-six states illustrated "the tendency to extend state intervention." In the third edition, published in 1895, the tables were dropped – perhaps because the laws and topics had become too numerous to list in this way – but the examples had become more numerous.[2]

Bryce had had considerable difficulty in obtaining accurate information about state legislation. He corresponded with Herbert Baxter Adams at Johns Hopkins about the lack of literature on the subject and suggested that one or more political science graduates might study laissez faire in the states. The outcome was that in November 1888 Albert Shaw, later to achieve distinction as editor of the *American Review of Reviews*, sent an article to Bryce for comment and in hope of publication in an English journal. Bryce suggested amendments to make it more comprehensible to English readers, secured its acceptance by the *Contemporary Review* with the title "The American State and the American Man," and acknowledged his debt to Shaw in a footnote to his chapter on laissez faire.[3]

[1] *The American Commonwealth*, 1st ed. (London and New York, 1888), 421.
[2] *Ibid.*, 3rd ed.
[3] Letters from H. B. Adams about Shaw and from Shaw to Bryce are in the Bryce Papers, Bodleian Library, Oxford. Shaw was born in 1857 and died in 1947. He was a prolific writer, became an authority on municipal enterprise, and was the first editor of Woodrow Wilson's messages and papers. He was intimate with Wilson when *Congressional*

1

Shaw began his article by observing that American economic literature and the prevailing tone of the press might "sanction the opinion that the laissez faire policy is pretty consistently practised in the United States." College texts and articles by leading publicists reinforced this view: "They teach an easy, axiomatic, *a priori* sort of economic doctrine that captivates the young student of the Tariff question and enchants the country schoolmaster by its lucidity and completeness."[4] The "neat, clear syllogisms of the laissez faire economists" seemed to have triumphed everywhere over rival doctrines and especially over the protectionist tradition of Alexander Hamilton, Henry Carey, and Horace Greeley; but this victory was illusory since Americans had a unique capacity for living "in one world of theory and another world of practice." For verification of this paradox Shaw pointed to the "astonishing quantity of legislation" passed every year in the American states, and observed that "the one common and striking characteristic of this huge collection of new statutes was its utter disregard of the laissez faire principle." In his *American Commonwealth* chapter on "Laissez Faire" Bryce argued that while there was a strong emotional commitment to laissez faire, there was no widely accepted philosophy of non-intervention. Americans believed that they could do most things for themselves, but when they encountered something that could not be accomplished without government action they had no hesitation in pressing for it, and no theoretical objections were likely to be raised.

Misconceptions might be reinforced if one looked at the federal government, where theoretical objections to intervention coincided with constitutional restraints; but the lives of the ordinary citizens told a different story. It was, wrote Shaw, "in the individual states and in the very home of the citizen that the subject of Government interference must be examined."

Shaw went on to cite examples from Minnesota. In the interests of farmers the state had established a Dairy Commission, prohibited the manufacture or sale of "butterine" (margarine made with one-third dairy products), set up a Bureau of Animal Industry, employed "State veterinarians," and imposed strict quarantine on animals brought into the state. In the lumber industry "not a log is floated down stream from the woods to

Government was being planned and written. He became editor of the American edition of *The Review of Reviews* in 1891, and subsequently of the autonomous *American Review of Reviews*. See Lloyd J. Gaylor, *Albert Shaw of the Reviews: an intellectual Biography* (Lexington, Ky, 1974).
4 "The American State and the American Man," *Contemporary Review*, 51 (1887), 695–711. Quotations in this and the following paragraphs are from 696–8, 699–700, 701–4, 705.

the saw-mill . . . without official cognizance." There was an Insurance Commission, an Oil Inspector, a Board of Medical Examiners (which licensed all new practitioners), a State Board of Pharmacy, and a new Board of Dentistry. The fish and game laws were "minute and exhaustive." Inspectors of steam boilers administered a law for testing and operating stationary steam engines; recent laws regulated telegraphs, the storage by railroads of unclaimed baggage and freight, the registration of trademarks, the prohibition of racial discrimination in inns and public conveyances, and the regulation of "offensive trades and employments." Other laws required the collection of statistics on crime and punishment. A Board of Health required every city, town, and village to maintain a local board of health; sanitary inspection was obligatory, bylaws could be issued by the local boards, and Shaw concluded that "This arbitrary power to invade private premises and issue peremptory orders in the interests of public health, is not hedged about or limited in any way; and it presents a striking example of the growth of State interference."

In common with most western states, Minnesota had been much exercised by questions affecting railroads and grain elevators, and almost the entire legislative session of 1885 had been occupied with these matters. Shaw believed that the only practical limit to regulation was the realization that services might be withdrawn if profits were cut too hard. The outcome was a regulatory statute, going into great detail and to be enforced by three commissioners. Discrimination between shippers was forbidden, the right to build warehouses on railroad land was to be freely given, railroad cars were to be supplied to all applicants, and reasonable services maintained; the commission was required to investigate all complaints and to institute prosecutions if necessary, and it had discretionary power to determine rates.

Just after the turn of the century Albert Bushnell Hart published a book on American government which amplified Bryce's general picture.[5] In all state governments "large executive powers" were exercised through boards and commissions, and by Hart's reckoning there were twenty-five railroad commissions, over thirty boards of health (with innumerable local boards exercising delegated powers), about twenty-five bureaus of labor, twenty fish commissions, and a very large number of gas, prison, and police commissions. Boards of education had long been found in local govern-

---

[5] Hart sent a copy to Bryce in which he explained that he was continuing the investigation of American institutions begun in *The American Commonwealth*. The book was *Actual Government* (New York and London, 1903). The quotations are from 145–6.

ment, but state boards had become common and very large sums of public money had gone into schools, teacher training, and state universities. Many states had boards of public charities with a primary responsibility for insane asylums, reformatories, children's homes, and special schools, but they often extended their nets into every area in which handicaps or extreme poverty made people dependent upon public support. This proliferation of boards, bureaus, and commissions meant that a very large number of men (and some women) were involved in state government. Hart believed that in Massachusetts alone over three hundred people belonged to these state agencies, providing unpaid but public-spirited services for the state. In addition to the voluntary members there were salaried secretaries and under them, in many instances, agents and inspectors. Here then was a whole world of activity that has been strangely neglected by historians.

Few of these state agencies existed before 1863. New York had a short-lived railroad commission in the 1850s. Weak railroad commissions in some New England states dealt with routine questions. There was a state board of health in Louisiana in 1855, but its character changed so much after 1870 that it re-emerged as virtually a new agency. The keynotes of the new era were sounded in Massachusetts where a board of public charities, a railroad commission, and a bureau of labor statistics were established between 1863 and 1870. Several railroad commissions followed in the 1870s, and by 1895 these were found in the great majority of states. Boards of public health were set up in most states between 1870 and 1890. Bureaus of labor statistics came into existence largely as a result of pressure from organized labor, and an added incentive came from the labor troubles that culminated in the violence of 1877; by 1885 they were found in most states where industry played a significant part and in a few others. They developed in two forms which were not always distinct, either becoming the major agency for the collection and assessment of industrial data or assuming the functions of a modern department of labor. Boards of state charities existed only in Massachusetts, Pennsylvania, and Ohio before 1870, but the increase in poverty, crime, and destitution following in the wake of the great depression led to their adoption in most eastern and midwestern states. Numerous other agencies that sprang up in the late nineteenth century were more closely related to needs of special groups or circumstances; such were dairy, forest, horticultural, livestock, banking, and insurance commissions.

In 1883 Governor Josiah W. Begole reviewed the situation in a message to the Michigan legislature:

Railroads and insurance, corrections and charities, education, agriculture, and health have been committed to State boards, whose valuable statistics and suggestions form a basis for legislation. The paupers and criminals, the fish that swim in our rivers and lakes, and the cattle that graze in our fields, are cared for by commissioners appointed by the state.[6]

He recommended the addition of a Labor Bureau to speak for "a large class of our citizens, who are seldom found in our halls of legislation to speak for themselves." This recommendation was adopted, thus recognizing that the establishment of a new agency was the appropriate way to represent an interest at the State Capitol.

Eight years later Governor Edwin B. Winans said that in Michigan there were fifteen boards composed *ex officio* of state office-holders and thirty others with unpaid members. The size of the latter ranged from three to six so that their total membership exceeded a hundred with the addition of salaried secretaries, clerks, and other officials. He recommended the rationalization and amalgamations of several boards, but the legislature did not act on his suggestion and his successor preferred to retain the existing structure.[7]

In 1891 Ohio had a Commissioner of Railroads, a Superintendent of Finance, and a Commissioner of Labor Statistics; an Inspector of mines, another for factories and workshops, and a third for oils; three commissioners for livestock, five for fish and game, and one for dairies and food; a Board of Health, a Board of State Charities, a Board of Pharmacy, a Canal Commission, a Board of Agriculture (which maintained an experimental station), a Forestry Bureau, and a Board of School Examiners. These were in addition to such traditional departments of the state government as the Boards of Public Works and of Pardons. At the close of the century Wisconsin had an equally long list of agencies and in addition a board of dental examiners, a lumber inspector, and a state veterinarian. California had, in addition to most of the agencies named above, a board of horticulture which also incorporated former boards of viticulture and silk. Other states in the north and west could tell a similar story. Agencies were less frequent in the southern states, but all possessed some.[8]

It is not to be expected that all these agencies were efficient, and some

---

[6] *Journal of the House of Representatives of the State of Michigan* (1883), 68.
[7] *Ibid.* (1891), 57.
[8] The word "agency" was used infrequently in the late nineteenth century. Here it is used for convenience to describe any autonomous body exercising a function on behalf of the state. For agencies in California see Gerald D. Nash, *State Government and Economic Development: Administrative Policies in California, 1849–1933* (Berkeley, Calif., 1964).

were kept so short of money that they never had an opportunity to develop professional services. Others were plagued by frequent changes in personnel dictated by political partisanship, by traditional attachment to rotation in office, or by a combination of both. The most effective agencies consisted of members appointed by the governors with the consent of the Senate for terms of four or six years, with holdover members to ensure continuity, and salaried officials holding office for several years. The least effective agencies had their members elected for two-year terms on party tickets, and their salaried officials subject to political patronage. Between these two poles there was room for much variation. Some agencies were purely advisory: they could do no more than investigate, recommend legislative action, and report infractions to the law officers of the state. At the other end of the scale were agencies with the power to make regulations with the force of law, whether by issuing general orders or by dealing with specific instances, and to prosecute offenders. Strong agencies of this kind might have the right to reach a final determination on matters of fact, provided that certain procedural rules had been observed, though their relationship with the courts might occasion much dispute. In the last resort a court might find that the statute conferring power was unconstitutional, and short of this action by an agency might be halted by an injunction. The general trend in the courts was however toward very broad interpretation of what was called, though not with uniform implications, "the police power." When there was a serious threat of disease a board of health might take immediate and summary action, even though this involved serious loss of property; on the other hand a bureau of labor statistics with responsibility for enforcing a factory law might well find its way encumbered by judicial intervention. Railroad commissions might find that rates ordered were suspended while court action to test their validity was awaited, but increasingly state law threw the burden of proof on complainants and required orders to remain in force until the decision of the court was made known.

It often happened that after a period of controversy an agency slipped out of the public view. As an agency became more professional, more immersed in detail, and more concerned to see that the system worked equitably for all parties, its role as an advocate became less evident. Many agencies came into being as a result of pressure from a group or interest, and moves to the position of arbiters or toward becoming impartial experts were likely to disappoint their original sponsors. Railroad commissions often emerge as a result of intense agitation against the corporations; but by the close of the century it seemed from the outside that many were acting as advisers to the railroads on operational details and securing general acceptance for improvements that the powerful companies wished to adopt. Complaints were still heard, but the commissions refused to presume guilt on the part of the companies. Most bureaus of labor statistics continued to believe that their function was to see that justice was done to labor, and gave a sympathetic hearing to organized unions; but more and more of them came to believe that the road to justice was paved with tables of statistics which meant little to working men and women. A board of health might come into the limelight when an epidemic struck, but steady progress in the fight against disease meant that it was more likely to be concerned with a host of minor regulations and with sponsoring scientific work than with medical drama. Absence of controversy might mean that an agency had become inert, but might also mean that its usefulness was recognized and its permanence accepted.

When all qualifications have been made, the growth of state agencies between 1865 and 1900 remains impressive. Their simple enumeration is enough to show that a great change in government had taken place. The record becomes more impressive when one considers the collateral effects of this extended public responsibility. Though the record across the nation was uneven, the trend is clearly marked. In addition to the agencies themselves new professions came into being. There were inspectors for factories, mines, railroads, food, sanitation, prisons, poorhouses, and children's homes. Statisticians collected and processed the data without which modern administration would be impossible. The standards of old professions were raised as physicians were licensed, pharmacists were regulated, and definite educational standards were required for both. Above all, in numerous walks of life statutory bodies had the right to investigate and the duty to report.

Even an agency with ostensibly weak powers might be given, or soon acquire, the right to subpoena witnesses, call for business records and accounts, and take evidence on oath. This might be weakened by a proviso that a man could not be compelled to give evidence about his private affairs, but officers of corporations were normally required to answer. These powers in the conduct of hearings were often extended to include the right to enter premises, to inspect machinery and buildings, and to suggest changes. In states with child labor laws, inspection could demand lists of employees, verify ages, and carry out educational tests. The findings of hearings and inspections could be published in the regular reports, or might be communicated more directly to the press. Most agencies in Massachusetts never had or sought greater authority than this, yet they were by all accounts amongst the most effective in the country. It was not however a pattern that was everywhere acceptable. An advisory agency depended for success upon being able to mobilize opinion by publicity; but this could succeed only if there were groups and interests ready to respond and to bring pressure to bear upon the parties concerned or upon the lawmakers. In simpler societies the agencies sought the power to issue orders having the force of law.

It is possible to construct a model to illustrate the development of a state agency. Not every stage will be found in every example, and in some two or more stages may be conflated; but the study of numerous agencies reveals a sufficient number of common factors to make the exercise worthwhile.

Stage 1. Identification of a need and proposals for action

A group becomes interested in the extension of public responsibility in a particular area. This group may be a professional, trade, labor, or philanthropic association. Its character will vary according to circumstances or objectives, but it is certain that without it nothing is likely to happen. Its objective is to secure the passage of a law, and to this end members of the promotional group will seek publicity and attempt to influence individuals connected with the state government and legislature. As the prospect of legislative action brightens, the leaders will probably come forward with a draft bill and in due course this will be considered by the appropriate legislative committee.

Stage 2. The agency established

A statute is passed setting up the agency and defining its powers. It is almost certain that this will fall short of what the promoters want, but they now have official recognition with the right to investigate in the name of the state and to report. Some members of the original promotional group are likely to become members of the agency, and will carry into its activities the enthusiasm, optimism, and aspirations of the earlier phase. One of them may well be appointed as full-time secretary and on him will fall the responsibility for successful administration. The members will be aware of the need to make an impact, justify their existence, and win greater power; the first topics chosen for investigation are therefore likely to be acknowledged evils which can be studied with the limited time and resources available.

Stage 3. The struggle for wider responsibility

The contents of the early reports are predictable. The topics selected for investigation will be reported with an eye to publicity, and will be strong in presentation even if weak on facts. It will be intimated that important and wide-ranging tasks lie ahead, and the agency therefore requests more money and an increased staff. Some defects in the investigatory system will be exposed. The agency may have no money for personal visits by its officers, have to rely upon information collected by mail, lack the legal power to hold effective hearings, or have no right to enter premises. As the legislature is very unlikely to grant everything that is needed at one time, these requests or variants upon them will recur in report after report; but expansion also feeds expansion as investigations reveal new needs and suggest new methods. Concurrently with pressure for improving its own machinery, the agency will recommend new regulatory laws, with the same history of partial success followed by renewed recommendations and further requests. The techniques of lobbying, developed in the first phase, must be refined, strengthened and accepted as a permanent responsibility by board members and their secretary.

Stage 4. Consolidation and expansion

The agency is accepted as a permanent part of state administration. The original promotional group has won adherents, and some interests in the state have become committed to the agency's efficient operation. Though there is still pressure for improvement, the original defects in the laws have been corrected. There is a tendency toward specialization within an agency (for instance, a board of health may develop sections with special responsibility for sanitation, water supply, and the administration of laws against the adulteration of food). The circulation of reports will lead to greater awareness of what is being done in other states, and it is probable that national associations will be formed.

Stage 5. Professionalization of the service

This may be difficult to separate from the preceding stage, which will have seen a significant increase in the numbers of men and women serving for many years in the agency; but in all agencies there comes a point at which the momentum is being maintained by its full-time experts rather than by unpaid voluntary members of the board or by political appointees. The beginning of this phase often coincides with the withdrawal from public life of those who were members of the original promotional group. The work of the agency has ceased to be a crusade and become a career. Agencies which had been charged with advocacy act more and more as expert advisers, and though the power to enforce must be present if the agency is to remain effective it will be used less and less. A greater part of the agency's time will be taken up with the undramatic settlement of issues by informed discussion, and the reports will become more technical and more concerned with detail. The massed power of professional administrators and inspectors should not however be underestimated; the pressure for expanding and refining their responsibilities is constant, while on occasions they can produce the evidence for major new advances in their field.

Stage 6. The function becomes institutionalized

The agency and its work has become an accepted and normal part of government. Business is voluminous but attracts little attention. Rules and precedents have been evolved which enable the agency to work tolerably well even with slack leadership. An increasing number of specialists – engineers, scientists, or social workers – are employed. There is a danger of inertia, but the drive for greater efficiency often comes from these specialists. The agency can still be a major innovative force if the political will exists to bring it into play.

This sequence will be observed in the history of several agencies described in later chapters; here the early history of one small agency may be reviewed to illustrate the pressures which increased the responsibility of government. This is the Wisconsin Dairy and Food Commission established in 1889. Dairy farmers were politically important in the state and had been pressing for laws to prohibit the manufacture and sale of oleo-margarine, and in 1888 William D. Hoad had been elected governor with a promise to legislate in this field. A much smaller group was interested in legislation to prevent the adulteration of food, and hoped to latch their own cause onto that of the farmers.

Hoad prepared for the law which he intended to recommend by

corresponding with dairy commissioners of other states, in order to draw upon their experience. H. D. Sherman, the Iowa commissioner, sent a copy of his state's law with a note that he would have preferred a Dairy and Food Commission but that his legislature would not sanction the dual function. Sherman also commended an Ohio law which made it illegal to color oleomargarine to make it resemble butter. He wrote that "there is no good reason why lard should be tripled in value because it is made to appear like butter and thereby obtain a fictitious value as a result of deception and fraud."[9] The point of interest here is that, even before the Wisconsin law was enacted, pressure was being exerted to widen its scope and to shift the emphasis to the protection of consumers. These principles were then incorporated in a law establishing a Dairy and Food Commission with unusually wide powers. It was to enforce all laws relating to dairy products, administer laws against the adulteration of food, inspect premises where food was produced or sold, and prosecute anyone obstructing its work. The law also recognized at the outset that the agency must bring science to its aid and authorized it to establish, maintain, and staff a laboratory.

As soon as it had been inaugurated the commission began to prepare the case for enlarged power and improved laws. Hoad wrote that "we have got the machine started and are in hopes that we shall be able to secure some good legislation next session."[10] One early discovery was that the laws against adulteration were few and defective, while consumers in search of cheap food were only too easily taken in by cheap items offered for sale. In its first report the commission enunciated the important principle that consumers should be protected against the consequence of their own ignorance.[11] Its recommendations secured some improvements in the law, and this brought on the demand for further staff. In 1892 the commission sought to stimulate public interest in the work that it was doing "for the direct benefit of the people," and in 1898 the duty to protect the consumer was again emphasized.[12]

---

[9] H. D. Sherman to Hoad, June 16, 1889, *W. C. Hoad Papers*. Wisconsin Historical Society.
[10] Hoad to T. W. Clark, Aug. 21, 1889, *ibid.*
[11] Wisconsin Dairy and Food Commission, 1st Report (1890), 7.
[12] 2nd Report (1892), 27. The commission was anxious to dispel the idea that it existed only to protect the interests of dairy farmers and that it was similar to a trade association: "Until little over a year ago it was not generally understood that this work was being done for the improvement of the dairy and food supply and was being paid for by the State of Wisconsin." By 1892 a growing demand for analysis by the commission's scientific staff showed that this notion was being corrected. In its report for 1897–8 the commission said that "the law is primarily intended to protect, and does protect, the purchaser of dairy products from the imposition of a counterfeit."

In its fourth report the Wisconsin commission emphasized again the need for expansion. It pointed out that almost all of its time was occupied with milk, milk products, and margarine, and that not enough time or expert study could be devoted to evils attendant upon the adulteration of food. Finally, in 1897, a new law, modeled on that of Massachusetts, provided the means and men to counter adulteration. So far most of the pressure for expansion had come from the commission itself and the small number of people who were informed and alarmed about the dangers of adulterated food; but the commission was also working to stimulate awareness of the problems amongst the people at large.

In 1902 the commission requested an appropriation to issue quarterly bulletins, so that storekeepers might be warned quickly of adulterated food, and strict control over the use of stencils, which it issued to approved factories for labeling their cheeses. In addition there was the expected request for increased staff, with the claim that the dairy industry had trebled in the past decade and therefore at least five inspectors, a chemist, and an assistant chemist were now required. To direct the attention of the legislature and to win public support for new laws the commissioners included in their report an eloquent passage on the evils of adulteration:

The universal demand for cheap things brings a supply. Wheat flour is adulterated with corn flour; buckwheat with wheat middlings. Vermont maple syrup is made that never saw Vermont, and is made from the sap of trees that grow in the heart of Chicago. Glucose has dethroned cane syrup. Cider vinegar is distilled from grain. A good portion of the strained honey of commerce never produced any strain upon the bees. Milk is robbed of its cream, filled with lard, and sent all over the world to ruin the reputation of American cheese. Borax and formaldehyde go into milk to kill babies and weaken invalids. Oysters are partially embalmed with chemicals. Lemon extracts are made without lemon oil and vanilla extracts without vanilla. The hogs of the North compete with the cheap cotton-seed oil of the South and mix in the same tub under the banner of lard. Artificial smoke is made for hams out of poisonous drugs. Jellies colored in imitation of the natural fruits and sold as fruit jellies flood the market, although they are almost as destitute of fruit juice as a bar of iron. Canned fruit is preserved with antiseptics that delay the digestive processes. Baking powders under misleading names crowd the markets. Spices enriched with pepper hulls and ground coconut shells are sold by the ton.[13]

The momentum of pressure, legislation, regulation, expansion, and widening responsibility was fully established in this agency. The rapidity of the Wisconsin commission's growth can be explained in part by the initial enthusiasm of W. D. Hoad and in part by its late entry into the field of food control, which enabled it to draw upon the accumulated experience of other

[13] Wisconsin Dairy and Food Commission, 7th Report (1901–2), 56.

states. Yet it also displays features found in other agencies which took longer to reach maturity. From small beginnings it had become a powerful body with experienced administrators, trained inspectors, and scientific experts. Its concern for the public and its willingness to assail unscrupulous business gave it the hallmarks of the progressive spirit; yet it grew naturally from momentum acquired in earlier years. The same could be said of the hundreds of other state agencies which came into existence during the last thirty-five years of the nineteenth century.

The true measure of the change that had taken place was the number of agencies, the amount of money appropriated to their use, and the men and women engaged in their activities. In many agencies the overall responsibility still lay with unpaid members of a state board, but acting under their command were great professional armies of secretaries and assistant secretaries, statisticians, inspectors, scientists, analysts, superintendents of state institutions, railroad and sanitary engineers, and experts in every field. Let the list be compared with the situation as it had been at the close of the Civil War, and the magnitude of change can be recognized. One may hesitate to use the overworked word "revolution," and perhaps some other term is necessary; but the change which added in this way to public responsibilities is evidence of altered assumptions about the character of government itself.

Why have these major changes in the concepts and practice of public responsibility received so little attention? One answer is that they received little notice from the contemporaries whose work has been most read and admired. Nothing of their history can be gleaned from the pages of *The Nation*; prominent reformers such as George William Curtis focused their attention on national affairs; state administration was far beneath the philosophic gaze of Henry Adams, though his brother headed the Massachusetts Railroad Commission for several years. Controversy over the currency and the gold standard left as their legacy an enormous volume of closely argued pleas, but there was no counterpart in labor legislation, public health, or the means of dealing with distress. A scholar can be well versed in the literature of the period and remain unaware of all this activity in the states. Railroad regulation was a partial exception to this rule, but largely because it was erroneously linked with agrarian radicalism; and comment was almost exclusively confined to the subject of rates, with nothing to say about the many other ways in which the states intervened to insist upon adequate standards for safety and service.

More might have been heard of the state agencies if the contemporary critics who attracted so much attention during the progressive period had paid attention to these examples of government activity. Lester Ward gave them hardly a thought. His vision of what government ought to be contrasted so sharply with what it was that there was little point in considering its administrative structure; government ought to be "the protector of all true civilizing agencies" but was in practice "a barrier to their normal development." For Ward, government emanated always "from the few seeking power, never from the many seeking protection," and there was a perennial struggle between the ruling minority and the majority seeking to be governed less. Modern governments might be compared to great corporations in which many held minute portions of stock and the directors managed things as they wished, and "those who imagine that representative governments form an exception to this rule, simply illustrate the ease with which the stockholders are deceived."[14]

A revolution was necessary before government could take on the tasks which Ward believed it should perform. The revolution need not be bloody, but neither could it result from small changes, however numerous, in aims and procedure. Government by classes, interests, and professional politicians must give way to "a truly progressive agency which shall not only be a product of art, but shall itself be an art." Many years after the publication of his *Dynamic Sociology* in 1883 Ward still regarded such a fundamental change as the necessary prelude to implementing the true science of government. Legislation, under this new dispensation, would become "a merely formal way of putting the final sanction on decisions that have been carefully worked out in what may be called the sociological laboratory," and would incorporate the results of "a series of exhaustive experiments on the part of true scientific sociologists and sociological inventors working on the problems of social physics from a practical point of view." The aim of these "experiments" would be to solve "questions of social improvement, the amelioration of the conditions of all people, and . . . in short the organization of human happiness."[15] Clearly this lofty vision could only be impaired by taking into account the halting ventures in social administration undertaken by well-meaning men and women in an imperfect civilization.

Richard T. Ely, favorite economist of the progressives, was trained at Johns Hopkins to seek out empirical bases for generalizations, and might have been expected to accompany his plea for active government on ethical

---

[14] *Dynamic Sociology*, 2nd ed. (New York, 1883), II, 224, 242.
[15] *Ibid.*, 251; *Applied Sociology* (Boston, Mass., 1906), 339.

principles with a diligent inquiry into what was done in the states.[16] His instinct, fortified by German influences, pushed him in the opposite direction toward sweeping theories, supported by evidence when possible but without when it was not readily available. While often preoccupied with problems of individual social responsibility he could also slip frequently into writing of "society" as a single entity without analyzing the institutions of which it was composed, and among his omissions were the boards, bureaus, and commissions of the states. In his *Studies in the Evolution of Industrial Society*, published in 1903, he did suggest that there was "some ground for thinking that the states are again becoming of greater importance in our general studies of government." To support this statement Ely observed that expenditure in New York had more than doubled in twenty years, and that some western states had brought into being great educational systems, taken a lead in forest development, and set up Departments of Forestry. The paucity of examples indicates lack of awareness rather than deliberate intention to ignore the torrent of laws with which the statute books of all states had been loaded since the Civil War.[17] The agencies of the states published voluminous reports, but outside their own states they were little read save by people with professional interests in their respective fields. Ely did refer to reports of the Massachusetts Bureau of Statistics, but only for figures to support his argument that the wage system led to a very unequal distribution of rewards even among men in similar occupations. He does not seem to have noticed the considerable amount of data on labor law and conditions included in Carroll D. Wright's *Industrial Evolution of the United States*, published in 1896.

Publicists of the progressive period were not much interested in the descriptive work that was beginning to take hold in the new schools of government, and a void existed where state administration took over. In 1909 Herbert Croly wrote, in his enormously influential *Promise of*

[16] Ely was an admirer of Lester Ward and acknowledged his debt to him (Ely to Ward, Dec. 11, 1886, Lester Ward Papers, Brown University). He put Ward in touch with A. W. Wallace, the English biologist, whose views of evolution reinforced those of Ward. This is examined further in the next chapter.

[17] *Studies in the Evolution of Industrial Society* (New York, 1903), 328. Ely's neglect of state activity is the more surprising as he would certainly have studied carefully Bryce's *American Commonwealth*, would have been directed from there to W. A. Shaw's article in the *Contemporary Review*, and should have had an opportunity to read Hart's *Actual Government* before his *Evolution of Industrial Society* went to press. Like other academics before and after him, Ely was guilty of blindness to inconvenient evidence, and it would be unnecessary to make these points if he had not received something more than his fair share of praise as a critic of ideas and institutions in his day.

American Life, that "the Federal Government has done much to ameliorate the condition of the American people, whereas the State governments have done little or nothing." Conceding some advances in education by the states, he added the grudging comment that they had not been "as intelligent and well-informed as they had been well-intentioned." He concluded that all the major functions of social and economic policy and "the still more radical questions connected with the distribution of wealth and the prevention of poverty" should be left exclusively to the central government or, if local administration was preferable in some instances, the states should be no more than agents of central government.[18]

It was natural for reformers to emphasize the defects of existing institutions, to deplore the lack of vision shown by their predecessors, and to dwell upon opportunities missed rather than progress made; but when these judgments became a part of historians' orthodoxy the past was seriously distorted. A serious reappraisal of the late nineteenth century will not rush to extremes and discard all contemporary criticisms; but it must look at the record and deal both charitably and realistically with these early attempts to grapple with problems that still remain unsolved.

Progressive contempt for state governments and what they had achieved was reinforced by widespread distrust of all politicians. For over thirty years it had been part of the stock-in-trade of those who wished to improve society to condemn politicians for their ignorance, self-interest, and corruption, and to assume that with few exceptions the most venal and most likely to betray the public interest were found in the states. It had become axiomatic that no good could come out of state legislatures and little from their executive departments. Reformers of the progressive period often shared these assumptions with the elite of the eastern seaboard who had long proclaimed – privately if not publicly – their alienation from the political system. Ward's contempt for representative government as practiced in American did no more than express in compact form the doubts which clouded the hopes generated by union victory in the Civil War and by destruction of the slave system.

E. L. Godkin moved from qualified approval of democracy (despite

---

[18] *The Promise of American Life* (New York, 1909), 317, 350. In an argument that was not entirely consistent Croly also said that reform had made matters worse by imposing more and more constitutional checks on legislative discretion: "The legislatures have been corrupt and incapable, chiefly because they have not been permitted any sufficient responsibility" (*ibid.*, 321). Yet his own prescription would have reduced their responsibility still further, even though this was to be done by the concentration of more functions in the federal government rather than by reinforcing constitutional checks.

some dangers which could be foreseen) to extreme pessimism about its future consequences. William Graham Sumner, disillusioned by the persistent appetite of democratic majorities for preservation of the less fit, moved from didactic precepts to defend the truth as he saw it, and finally to despair of the future. Henry Adams, who had been ready to play his part in national politics, left his own testimony of alienation from the mores of American political life. Face to face with men at the head of national affairs, Adams decided that they were narrow, self-interested, and often corrupt. He settled debts with the national political establishment by writing his anonymous *Democracy*, which left the reader with no illusions about the leaders who competed for their votes. Godkin, Sumner, and Adams formed their judgments through close observation of national politics; state politics they judged to lack any serious claim upon the attention of scholars and gentlemen. George W. Curtis, who made an effort to come to grips with New York politics, retired bruised and disillusioned. Yet it was in the states alone that the condition of men could be improved, and rejection of state politics cut off many humane and civilized men from the only available means of dealing with the social problems of the day.

The dilemma of men who criticized the prevalent political mood, yet despaired of reforming it by existing political methods, is well illustrated in a letter which Charles Eliot Norton addressed to Godkin in November 1871. Residence abroad had given him the opportunity to reflect upon the way in which things were moving or drifting in America and to conclude that "we have come pretty near to a deadlock with our system of individualism and competition." The erection of selfishness into a rule of conduct had meant a decline in moral standards and bred social conflict; and, whatever scorn economists heaped upon the belief that the rich grew richer and the poor grew poorer, it was essentially true.

The social progress of mankind depends on men learning that they are primarily social, not individual beings; that the principle of self-interest is not the first in the scale of rules of conduct; that duty and the performance of duty precede rights and the exaction of rights and that the claims of the community are always superior to the interests of the individual.[19]

No social gospeller or new economist, writing a quarter century later, could have said more, and in common with these later reformers Norton turned immediately from social morality to a bitter comment on American

[19] Norton to Godkin, Nov. 3, 1871 (written from Dresden), Godkin Papers, Houghton Library, Harvard University.

politics. Like New York, he said, the whole country was in the hands of the "Ring" and willing to let things grow worse, until improvement would be impossible without a "complete upturning of the very foundations of law and civil order."

> The *Nation* and Harvard and Yale Colleges seem to be the only solid barriers against the invasion of modern barbarism and vulgarity. There is no concentration of the forces of the upright and thoughtful part of the community, – rather a general indifference as to the results of conduct and character.

Before the Civil War the "upright and thoughtful part of the community," with which Norton identified himself, had shared common hopes with anti-slavery politicians and had been prepared to join in their endeavor. Now the bonds were broken.

The revolt against politics by American intellectuals is a familiar aspect of late nineteenth-century America, but its full implications have yet to be explored. If a society whose intellectual core was a set of political beliefs rejected politics, what remained? How could one defend representative government if the fact of being elected to office deprived a man of trust and respect? "The battle of the day," stated an editorial of 1882 in *Christian Union*, "is not between Free Trade and Protection; it is between the professional politician and the people."[20] If this was true, how could the American political system be defined? It was not a republic, declared one writer in 1890, because the representatives were not chosen by the people; it was not a democracy, because there was no effective way in which the people could bring government to account; it was government by a class but was not an aristocracy. The ruling class was not recruited on merit or possessions but solely by rewarding with power those who could control the party organization and get electors to the polls.[21]

The shadow of Boss Tweed and his Tammany organization hung over much political discussion, and too often it seemed that all the world was New York City. George William Curtis, the political reformer, told how a New York politician had said to him: "This is a nasty state, and it takes a great deal of nasty work to carry it. I trust we have nasty agents enough to do it." Patronage poisoned the system, said Curtis, and political control was falling into the hands of "paid stipendiaries of the State and Nation."[22]

[20] *Christian Union*, 26, No. 16 (Oct. 1882).
[21] *Forum*, 9 (Apr. 1890), 113–32. The article was called "The Degradation of Our Politics" and the author was F. A. P. Barnard who was president of Columbia University from 1864 to 1889. He was a pioneer of educational reform and an advocate of the rights of women in higher education. Barnard College is named after him.
[22] G. W. Curtis, *Machine Politics and the Remedy* (New York, 1880), 4.

How relevant was this for the hundreds of ordinary American citizens who were elected to serve for short periods in state legislatures? It will be argued in the next chapter that plenty was wrong with the state legislatures, but that wholesale corruption was not one of them. Legislatures which operated under constitutions deriving directly from eighteenth-century forms might be less than efficient when called upon to tackle the problems of modern society, but by and large the representatives struggled to put into law the wishes of their constituents. If they often failed there was little constructive criticism to tell them how it should be done.

Contempt for the states voiced by intellectuals was reinforced by the opinion of most educated men in the north and west who had been brought up to look with suspicion upon anything that savored of state rights. Corporation lawyers were not the only men to argue that curbs placed upon the states by the fourteenth amendment should be extended to cover more than civil rights. It was therefore appropriate that the most comprehensive exposition of state power should come from a young political scientist bred in the south. In *The State: Elements of Historical and Practical Politics*, published in 1889, Woodrow Wilson reminded his readers that the states were "the chief creators of law among us."[23] Indeed one could go further and recognize that "all the civilized rights of our citizens depend upon state legislation." In addition to punishment and prevention and the laws that governed domestic relations, family life, and inheritance, the states were responsible for the whole body of law governing commercial activities, corporate charters, and financial transactions. Subject to the undefined constitutional restraint that they must not "impair the obligations of contract," the states controlled "the possession, distribution and use of property, the exercise of trade, and all contractual relations." At a time when so many reformers and academic critics wrote as though the states could be ignored, this catalog of state powers provided a timely reminder of the real facts of political life. Whatever the moral character or administrative efficiency of state governments they would continue to exercise responsibility for most things which affected the daily lives of their citizens.

However, the authority of the states was diffused and limited in another

[23] Woodrow Wilson, *The State: Elements of Historical and Practical Politics* (Boston, Mass., 1889), 470, 473. This passage was given greater currency than might be expected for a college text because it was quoted by John Fiske in his *Civil Government in the United States* (New York and London, 1890). Fiske was at the height of his reputation while Wilson was little known outside professional academic circles.

way, for beneath them there existed a proliferation of local governments with almost unlimited power to obstruct or simply to ignore directives, even when embodied in statutes. Counties, municipalities, towns, townships and school districts added up to an incredible total of more than 150,000 units of government in the United States; all were controlled by elected officials, most had the right to levy taxes, and in many states their powers were enshrined in the constitution. Except in a handful of larger cities there had been little attempt to subject local government to critical scrutiny, and there was no single source to which one could turn for information. Very few states published any information about local government or sought to disentangle the web of responsibilities, which depended as much upon ancient custom as upon statute law. As late as 1917 a scholar who essayed this task described county government as "the dark continent of American politics," and thirty years later the foremost authority on state political systems agreed that the phrase was still apposite.[24]

Counties existed in all the states, and in the south they were the major instruments of local government, with few subordinate units. In New England, on the other hand, the counties were little more than administrative units for assessing and collecting taxes and all the real authority was exercised by the towns (of which the majority were rural in character). Midwestern and western states combined both systems, with counties as the major administrative unit but with important responsibilities delegated to the townships (which was the more common designation outside New England). The number of counties varied greatly from state to state; there were three in Delaware and over 250 in Texas. Massachusetts had thirteen counties and over three hundred towns; Minnesota, with a much larger area but a much smaller population, had 87 counties and over eighteen hundred townships.

If popular representation were the sole test of government these local governments would present an epitome of the democratic ideal. Thousands of officials were elected individually and responsible only to the people; frequent elections ensured strict accountability; most functions of government were carried out under the close scrutiny of men who were intimately aware of the character, reputation, and record of the office holders. In a county the principal authority (at least on paper) was the board of county commissioners, which might be a very large body with representatives from

---

[24] Henry S. Gilbertson, *The County: the Dark Continent of American Politics* (New York, 1917); W. Brooke Graves, *American State Government*, 3rd ed. (New York, 1946), 809–10.

every township or a smaller body with members elected by a county-wide vote. In addition, and separately elected, were the sheriff, treasurer, coroner, and county attorney; sometimes appointed by the commissioners but more often elected were superintendents of the poor, county surveyors, health officers, tax assessment officers and collectors. The school boards, of which there might be several in a county, were also elected, determined their own expenditure, decided what tax should be levied, and requested this amount from the tax collector. All these offices were of short tenure and poorly paid – often drawing no more than a per diem allowance while attending to duties which were not expected to consume much time; they commanded a little influence, and election might be a mark of local respect, but there was little incentive for busy and ambitious men to offer their services. It was not uncommon for the county officials to include few who had got beyond elementary education, and their experience was most likely to be confined to farming or small business. Even in parts of the south where justices of the peace had important administrative as well as judicial functions, the holders of these ancient and honored offices were no longer the leading men in the district. There is no need to doubt the honesty of local officials, but their educational attainment was low and their experience limited.

The spirit which permeated the whole system of local government was the belief that the purpose of representation was to provide a bulwark against authority of any kind, and particularly against the propensity of all in authority to spend too much and tax too heavily. The very idea of a chain of command – with ultimate decisions vested in some remote official in courthouse or statehouse – was abhorrent. The revenue of state and local governments was derived very largely, and in most cases exclusively, from property taxes, so it was the owners of property who were immediately affected by any proposals for increased expenditure; and, though every adult male could vote if qualified, it was often only the tax-payers who bothered to do so. Local government was very much a government of, by, and for the owners of property. Few examples of outright corruption were recorded; there might be petty malfeasance, but most local office holders were honest according to their lights. These lights did not include sympathy for anyone who became a burden on the community, understanding of new ideas on health or sanitation, or readiness to commit capital for long-term improvements. There was one notable exception to parsimony and horror of becoming indebted: many communities, and particularly in the more thinly populated states, were ready to raise quite large sums and borrow heavily if there was any prospect of persuading a railroad to construct a branch, or, better still, route their main line, so that the county or city would be served. In most states there were statutory limits upon bond issues by local governments, and many of the bills which crowded in upon the state legislatures were intended to authorize borrowing in excess of the legal limit. Apart from these and a few similar exercises to promote economic prosperity, local governments showed a resolute opposition to any change which meant spending money. Resistance was unlikely to be open, for it was much easier to ignore a suggestion, recommendation, or law, and to go on in the accustomed way.

These characteristics meant that local governments were hardly the best-constituted authorities to control poor relief, maintain almshouses, care for the aged or indigent sick, look after the feeble-minded, or safeguard the interests of orphaned and abandoned children. Nor were they enlightened managers of county jails. Counties which contained manufacturing establishments seldom exerted any supervision over them, except perhaps when the most obvious threat to the comfort and health of neighbors caused the traditional power to compel the removal of a "nuisance" to be invoked. Mine operators had little to fear from county officials, even if the law of the state enjoyed safety standards. Counties might be impelled to take action if one of the more dangerous epidemics struck the district, but normally their health officers were local physicians who attended irregularly to poorly paid part-time duties.

The work of the state agencies in the late nineteenth century must therefore be seen against this background of local apathy and incompetence. Lack of enthusiasm for change may be characteristic of any society, but it was all the stronger in the United States because it was embodied in local institutions which had behind them both the weight of tradition and added authority as the authentic expression of popular will. Direct and frequent elections, short tenure and rotation in office, the accountability of public officials, and the containment of authority within a mesh of checks and balances were all present; and all would be supported, if the need arose, by appeals to the most revered principles of American democracy.

It is no wonder if, in some fields, improvement was painfully slow. Yet it can also be asked whether improvement would have come at all, if some dedicated men and women had not been ready to take the initiative, seek to clothe themselves with the authority of the State, and then to use that authority to advance, step by step, the cause of public responsibility. The movement to regulate railroads operated from a somewhat broader base than attempts to improve the lot of the destitute or afflicted, but both shared the common assumption that it was the duty of the State to remedy those defects in society which individuals alone could not overcome. The case for giving serious attention to these state activities is therefore complete, but before the nature of their work can be studied there are certain questions to be answered. How did the men and women who promoted and staffed the agencies of the State regard their duties, and how far did they run with or counter to the ideas of the age about government intervention in social and economic affairs? What political obstacles did they encounter, and how did they obtain results from a political system that has been so widely criticized? How could these new activities be fitted into the framework of law, and how far did the judges help or hinder the process of putting the new wine of public responsibility into old constitutional skins? These are the problems to which the next two chapters will be devoted.

2

THEORY AND PRACTICE

The great majority of those who administered the agencies of the State were of north European descent, Protestant, and nurtured in business or professional environments. Unpaid members of boards were likely to be middle-aged or elderly, in affluent or comfortable circumstances, and to have behind them a successful career in business or a profession. Clergymen were often found on the boards of state charities, while the majority of members on a state board of health were usually required by law to be doctors with good medical qualifications. The salaried officers were likely to be younger, though the early secretaryships often went to veteran campaigners in the cause. As time went on, an increasing number of executive officers, agents, experts, and inspectors would be looking for a career in the service of the agency; but the great majority of them continued to be drawn from the same ethnic and religious environment as the older men. A partial exception was found in some bureaus of labor statistics, where the first appointees were often men who had been prominent in labor organization, but the trend was always away from graduates of the workbench and toward the recruitment of men who expected to make a career in statistical investigation or factory inspection. Another partial exception was found in the railroad commissions in states where the members were elected. In states where they were appointed they were most likely to be men with business and preferably with railroad experience, and even on elected commissions the trend was to seek for nomination men with this kind of qualification. Few lawyers seem to have served in these state agencies, though there would have been many occasions on which legal advice would have been sought. Women frequently served on boards of state charities, and in the later years of the century several were employed as factory inspectors.

Social background and experience were more important than party affiliation. Railroads became a hot political issue, but the argument was bipartisan on both sides of the question. Temperance legislation tended to divide men on party lines – with more Republicans favoring prohibition or at least restraint on sales and more Democrats supporting the freedom to drink – but most other social issues were so novel that there were no ready-made party attitudes and no familiar rhetoric to obviate the need for information. Promoters of public responsibility had many difficulties to contend with, but predetermined party attitudes were not among them. The intrusion of partisan politics into the affairs of an agency was usually resented, but more because of the frequent changes and the appointment of inexperienced men than because a change in party meant a change in purpose. Nor did friends of the agencies have to overcome the corrupt influence of vested interests as often as might be supposed from much contemporary comment or subsequent generalization. Parochialism, parsimony, and ignorance were more frequent foes of public responsibility than the massed battalions of capital. There were of course occasions on which railroad corporations, mineowners, and manufacturers lobbied the legislatures; but so did merchant associations hostile to railroads, organized labor, dairy farmers, doctors, and the agencies themselves. The protagonists in all causes shared common experiences, traditions, and beliefs which provided the vocabulary for the discussion of public issues and crossed the lines of party, class, ethnic origin, and economic interest.[1]

The majority of men who were in positions of leadership around 1870 had been young when Jackson was in the White House; in their formative years they had been touched by the ferment of reform and by the great controversies over territorial expansion, sectional conflict, and slavery. They might have been too old to fight in the front line during the war, but all had been profoundly affected by it, and many had shouldered wartime responsibilities. The rising generation of 1870 therefore included men with first-hand experience of a war which had called forth organization on an unprecedented scale, leadership, and collective purpose, as well as realization that nothing was achieved without will, effort, and shrewd planning. Self-reliance was an essential virtue on the field of battle, but anyone who had fought in a long campaign knew that undisciplined individualism was the surest road to defeat. These young men of the war generation would dominate public life until late in the century.

[1] Ballard C. Campbell, *Representative Democracy: Public Policy and Midwestern Legislatures in the Late Nineteenth Century* (Cambridge, Mass., 1980), Chapter 3, has an excellent analysis of the composition of legislatures in Illinois, Wisconsin, and Iowa. The subject has not attracted much attention elsewhere.

Every war has its seamy side, and for many participants the lesson was that ruthlessness, lack of scruple, and a large slice of cunning formed the recipe for worldly success; these characteristics would be all too evident in the post-war age, but a picture which presents them alone is one-sided. War also played upon ideals, and left an abiding conviction that something had been gained that should not be sacrificed. Beside the men on the make an unexpected number were prepared to devote time and energy to unpaid public service. Others, lacking financial security, provided recruits for the new army of administrators, agents, and inspectors.[2]

Next to the impact of war the most telling influence upon men of the late nineteenth century was the experience of unprecedented economic change. Men who had first known the railroad as an interesting novelty lived to see the completion of the national networks. Industry grew beyond the range of earlier imagination. Cities with population that had not risen above 50,000 came to be numbered in hundreds of thousands, so that not only the scale but also the quality of urban life changed out of recognition. The war demonstrated how decisions could be quickly translated into action by the telegraph, and before the close of the century typewriters and telephones were transforming the conduct of business. Population doubled and immigrants continued to swarm in with all their attendant problems of assimilation and urban congestion. Writing in 1889 David A. Wells, who had reflected upon economic problems for over thirty years and had played his part in molding public policy, grasped the extraordinary impact of change upon the human mind:

When the historian of the future writes the history of the nineteenth century he will doubtless assign to the period embraced by the life of the generation terminating in 1885 a place of importance, considered in its relation to the interest of humanity, second to but few, and perhaps to none, of the many similar epochs of time in any of the centuries that have preceded it.

During these years, he continued, men had attained unprecedented control over the forces of nature, contrived to produce more in less time than in any previous age, and provided opportunities in education, culture, and the use of leisure that could hardly have been anticipated. If labor discontent caused disquiet one should see it in the context of "an increase in

---

[2] There is no comprehensive study of the effects of the Civil War on individual characters and careers, but Morton Keller, *Affairs of State* (Cambridge, Mass., 1977), Chapters 1, 4, and 5, has perceptive comments on the legacy of war.

knowledge and a rise in expectations." Optimism might be the mood but the lesson was that "civilized society in recent years . . . has become a vastly more complicated machine than ever before."[3]

The response to these forces was conditioned by the religious and educational background of the men and women who shouldered public responsibilities. Lord Bryce noticed the absence of any coherent and philosophical theory of laissez faire; the other side of the coin was the wide acceptance of attitudes based on quite different premises about the relationship of man to society and deriving, in one way or another, from the Calvinist teaching which underlay that of most Protestant denominations. From this starting-point social attitudes had developed along two roads marked by the evangelical enthusiasm which had inspired so much earlier reform, and by the modifications of Calvinist determinism introduced by the Scottish philosophy which dominated American college teaching.

Protestantism, especially in its Calvinist form, was concerned primarily with the relationship of the individual to God; yet the individual was always in a community, belonged to a congregation, and had explicit duties to perform. Ernst Troeltsch, the great historian of Christian social thought, wrote that Calvinism gave to the individual "the possibility of an extensive co-operation with and a claim upon the whole." Men with privilege and power were "laid under heavy obligations to the community," while those without these advantages could accept a more humble station in the knowledge "that all inequalities were swallowed up in a system in which the powers of all were engaged in a mutual effort for the good of the whole community." Riches did not give a man the right to judge another or prescribe the rules for society, but indicated merely that God had called him to perform certain tasks. It was the duty of the Church to point where charity, self-sacrifice, or collective effort were required; and, if this necessitated law, the civil government must do its duty. Americans who cared to contemplate these precepts could find them exemplified in the early history of New England colonial societies, for in these uniquely successful experiments in "social engineering" there had been constant public involvement in relief of distress, care for the sick and old, education of the young, provision of employment, and protection against moral depravity. There if anywhere had been demonstrated the truth of Troeltsch's dictum that in a Calvinist society "every individual member should receive his

---

[3] David A. Wells, *Recent Economic Change* (New York, 1889), Preface, v.

appointed share of the natural and spiritual possessions of the community."[4]

This Protestant social philosophy could inspire altruism but seldom degenerated into sentimentality. Charity was balanced against the ever-present knowledge of the power of sin in the world. Physical deformity, disease, and old age lay beyond the range of censure, and in growing cities it was becoming evident that the environment exposed men and women to temptations which they lacked the strength to resist; but there was also the conviction that the worst misfortunes could be borne with fortitude and that defects in moral character multiplied every ill. Alcohol, crime, immorality, and idleness turned a vicious wheel of evil which lowered whole families into the slough of destitution. Charity must always be guided by the hard-headed determination to help the truly unfortunate without encouraging the degenerate, depraved, and unregenerate; indiscriminate charity so weakened the will of the recipients that they slipped down further into what was known as the "dangerous class." At best these attitudes amounted to social realism informed by experience, and they should be sharply distinguished from the modern travesty which accuses earnest humanitarians of assuming that poverty was a crime.

Individual responsibility to God, and to society as part of God's purpose in the world, did not stop with the duty of charity, for no man had a right to make others suffer or to place anyone in a situation where sin might claim another victim. Nor should help for others be regarded as a departure from the real business of life. The necessity of benevolence was the particular contribution of the Scottish philosophers whose acceptability in American colleges was heightened by the knowledge that so many of them were ordained Presbyterian ministers.[5] Political economists might find it expedient to imagine a world in which all men were guided by rational calculations of profit to come, but fortunately these were not real men in the real world. In the eyes of Thomas Reid, perhaps the most influential of the Scottish philosophers, "the benevolent affections planted in human nature

---

[4] Ernst Troeltsch, *The Social Teaching of the Christian Churches*, translated by Olive Wyon (London and New York, 1931), Vol. II. Discussions on the social theory of Calvinism are found on 617–25, 641–4, 644–50, 652–4. Note especially the statement (648): "The capitalist is always a steward of the gifts of God, whose duty it is to increase his capital and utilize it for the good of Society as a whole . . . all surplus wealth should be used for works of public utility." Also (649): "Within Calvinism, in the face of the modern development of capitalism, there always has been, and still is, a tendency to merge into a form of Christian Socialism."

[5] For a general discussion of the influence of Scottish philosophy see Henry May, *The Enlightenment in America* (New York, 1976), 342–8.

appear . . . no less necessary for the preservation of the human species than the appetites of hunger or thirst." From this premise Reid pointed toward a comprehensive social philosophy:

No man is born for himself only. Every man, therefore, ought to consider himself as a member of the common society of mankind, and of those subordinate societies to which he belongs, such as family, friends, neighbourhood, country, and to do as much good as he can, and as little hurt to the societies of which he is a part.[6]

Though the general principles of "systems of morals" were easily understood, their application extended "to every part of human conduct, in every condition, every relation, and every transaction of life." They formed "the rule of life to the magistrate and to the subject, to the master and to the servant, to the parent and to the child, to the fellow-citizen and to the alien, to the friend and to the enemy, to the buyer and to the seller, to the borrower and to the lender." These principles were compared by Reid to "the laws of motion in the natural world, which though few and simple, serve to regulate an infinite variety of operations through the universe."[7]

Teaching of this kind could, it was true, degenerate into pious platitude, but it would be wrong to dismiss its influence and equally wrong to overlook the way in which private duty taught in this way involved public responsibility. A case in point is the long-sustained argument over prohibition. Nothing required a greater degree of interference by government with human freedom – affecting not only those who indulged excessively but also respectable imbibers and all who made or sold alcohol – but temperance advocates did not hesitate to argue that government had a moral duty to act. Even those who drew back from complete prohibition were ready to accept licensing laws which drastically reduced the freedom to sell and to consume. In long and often angry arguments over this issue there was seldom dispute over the right of government to act, but only over the proprietary and possible consequences of intervention. Anyone engaged in this battle became acutely aware of the wide ramifications of the principle that government was responsible for some aspects of social behavior.

To men trained to think in this way the attempts to translate an individual's belief that he knew his own interest best into a social philosophy appeared facile and often inconsistent. A glance at some attempts to express these ideas as a guide to human behavior demonstrates

---

[6] Thomas Reid, *Essays on the Active Powers of the Human Mind*, ed. Barach A. Brody (Cambridge, Mass., 1969), 365.
[7] *Ibid.*, 374.

their poverty when contrasted with the subtle distinctions of traditional Christian teaching. Francis Bowen, who was teaching economics at Harvard until 1871, was typical.[8] In his *American Political Economy* he wrote: "Let the course of trade and the condition of society alone, is the best advice which can be given to the legislator, the projector, and the reformer." This assumption that both trade and the condition of society should be governed by the same rules became even less tenable when Bowen warned that, if men must concern themselves with wrong, hardship, or suffering, they should confine themselves to individual cases and not "meddle with the great laws of the universe." Any man with a sprinkling of moral philosophy could point out that the "great laws" were nothing more than fictions lacking substance or proof. Bowen argued that when men found co-operation necessary it would come about as spontaneously "as [among] bees in a hive and with as little conscious perception of what they are doing." If this was a true forecast, there must come a time at which men would demand legal sanction for their co-operative endeavour and coerce those who broke its rules; one had to ask at what point the "great laws of the universe" should then be invoked, and by whom.

Simon Newcomb, a good astronomer and an enthusiastic but indifferent writer on economic questions, realized that popular preferences well might come into conflict with the "let alone" principle and was thus led to reject the view that "the principal object of government is to enable the majority to carry out its views." A majority might want protective tariffs, limitation on the hours of work, regulation of prices, and legal tender laws that compelled creditors to accept payment in depreciated currency; but these were policies which should never prevail in a well-ordered society.[9] So "let alone" did not mean allowing people to do what they wanted, but applying arbitrary curbs to popular demands.

Edward Atkinson, a Massachusetts manufacturer and prolific propagandist against intervention, deplored the consequences of limiting by law the hours worked by women and children in factories. This law was "but one of many . . . by which it is attempted to enlarge the functions of statute laws, so that by means of a statute morality shall be imposed, leisure shall be inflicted, and prosperity shall be enforced." If it were proved that shorter hours increased productivity the manufacturers would limit them of their

---

[8] *American Commonwealth*, 3rd ed., II, 537–8. Bowen's economic views are discussed in Joseph Dorfman, *The Economic Mind in American Civilization*, 4 vols (Chicago, 1947–9), II, 835–44; III, 63. The extract which follows is from *American Political Economy* (New York, 1873; rep. 1969), 18–19.

[9] "The Let Alone Principles," *North American Review*, 226 (1870), 2, 5.

own free will, and if one of them objected "the self-interest of employers as a body will counteract the selfishness of individual men who compose their number." What he suggested was improbable, but should it ever be realized still more perplexing questions would arise. Would the manufacturers obtain the compliance of recalcitrant associates by private action outside the law, or would government be called in to effect this purpose?[10]

Similar questions were raised when in 1871 *The Nation* expressed its editorial opposition to laws restraining or prohibiting the sale of liquor.[11] A law, it argued, could never be a substitute for education, but one might be enacted when a majority had learned temperance by self-discipline and only a minority objected. Was there then a point at which freedom could be restricted by majority decision, and were there no universal laws of non-interference, but only advice that coercion must wait until enough people demanded it? If so, what safeguard existed against all those popular but unfortunate policies which *The Nation*, like Newcomb, detested?

Given the weakness of this kind of argument, it is no surprise that it made little impression upon the deeply rooted traditions of Calvinist social theory. Nor is it hard to understand why the advocates of laissez faire said less and less about universal laws. Increasingly they proclaimed what ought to be rather than providing a descriptive analysis of society as it was. Moralism took the place of social mechanics. Moreover, from the end of the great depression of the 1870s, America prospered despite laws regulating railroads, setting safety standards for factories and mines, sanctioning summary intervention in the interests of health, imposing sanitary codes, and curbing the freedom to adulterate food and drink. Under these circumstances it became more plausible to lament the loss of moral vigor rather than economic perversity. "Paternalism" became the enemy.

The theory of social evolution as presented by Herbert Spencer seemed at first to rescue laissez faire theory from these dilemmas. Spencer's exposition of evolution as nature's way of improving the condition of man appeared to substitute science for rhetoric. It was powerfully reinforced by Darwin's principle of natural selection. No more need moral law be invoked, because there was a law of nature which had been scientifically demonstrated. William Graham Sumner put in its bleakest form the only choice open to men: "The law of the survival of the fittest was not made by man and cannot be abrogated by man. We can only by interfering with it

[10] *The Inefficiency of Economic Legislation* (Cambridge, Mass., 1871), 1, 3, 8.
[11] *The Nation.*

produce the survival of the unfittest."[12] Spencer was, in fact, a good deal more subtle than this. While believing that government intervention could never be justified because its full consequences could never be foreseen, he realized that in a complex society men would be called upon to make all kinds of decisions including the definition of "fitness." If self-interest were the main spring, it generated moral codes, social obligations, and means for mitigating the rigors of unrestrained competition. Ethics and aesthetics were as much the products of evolution as were skill and efficiency. In America it was however the materialism and primitive mechanics of Spencer's early work on *Social Statics* that attracted attention and limited his influence.

These points must be made to counteract the notion that laissez faire and social Darwinism dominated American thought during the late nineteenth century. If this had been true much that happened would have been inexplicable. In practice the prevalent and common-sense view was expressed by the Reverend Frederick H. Wines (perennial secretary of the Illinois Board of Public Charities and a Presbyterian minister trained in Princeton orthodoxy) in one of his early reports: "In case of conflict between humanity and self-interest, humanity ought to prevail. But there is no real conflict of interest among men. The conflict is in appearance only. It is our selfishness which makes us think otherwise."[13] In his philosophic first report he wrote that society must be viewed as a whole and that its success depended upon the vitality of every one of its members. It followed that weakness in one part damaged all, and help for the distressed was not sentimentalism but a rational necessity. If government intervened to prevent the spread of pauperism it did so in the interest of all.[14]

Social philosophy derived from the Protestant stem did not find it difficult to assimilate evolutionary theory. Charles Loring Brace, founder of the Children's Aid Society of New York and for many years its guiding spirit, was an early convert to evolution. In articles published in the *North American Review* and *Christian Union* he argued that there was no essential difference between "the Darwinian conception of the Creator" and Christian doctrine. So far from contradicting it, the new theory confirmed the old by teaching that "the current of all created things, or of all phenomena, was towards higher forms of life."[15] Natural selection was "a

---

[12] "Sociology," *Princeton Review*, 4 (1881), 308, 311.
[13] Illinois Board of State Charities, 1st Report (1870), 19.   [14] *Ibid.*
[15] *The Life of Charles Loring Brace . . . edited by his daughter* (New York, 1894), 285 (letter to Lady Lyell, Dec. 23, 1866). (See also (297) letter to Henry Ward Beecher, 1869: "The Idea of this age is of slow growth, especially of moral things.")

means of arriving at the best," of evolving toward man in the image of God. This gave no ground for believing that men temporarily at the head of a society should be treated with exaggerated respect, for it was no glory to lead in an imperfect world; evolutionary improvement would soon pass them by. The logical conclusion was that eventually there must emerge "a race . . . in which the highest inspiration and capacity for nobleness shall be embodied and transmitted and perpetuated." In a reflective work on Christian life, written in 1881, Brace argued that history provided abundant evidence for the survival, by natural selection, of superior moral qualities, and that continuation of this process would lead to "a new principle in the distribution of wealth" according to which surplus riches would be "continually distributed by means of education, of wise charity, and of public improvement."[16] These forces could even be seen at work in the labor conflicts which so many of his class and time deplored. In 1877 he said: "There is something always impressive in these blind passionate movements of the laboring classes for a larger share of the goods of life . . . The gradual settlement of values is going to bring about many such outbreaks. The great problem of the future is the equal distribution of wealth, or of the profits of labor (under the guidance of brains)."[17]

Another Christian convert to evolution was Henry Ward Beecher, brother of Harriet Beecher Stowe, and one of the most influential preachers of the day. There was, he insisted, no conflict between religious and scientific truth. The Bible recorded "the gradual and progressive unfolding of human knowledge in respect to social and spiritual things throughout vast periods of time."[18] This may well have been a paraphrase of a letter written to him by Charles Loring Brace, asserting that "The idea of this age is of slow growth, especially of moral things. We doubt sudden changes, or, at all events, we consider them only feeble beginnings of long-working changes . . . influenced by ten thousand imperceptible causes, and salvation is the slowest of all things."[19]

At Princeton the heights of Presbyterian thought were commanded by James McCosh, president of the university and foremost American exponent of Christian philosophy.[20] In 1871 he published a series of

[16] *Gesti Christi: or, A History of the Progress of the Human Race under Christianity* (New York, 1882), 471.　　　　[17] *Life of C. L. Brace*, 854–5.

[18] Quoted from Beecher's *Evolution and Religion* by Paul F. Boller Jr, *American Thought in Transition: the Impact of Evolutionary Rationalism, 1865–1900* (Chicago, Ill., 1969), 33.

[19] The letter from Charles Loring Brace is from the *Life of C. L. Brace*, 297.

[20] McCosh was born in Scotland in 1811 and educated at Glasgow and Edinburgh Universities. He was professor at Queen's, Belfast, 1852–68, and president of Princeton 1868–88. He introduced elective studies, promoted scientific teaching, fostered graduate studies, and was a prolific writer on theological and philosophic questions.

lectures on Christianity and Positivism in which he commended biologists
for having directed attention away from a golden age which never existed to
a real world of conflict; but material survival was only part of the truth and
change was not the product of blind chance. There were "clear proofs of
contrivance and wisdom and kindness, and evidence that good was being
brought out of evil." Man's existence was not merely a struggle against
nature but also a contest between the spiritual and the natural. There was
no cause to sit passively by if "nature" produced unhappiness, distress, and
suffering; in the cause of true religion and justice the Christian should not
let things alone.[21]

McCosh believed that it was a special task of religion to ensure that man
was not degraded and reduced to the level of animals. Darwin had
demonstrated how in nature "the strong live and multiply, while the weak
die, give way and disappear;" in human history this applied to primitive
society with "the powerful tyrannizing over the feeble, men making women
do all the menial work, and the great body of the people . . . slaves to the
few"; but human evolution was moving away from this condition, and
there were "indications that intelligence is to prevail over unreasoning
force." The danger in Darwinism was that it encouraged the superficial
conclusion that "the poor and helpless need not be protected or defended,
but may be allowed to perish," and this was a doctrine to make "the
shadow on the dial of time go back for ages."[22] The Pennsylvania Board of
Charities made a similar point about progress in its report for 1872 when it
argued that both private individuals and governments should make justice
and charity, humanity and civilization, morality and religion their guiding
principles.[23]

Another clerical and academic critic of materialist philosophy was John
Bascom, president of the University of Wisconsin, and a frequent writer on
economic questions. In 1872, in the *Princeton Review*, he criticized Spencer
for having failed to explain phenomena which could be observed empiri-
cally, the foremost of which was human capacity for rational thought. The
assumption that mental facts could be explained in the same way as
physical motion was unscientific and erroneous. Spencer, said Bascom,
wrote as though human behavior could always be explained as "will
flowing along the line of least resistance," with men seeking the best market
with the same necessity "as water flows downhill, or the cow is attracted by
the greenest grass"; but this left unexplained other deeply rooted mot-

---

[21] James McCosh, *Christianity and Positivism* (New York and London, 1871), 71.
[22] *Ibid.*, 76.   [23] Pennsylvania B. of St. Ch., Report for 1872, cxx.

ives.[24] Bascom may also have been the author of an earlier *Princeton Review* article criticizing Spencer's thesis that social life followed an evolutionary progress from homogeneous to heterogeneous organisms. Some aspects of society did see men drawing apart in their specialized pursuits, but political democracy and technical improvements worked in the opposite direction. "The same locomotive that draws the rich draws the poor," while education and intelligence crossed the barriers of class and worked to "make the lower classes homogeneous with the higher."[25]

These views are implicit in many reports of the state agencies, and explicit in some. In 1870, in the first report of the Illinois Board of Public Charities, it was claimed that the efforts of private voluntary societies could never be sufficient to deal with the problem of pauperism: "There must be interference on the part of the governing power . . ." Indeed the highest function of any government was "the elevation of the lower classes."[26] Thomas Logan, first secretary of the California Board of Health, wrote in 1873 that the difference between lower and higher civilizations was that in the latter there was "more perfect adaptation to and control over our own surroundings."[27] Greater knowledge of the laws governing natural phenomena enabled men to promote the beneficial and suppress the harmful tendencies. There was no conflict between "nature" and man's efforts to control it to his own advantage. In 1873 the Illinois Board of Public Charities brought in evolutionary theory to support its attack on the system of county jails with the argument that "in Society, as in any individual organism, up to a certain point, structure is necessary to growth; and beyond a certain other point it arrests growth."[28] Local responsibility for county jails had been necessary when population was sparse and communication bad, but circumstances had changed and central control was now essential if they were to be improved. In 1880 the Connecticut Board of Health printed an essay by Professor W. H. Brewer of Yale in which he pointed out that the growth of cities necessitated greater control over disease; if pestilence struck it was due "either to official ignorance or

[24] "Evolution as Advocated by Herbert Spencer," *Princeton Review*, N.S. 1 (1872), 496–515.
[25] "Herbert Spencer's Philosophy," *Princeton Review*, 37 (1865), 243–70. Bascom's authorship is suggested because the argument that democratic society tends to become homogeneous also appears in the later article. Late in life he also wrote *Evolution and Religion: Faith as a Part of a Complete Cosmic System* (New York and London, 1897). In the introductory chapter he wrote (3): "Evolution . . . gives a perfectly open, and an absolutely complete, field to empirical enquiry . . . In no direction is this search unfruitful; in none do we put upon it any final limits."
[26] Illinois B. of St. Ch., 1st R. (1870).
[27] California B. of Public Health, 2nd R. (1873), 5.
[28] Illinois B. of P. Ch., 2nd R. (1873).

public neglect." Social evolution meant more government intervention not less.[29]

Support for the assimilation of science to traditional Christian beliefs came from the new science of statistics. Faith in statistics epitomized the rationalist belief that man was master of his world provided that he first understood it, but it was also consistent with the use of reason to explain God's purpose. A method which divested itself of preconceived theory, concentrated upon the collection of data, and presented the results objectively was conceived as the essential instrument of material and moral progress in nineteenth-century civilization. With the help of figures one could trace long-term movements in social evolution instead of merely talking about them, and show how wealth was produced, distributed, and used; while vital statistics demonstrated the incidence of morality, the survival of infants, the effects of disease, and the influence of unhealthy environment or occupations. Statistics could establish what was normal, detect fluctuations, and perhaps identify causes.

It is ironical that a science which claimed complete objectivity should have been given its most decided impetus by labor demands for fair treatment. The explanation lies in the fact that labor leaders shared the common belief that the facts would speak for themselves, and, in this instance, demonstrate the justice of labor's case; but after a short period of advocacy the first bureau of labor statistics came under the control of Carroll D. Wright, who was to become the leading proponent of scientific objectivity in statistical work. The statistician served no master save the truth. Yet at the end of his long and distinguished career Wright claimed credit, on behalf of the bureaus of labor statistics, for a long list of improvements in the law: there were factory, mine, and housing regulations, there were safety, child labor, and employer liability laws, and across the nation were inspectors enforcing this legislation.[30] No doubt he would also have claimed a good deal of sense knocked into the heads of labor leaders, and he certainly looked forward to a time when investigation of strikes would prove their folly and lead to compulsory arbitration. So the overall result of all this patient investigation had been and would continue to be the affirmation of public responsibility for conditions in industry.

Statistical inquiry also discounted attempts to discover general causes

---

[29] W. H. Brewer, "Some Relations of Modern Health Boards to the Material Prosperity and Wealth of a Country," Connecticut St. B. of H., 3rd R. (1880), 30.

[30] *The Industrial Evolution of the United States* (London, 1896), 276–8, 287–9, 291.

and pronounce dogmatically upon them. In the first report that he issued as federal commissioner of labor in 1886 Wright commented wryly upon attempts to "explain" depression.[31] He had found that bankers invariably attributed it to financial dislocation or unfavorable trading conditions, clergymen blamed moral decline, manufacturers were confident that it was caused by "industrial conditions," labor laws, and the demands of working men, while wage earners themselves blamed combinations among capitalists, long hours, low wages, machinery, and other factors affecting conditions at work. Politicians blamed the folly of past or present administrations. "The fact that, as a rule, [a man's] opinion can be foreseen by knowing his calling in life, vitiates to a large extent the value of causes alleged." It might follow that the course of wisdom was to discount all theories, investigate the facts, and hope that the evidence would suggest better laws. Empiricism, not a priori theory, should guide action. No legislative remedy should be proscribed provided that it was suggested by facts, but the way to improve social life was to deal with each issue as it was revealed and not to seek sweeping solutions for all problems. If statisticians had little faith in the capacity of society to regulate itself they had even less in radical panaceas.

One organization attempted to draw together the theoretical, moral, and practical aspects of social policy. This was the American Social Science Association, founded in Boston in 1865.[32] Its object was to promote "discussion of those questions relating to the sanitary conditions of the people, the relief, employment and education of the poor, the prevention of crime, the amelioration of the criminal law, the discipline of prisons, the remedial treatment of the insane, and those numerous matters of statistical and philanthropic interest which are included under the general head of 'social science'." Significantly the idea originated with the Board of State Charities, and the initiative was taken by Franklin Benjamin Sanborn, who provides a link between earlier and later reform. He was a friend and admirer of Emerson, an active abolitionist who had been involved in the secret committee to aid John Brown, would be for many years closely

---

[31] Commissioner of Labor, 1st Annual R. (1886), 76.
[32] For a review and analysis of the association's work see Thomas L. Haskell, *The Emergence of Professional Social Science: the American Social Science Association and the Nineteenth Century Crisis of Authority* (Urbana, Ill., 1977); and Mary O. Furner, *Advocacy and Objectivity: a Crisis in the Professionalism of American Social Science, 1805–1905* (Lexington, Ky, 1975).

associated with the Massachusetts Board of State Charities, and survived to correspond with young reformers of the progressive period.

The new association was a monument to the nineteenth-century hope that accumulated knowledge scientifically recorded, would provide answers to the most pressing problems of the age. Its avowed objects were to organize research, correspond with all parts of the country in search of information, bring together theoretical and practical exponents of social policy in annual conventions, and publish the results. The emphasis was on investigation: "We must know what our own condition is; and to those who have had their attention drawn to the matter, it will be surprising to learn how little we know in America of the actual circumstances of the people."[33] Horace Greeley, invited to address the 1869 meeting of the association, stressed the need for "concise but comprehensive treatises of practical consequences." With confidence characteristic of the age, he believed that it should be possible for such brief publications to embody "all that is known beyond dispute in the domain of natural, intellectual, and moral science."[34]

The association did not attempt to produce a library of useful knowledge, and membership was never large (about 300 in 1873), but its meetings brought together men and women united by the common conviction that all was not well in American society and that active effort was necessary to remedy its defects. The work was organized in four "departments" – health, finance, jurisprudence, and social economy – of which the last was by far the most productive in papers and discussion. Opponents of intervention had their say at the annual conventions but, at an early date, there was a tendency for men with practical problems on their hands to seek separate sessions to exchange views, and though luminaries from the eastern establishment tended to dominate the platform at public meetings there soon developed demands for more specialized subsections. In course of time these become the parent bodies of several national professional associations.

In 1890 Sanborn looked back on twenty-five years of the association. By then the original enthusiasm had waned, meetings were poorly attended, and there were more signs of life in the successor associations. Nevertheless Sanborn reaffirmed his beliefs in the original aim:

It is to discover and amend what is wrong in the habitual life of men that social science applies itself most usefully – not to promulgate broad theories or insist upon

[33] "Report by the Secretary," *Journal of Social Science*, 6 (1873), 37.
[34] *Ibid.*, 39.

ambitious panaceas for every human ill, but to consider the ailment and apply the remedy patiently and repeatedly, as a mother tends the hurts of her children.[35]

The nature of this program meant that early hopes of a universal science of society had not been fulfilled. Indeed those who attempted too much had ended with least influence, and "whoever has ventured much in the experiment of setting right the disjointed times in which he was born, with the hope that he should receive even thanks for his praise, will certainly be disappointed, as he deserves to be." Sanborn believed that the real measure of the association's work was to be found in the National Conference of Charities, the National Prison Association, the American Public Health Association, and the Economic Association – all of which had been first planned and promoted at meetings of the parent association. Across the nation were now organized professional societies, largely composed of men who were making careers in a particular branch of social work, often with journals of their own, certainly with state and national conventions, and who were engaged in the continuous circulation of information. One could add other groups which held regular meetings and which, though not offshoots from the Social Science Association, imitated its methods; these included officers of the bureaus of labor statistics, factory inspectors, and railroad commissioners.[36]

The development of social science and professional associations suggest that the men who promoted, planned, and led the agencies of the State were not living in an alien intellectual world but obtained a ready hearing for their pleas. The shallowness of social philosophy in the pages of *The Nation*, so long as it was controlled by Godkin, has often been remarked. Other periodicals edited from Boston and New York were little better and by the mid-1880s there was a demand for a new journal that would open its pages to more wide-ranging discussion of social and economic problems. This need was met by *Forum*, which first appeared in 1886 under the editorship of L. S. Metcalf.[37] It was characteristic of the journal that the

---

[35] F. B. Sanborn, "The Work of Twenty Five Years," *Journal of Social Science*, 23 (1890), xiv.

[36] For references to these and other associations see Furner, *Advocacy and Objectivity*.

[37] For an account of *Forum* see Frank Luther Mott, *A History of American Magazines*, Vol. IV (Cambridge, Mass., 1957). Note especially his comment (512–3) that "it would be difficult to find a better exposition of the more serious interests of the American mind, in the decade 1886 to 1896, than is afforded by the first twenty volumes of the Forum." Though it printed some articles from conservatives and conventional thinkers, the balance was strongly in favor of social criticism. The owner was Isaac L. Rice, who was a talented musician, master chess player, mechanical inventor, lawyer and successful businessman. The first editor was the autocratic Lorettus S. Metcalf; he was succeeded in 1891 by Walter Hines Page, then at the beginning of a career of great distinction. Burton J. Hendrick, *The Life and Letters of Walter H. Page* (New York and London, 1930), describes his successful editorship (48–53) but is unjust to his predecessor.

editor believed that most of its readers were church members, and there was conscious sympathy with the "social gospel." In 1887 John Bascom contributed an article on "the gist of the Labor question" in which he argued that "competition or strife prompted by self-interest" was an inadequate guide for social science; rather there was a "demand for intelligence and good will." Working men should not be made to suffer "the pitiless punishment of unwise competition," and the fact that they might be weak or ignorant made them "proper subjects of the collective good-will of society, seeking to organize itself in the light of its own ideas." In a competitive world the strongest might survive but they were not necessarily "the fittest in that moral world to which we are hastening." The benefits of competition were not to be ignored, but it should not be treated as the sole manifestation of Divine law.[38]

In the following year *Forum* printed an article by Bishop J. L. Spalding which expounded a similar social philosophy. In industry, he said, power was in the hands of shrewd and capable men whose only motive was personal gain; their effect upon employees was "like malarial poison." It was this that had made pauperism chronic and fostered "what seems to be an irrepressible conflict, between the rich and the poor" which rose "like a cyclonic cloud on the horizon." The fundamental error of American society was in treating the accumulation of wealth as its primary purpose rather than in seeking a moral basis for life and law. "Character, not wealth or numbers, is our social ideal."[39]

New economic thought was represented by Richard T. Ely who wrote on "Labour Organization." He argued that there was no need to fear the rise of organized labor even if its leaders played a part in politics. The record showed that, so far from being irresponsible revolutionaries, they were "conservative forces, restraining the wild impulse of ignorant and less often vicious men." They encouraged temperance, promoted education, and would have a salutary influence upon legislation. They would, he believed, press for government ownership of railroads and the improvement of public education, but would not be interested in such fundamentally radical proposals as the nationalization of land. The implication was that if conservatives recognized their own best interests they would welcome labor leaders as allies against Henry George.[40]

In 1888 appeared an article by Lester Ward on "What Should the Public Schools Teach?" It included more than the title might suggest (though that

---

[38] *Forum*, 4 (1887), 87–95.
[39] "Is our social life threatened?" *ibid.*, 5 (1888), 16–26.   [40] *Ibid.*, 3 (1887), 124.

was wide enough), and was rather an essay on the essential aims of civilized society. He wrote: "To those who can rise to the contemplation of society as a conscious organism of the highest and most complex character, and who understand what its progress consists in . . . it must be obvious that the most eminently practical of all things is the subjugation of nature to man."[41] Another well-known contributor was the Reverend Washington Gladden. His article on "Socialism and Unsocialism" declared that individualism had been "a good club wherewith to fight feudalism" but was a poor foundation for society. The doctrine that individual wishes should never be thwarted save when they inflicted direct damage on others had left Americans confused and unhappy; a society in which every individual was encouraged to seek the greatest personal gratification was diseased.[42]

Another voice was added to this critique of laissez faire when, in 1887, Henry Carter Adams published *The State and Industrial Action*.[43] In it he pronounced that the error of English philosophy had been to regard the State as a necessary evil, while the error of German philosophy was to regard the State as "an organism complete in itself." Society, composed of individuals under government, should be the subject of all social inquiry. It was pointless to introduce universal rules unrelated to social reality and then to invest them with moral attributes: "Competition is neither malevolent nor beneficent, but will work malevolence or beneficence according to the conditions under which it is permitted to act." If one wished to introduce morals one should begin by realizing that in a competitive society business morals were on a lower plane than the ordinary conceptions of what was right. The State need not destroy competition in order to prevent it from damaging society; for instance, factory laws did not prevent capitalists from competing but did prevent them from competing in particular ways. Laissez faire doctrine had condoned monopoly *against* the public while denying to society the right to organize public control.

The attempt to present natural selection as an effective argument against intervention had been challenged at the outset by McCosh and Bascom,

---

[41] *Ibid.*, 5 (1888), 574–83. In an article on "False Notion of Government" (*ibid.*, 3 (1887), 364–72), Ward wrote: "The working people should realize that the government is their own, and it will be just what they make it. They should learn to work upon it as a creature of their will. They should cease to fear and distrust it, and should seek to mold and shape it."

[42] *Ibid.*, 3 (1887), 124.

[43] *The State and Industrial Action*, Publications of the American Economic Association, I, no. 6 (1887). 465–549. Citations in the paragraph are from a reprint, ed. J. Dorfman (New York, 1969), 82, 88, 89–90.

and in 1889 their arguments received indirect endorsement from no less an authority than Alfred Russell Wallace, the English biologist, who had come near to anticipating Darwin in a public presentation of basic evolutionary theory. In 1889 Wallace published *Darwinism: an Exposition of the Theory of Natural Selection*.[44] Writing as an "advocate of pure Darwinism" he nevertheless made important qualifications when applying the principles to human evolution. The conclusion that could be drawn from Darwin's *Descent of Man* was that moral conscience developed when there was a conflict between the interest of an individual and that of his tribe. Could this explain the evolution of man's capacity for abstract thought or aesthetic enjoyment? Wallace believed that these mental powers differed widely from those which were essential to man, and that "they could not, therefore, possibly have developed in him by means of the law of natural selection." The same argument might be applied to other mental attributes. Every civilization had produced a small body of priests, philosophers, or artists. This could not be explained on purely materialistic grounds, yet was not inconsistent with evolutionary theory; what it demonstrated was that at a certain stage in human history a new force entered into the evolutionary process. Conflict was the instrument of change, but there was more in life than competition for material well-being:

It is by unceasing warfare against physical evils and in the midst of difficulty and danger that energy, courage, self-reliance, and industry have become common qualities of the northern races; it is by the battle with moral evil in all its hydra-headed forms, that the still nobler qualities of justice and mercy and humanity and self-sacrifice have been steadily increasing in the world.[45]

This was in sharp contrast to the bleak choice offered by Sumner between the fittest and unfittest, without definition of fitness.

The citations in the preceding pages are not intended to review reformist activity in the late nineteenth century, but to demonstrate the existence of a strong current, near the mainstream of American thought, which favored government intervention to remedy social ills. The men and women who acted upon such principles owed little or nothing to such critics of the system as Henry George, Edward Bellamy, Lester Ward, or Henry Demarest Lloyd. Some of them were influenced by the social gospel movement, but usually through common sympathies and identification of the same evils rather than conscious enlistment in a crusade under the same

---

[44] Citation from the preface to the first edition (London, 1889), v, viii.
[45] *Darwinism*, 461–2.

leadership. Few were probably aware that the new economics, sponsored by Richard T. Ely and his friends, were pointing along the same road to active government, though they could be equally irritated by the tenacity with which so many academic economists clung to abstract theories which seemed to have so little relationship to real experience. As late as 1894 Edward W. Bemis, one of the new generation of economists, could lament the way in which senior professors at Chicago opposed any departure from classical economic theory; a gulf had grown up between theory, as expounded in their classrooms, and the conclusions drawn by men who faced the facts of social life. In 1881 Lester Ward told George Youmans, who was Spencer's most active American disciple, that interventionist views were far more popular in the country than those of men who opposed state action.[46] Ward may have been thinking primarily of the movement to regulate railroads, but his generalization could have been substantiated a hundred times over by the record of what was being proposed in the whole field of social policy.

Indeed the point was made with great cogency in a thoughtful review of Ward's *Dynamic Sociology* which appeared in the periodical *Science* in 1883.[47] Referring to writers who regularly expounded economic and social theory in such periodicals as *The Nation* the reviewer observed that "the publicists tell us we are governed too much; but the people are demanding more government, and, in obedience to this demand, law-making bodies are rapidly extending the scope of law." In every community, it was claimed, there was "a body of good and earnest people demanding reform, or devising methods for the improvement of mankind in diverse ways." They sought to relieve the unfortunate, educate the masses, diminish suffering and crime. "The energies of these people, exerted everywhere, in season and out of season, create a sentiment that law-making bodies cannot ignore. Yet in opposition to all this, the publicists ask for less government, and say 'Let society alone'." The reviewer went on to argue that, whatever Spencer might say about the nature of social progress being from more government to less, the facts spoke otherwise. Some writers looked only at the decay and final repeal of obsolete laws, without realizing

---

[46] Bemis to Ward, Mar. 13, 1894; Draft, Ward to Youmans; reply to letter of Dec. 7, 1881, Ward Papers, Brown University.

[47] *Science*, July 27, 1883. Clipping in Lester Ward Papers, Brown University. *Science* was in its first year of publication as a weekly journal. It was financed partly by Alexander Graham Bell, and Daniel C. Gilman, president of Johns Hopkins, was head of the publishing company. It attracted much attention and in 1900 became the official journal of the American Association for the Advancement of Science.

that the enlargement of knowledge called constantly for more legislation not less. An obvious example was found in the history of medicine: when disease was thought to be the work of evil spirits men could do nothing but make incantations, offer sacrifices, and burn witches, but once the causes were understood there followed a demand for sanitary laws.

Practical men, concerned with the day-to-day problems of business, paid little attention to academic opinion, and, whatever general support they might give to the "let alone" principle, had no difficulty in finding exceptions when their own interests were affected, and excellent reasons for limiting competition or controlling overmighty economic power would then be advanced. In 1885, when the Senate investigated railroad policy, very few railroad men were unequivocally opposed to regulation, and a majority wished to extend it. Stability seemed to be the watchword, and it was generally agreed that state commissions were more likely to secure it than private traffic associations or pools. It was however uncommon for any businessman to rationalize his attitude, and special interest attaches to the evidence of John H. Devereux of Cleveland before this committee.

Devereux had spent all his life in railroading, and had risen to be president of the Lake Shore and then of the Cleveland, Columbus, and Cincinnati Railroad.[48] He was receiver of the Atlantic and Great Western when it went into liquidation, and after reorganization its president. Significantly he had also had experience of administration on a large scale during the war when he was responsible for railroads supplying the Union armies in Northern Virginia. He was a friend of Vanderbilt and built for himself the mansion which now houses the Cleveland Art Gallery. Few men knew more about the practical details of railroad management, and he had personal experience of events in Cleveland which enabled John D. Rockefeller to exploit competition between railroads much to his own advantage. Devereux laid much blame for instability upon "the hostility, ignorance and indifference of the communities . . . served by roads." Intent

---

[48] Select Committee on Interstate Commerce, U.S. Senate, 49th Congress, 1st session, 819ff. There are Devereux papers in the Western Reserve Historical Society at Cleveland, Ohio. They include the paper which he presented in evidence to the Senate Committee. There are some verbal differences between the manuscript version and that printed in the hearings; some words in the printed version are obviously incorrect and must be printer's or stenographer's errors. On Apr. 7, 1881 a colleague blamed the misfortunes of the Atlantic and Great Western on "our early and continued reliance on the Erie for an eastern outlet, and the impossibility of making any binding contract with that corrupt company," and on the willingness of managers to give rebates by private arrangement with personal favorites (Devereux Papers, Western Reserve Historical Society). This experience may explain his striking attack on "survival of the fittest" and unregulated competition.

only upon securing cheap rates for themselves, they played off railroad against railroad regardless of long-term consequences, though the ruin of the weaker companies might end the competition from which they derived temporary advantage.

Devereux scorned the argument that "the survival of the fittest" was the principle that would restore order by eliminating the weak and inefficient lines. This was a "misapplied phrase of the scientist" which could not "furnish appropriate guidance for dealing with the commercial affairs of a people." It might explain the evolution of animals, but railroads were large and complex organizations upon which many were dependent for services or for the security of invested capital. If threatened with collapse railroads would indeed fight for survival, but weakness would augment their ability to pull down others with them.

Competition should not be a freebooter in this matter which enters into every material interest of the land and affects the welfare of all the people; nor is competition to be permitted to run amuck in the destruction of vested capital.

Only government could supply the corrective, and though Devereux relied mainly upon investigation, publicity, and recommendation he also recognized the need for coercive power in the background.

Few businessmen were so ready to put into words their rejection of the "let alone principle" or to articulate their views so forcefully, but there was tacit acceptance of the fact that government had a role to play. Most railroad men hoped that the influence of government would be used to impose stability and stop ruinous competition, rather than to back those who were trying to force down rates to ruinous levels; but most also recognized that this would be politically impossible unless government could also cut excessive rates, prevent discrimination in favor of large customers, and make regular scrutiny of railroad accounts. By the later years of the century they were ready to accept this degree of regulation and to concentrate their efforts upon establishing a good relationship with state commissions.

Argument about the theoretical wisdom of government intervention began to look unreal when the question was what a particular legislature could or would do; and practical obstacles in the form of procedural delays, overcrowded legislative timetables, and the inexperience of legislators were more significant than abstract arguments against the extension of public responsibility. Some state legislatures met every year, but the majority met biennially; and despite the enormous volume of business there was a tendency, when constitutions were revised, to shift from one- to two-year intervals. This was a strange departure from the belief of earlier generations that frequent elections and annual legislative sessions were the essential safeguards of liberty. It was becoming more common for people to assert that the more time politicians had on their hands the more mischief they would do; but this belief did not prevent individuals, communities and organized groups from pressing upon their legislators an extraordinary number of proposals for new law.[49]

Sessions were short. In a few states the session, which normally began in January, was allowed to run for three or four months; in others everything had to be done in six to eight weeks. The length was sometimes fixed by the constitution or, in some states, there was no formal limit to the length of the session, but legislators could be paid expenses for only a fixed number of days – they could continue to argue if they wished but at no charge to the public. Where there was no such constitutional limitation, the first duty of a legislature was to fix the day and hour at which they would adjourn; this was not expected to be too far in the future, and once agreed it was rigidly adhered to however much business remained unfinished. Members were directly elected, normally from small single-member districts, though in Illinois after 1870 and in Michigan after 1889 there were much larger multi-member districts. Either by law or by invariable custom the representatives were resident in their districts, well known locally, and not likely to forget that they must live the rest of their lives face to face with men who would not forget failure to serve them or their communities.

A study of three western legislatures reveals that an average of seventeen per cent of the members might be lawyers, thirty per cent businessmen, and thirty-three per cent farmers, though the latter might include men with substantial property and ramified business interests. The remainder included physicians, ministers of religion, newspaper publishers, and representatives of organized labor.[50] From one-third to one-half would be

[49] Bryce, *The American Commonwealth*, Vol. I, Part ii, remains one of the best accounts of the state governments at this period. He had made more effort than any other contemporary to gather information on this somewhat obscure subject. Despite his objectivity Bryce was influenced by his upper-middle-class correspondents (who were generally pessimistic). The groundwork, put together in the 1880s, remained intact in later editions. Later information can be gathered from A. B. Hart, *Actual Government*.

[50] Campbell, *Representative Democracy*, 38–9. Though valuable as a guide the figures must be used with caution, because an average – even in three western states – included such wide variation. For instance the figures for Illinois were 31% farmers, 24% lawyers, 11% blue collar or service, and 44% business and professional; in Iowa 47% farmers, 18% lawyers, 1% blue collar and service, 24% business and professional. Other information in this paragraph is derived from the same authority.

serving their first term in the legislature, and only a handful would have served more than two or three times. The Speaker was the most important member of the lower house and was normally chosen on a strict party vote, though within each party there might be stiff faction fights for the nomination. Almost invariably the Speaker was one of the longer-serving members, as were the chairman of the committees; between them they would have to consider every bill presented to the house or coming to it from the other house; they would report the bills which they approved (often in an amended form) and the great majority would pass as reported with little debate. If there was opposition it was more usual to refer a bill back to the committee than to attempt amendment on the floor, though clauses which aroused interest and controversy might have to be settled by roll-call vote. After passage a bill went to the other house, which might return it with amendments which required further consideration. Before it became law a bill had to have three readings in each house, be passed by both in an agreed form, and go to the Governor for signature; if vetoed it might return to the legislature for discussion and for a vote on re-passage by whatever majority the state constitution required.

These procedures had been well adapted to more leisurely days when the best government really governed least. By the later years of the nineteenth century the sheer volume of work, crowded into so tight a schedule, made for oversights, poorly drafted bills, ill-considered amendments, inconsistency, and confusion. In an article in the *Journal of Social Science* in 1881, Francis Wayland Jr discussed some of these shortcomings with material probably drawn from New England states and New York.[51] In one example three hundred bills were allocated 100 hours of committee time, and this made careful scrutiny impossible. Other distractions (for instance the election of a Speaker or a United States senator) might absorb much time so that the legislative timetable became even more contracted. The result was an extraordinary profusion of incompetent laws.

What shall we say of an act passed one day and amended the next; of an act passed and amended on the same day; of precisely the same act passed twice in the same session; of thirty-eight "dog laws" enacted in the same State during a period of forty consecutive years; of an act twice repealed; of an act amending an act which had long since been repealed; of several abortive repealing acts, appropriately indexed as "attempts to repeal, etc.," of six acts passed in a single session and repealed in the next as palpably unconstitutional; of a general corporation law placing no check on the objects for which corporations could be organized; of two independent statutes

[51] "On Certain Defects in our Method of Law Making," *Journal of Social Science*, 14 (1881), 1ff.

setting forth the same (and very heinous) offence and prescribing different penalties, and this blunder perpetuated in the revision of the laws; of an important section of a general banking law, so framed as to be absolute nonsense, and reenacted in a revision without changing a word?

As a remedy he suggested a permanent non-partisan commission of lawyers and businessmen to consider all proposed bills, hold hearings, and submit those approved to the legislature. There was not the slightest hope that such a constitutional innovation would be adopted, and it was indeed open to grave objections in any society which prided itself on being a government of the people by the people.

The history in 1881 of one Michigan bill which was not a party issue, aroused much sympathy, and offended no vested interest illustrates the time required for legislation.[52] The bill was to provide an additional asylum for the insane and to prevent the confinement of insane people for long periods in poorhouses or their own homes for lack of suitable accommodation elsewhere. The facts were not in dispute; the two existing asylums were overcrowded, some 350 insane persons were held in poorhouses, and perhaps another 300 at home. On this evidence no one disputed the statement of Governor David H. Jones that Michigan lagged behind other states in care for the insane or opposed his recommendation for immediate action. Even so it was not until February 21 that a bill was introduced in the House and referred to a special committee, which reported favourably on March 19. The reference to a special committee was an advantage as it obviated the chance of the bill being swamped by other measures before the standing committees. The committee of the whole house made no change and the bill passed its third reading by sixty-eight votes to four on April 12; the Senate made some minor amendments, these were accepted by the House, and the bill was signed on May 13. To summarize this brief history: four to five weeks were spent awaiting a place in the legislative calendar; some of this time may have been spent in drafting the bill, though its sponsors probably had it ready weeks before the session opened; the select committee took almost four weeks to consider the bill, and though no serious opposition was raised another four elapsed before it emerged from the lower house; the Senate had it for three weeks, adding a minor amendment, and a further week was spent on the final stages. It can be imagined that a bill which was controversial would have taken much longer; there was ample opportunity for procedural delays, any amendment of substance would hold up a bill, the day of adjournment would

[52] Abstracted from the journals of the House and Senate of Michigan for 1881.

become imminent, and the bill's backers would be hard put to it to find time to bring it to the vote. The last hours of every session saw an incredible scramble as the sponsors of bills competed for the few minutes of legislative time that would make them law.

Indeed a cursory reading of legislative journals makes one marvel that anything ever got done, let alone well done; but at this point of incredulity a look at the record may restore faith in popular government. The output was enormous. A. B. Hart reckoned that in 1899 forty-five states passed over 5,000 statutes.[53] A good many, perhaps, would have been open to criticism of the kind advanced by Wayland eighteen years earlier, but when all the errors and inconsistencies have been discounted, there must remain a substantial number sound in law and purpose. In 1881 the Michigan House considered 686 bills, while the Senate considered 330. Of the House bills 241 became law, and 128 of those initiated in the Senate. Every subsequent session but one saw an increase in laws enacted, and this experience seems to have been typical of all states.[54] Between 1891 and 1895 Massachusetts passed 2,986 statutes; New York passed 1,045 in the one year 1895.[55]

Many of these laws dealt with minor matters, settled some individual claim, or authorized small items of expenditure, but a good many were concerned with more important public questions. For instance a tally of bills initiated in the Michigan Senate in 1881 included several on the drainage of swamp lands, one to require superintendents of the poor to hold annual meetings, one to provide medical treatment for children in state homes, two to increase appropriations for the blind and for the deaf and dumb school, one to regulate life insurance, one to prevent the

---

[53] Hart, *Actual Government*, 137.
[54] Details abstracted from the journals of the House and Senate of Michigan. By comparison, in 1873 there were 428 bills initiated in the Michigan House of which 46 died in committee. The increase of 158 in five sessions was typical of the upward trend.
[55] Hart, *op. cit.*, Bryce, *American Commonwealth*, 3rd ed., I, 545–6, gives the following list of bills introduced and passed in the sessions of 1885 or 1886 in five sample states:

	Bills	Bills passed
Alabama	1,469	442
Kentucky	2,390	1,400
Illinois	1,170	131
Pennsylvania	1,065	221
New York	2,093	681

He also says that in 1889 in eleven states 10,838 public bills were introduced and 1,878 passed.

adulteration of liquor, and another to prohibit its sale to minors. There was also a bill to set up an additional asylum, another to improve the girls' reform school, and finally a bill to enable citizens to sue corporations chartered in other states or countries. There were far more on similar topics initiated in the lower house. These were not trivial or absurd questions but the very stuff of civilized government, and few critics of the state legislature suggested how else their business might be conducted; indeed most of them wanted not greater efficiency but fewer laws. Wayland closed his indictment by suggesting that his proposed committee of lawyers and businessmen, charged with recommending bills for consideration, "would naturally be led to consider with some care what subjects properly called for legislative interference, and concerning what subjects men may be more wisely permitted to regulate their own affairs."

The most fruitful source of legislative controversy was liquor. State-wide prohibition, local prohibition by counties, districts or cities, licensing laws, laws to punish intoxicated persons or prevent sale of liquor to minors, and further measures to enforce all these laws were fruitful topics. Sabbath laws and school laws were also hotly argued. These attempts to regulate behavior were the most likely to divide legislators on party lines, with Republicans claiming to be the party of morality and the Democrats defending personal liberty. Almost every legislature spent a great deal of time on railroads, but supporters and opponents of regulation were drawn from both parties. States where industry was a significant factor spent a good deal of time on factory laws, but again there was no party line on these issues though working-men representatives were more likely to be Democrats or belong to a minor party. Nor were health or sanitary laws party measures. In some states the officials in prisons, reformatories, poorhouses, and hospitals were political appointments, and this could cause party heat when measures for reform were under discussion; but it was only in a minority of states that this unhappy practice prevailed and in most the major obstacle to reform was indifference. From all this it follows that the development of social policy can be studied with little reference to party; change came in response to experience, general trends in opinion, and the hard work of men and women who dedicated themselves to these tasks.[56]

Anyone who wanted to get anything done had to lobby for it. This process, with all its sinister connotations, meant nothing more than having someone on hand, during sessions of the state legislature, to see individuals,

---

[56] For the matters referred to in this paragraph see Campbell, *Representative Government*, Chapter 4, *passim*.

explain issues, solicit support, appear in person before committees, and keep a close eye on the progress of bills so that – according to the nature of the lobby – an influential legislator might be primed to get a bill out of committee, secure its reference back, expedite proceedings, or move time-wasting amendments. Above all it was essential to work on the committee chairmen considering the bill. A lobby might represent a large interest or a small group; it might be promoting a sweeping change such as prohibition or railroad regulation or trying to promote a good cause which lacked popular appeal. Employers in industry lobbied, and so did organized labor. Farmers, especially large commercial farmers, were often in the lobby and, in alliance with dairymen, sought to outflank manufacturers of oleo-margarine. The anti-liquor men and women were always there, as were agents of brewers and distillers. The first lesson for members of the state boards, bureaus, and commissions was to learn how to lobby.

Lobbies with money to spend might offer cash bribes, but this was much rarer than is sometimes imagined; the cost could be exorbitant and the risk of exposure high. Presents of stock or favorable terms of purchase might sometimes be used, but probably only when a measure was thought to be of vital importance and even then it would be limited to key men. For the ordinary run-of-the-mill legislator, entertainment, drink, a little flattery, and a few favors would suffice. It was often much more important for an individual to get something for his district than for himself. Every lobby had to be on its guard against bills which were simply intended to wring further favors from the interest concerned, and to be aware that favors given too frequently might come to be regarded as perquisites.

A prime example of this truth was the railroad pass. In their arrogant days, before they were brought to heel by tough laws and *Munn* v. *Illinois*, the railroad companies undoubtedly hoped to win friends by the judicious issue of free passes for travel on their trains; but what had once been a special favor became an expected perquisite. In 1885 Charles Francis Adams Jr told the Senate Committee on Interstate Commerce that the pass system, especially in the western states, had become an outrage:

No man who has money or official position or influence – especially political or newspaper influence – thinks he ought to pay anything for riding a railroad. The company which issues passes right and left is "liberal", the company that refuses to do so is "stingy," and it shall assuredly be made "red hot" for it when the legislature meets.[57]

---

[57] Select Committee on Interstate Commerce Hearings, U.S. Senate (1885), 1,220.

Newspapers, he said, lost no opportunity of attacking a "stingy railroad" as "aristocratic" and "autocratic"; ill will would be manifest among legislators, passed on to shippers, and even influence courts of law.

Even the cost of entertainment and the time spent by employed lobbyists could become a burden. John O'Donnell, a New York railroad commissioner, told the same Senate committee a story about Chauncy Depew, president of the New York Central and for many years before that its leading attorney and lobbyist. Depew had told a New York committee that compliance with a ruling made by the commission had cost his railroad $200,000.

But he added *sotto voce* that it had not cost the railroad anything to go to the legislature to protect its interests for the last two years that the commission had been in existence. So on the whole perhaps he considers it about an even thing.[58]

The president of a western railroad told Bryce that he was obliged "to keep constant guard" at the state capital while the legislature was in session "and to use every means to defeat bills aimed at the railroad, because otherwise the shareholders would have been ruined."[59]

Lobbying could be tiresome for everyone except those who benefited from favors and hospitality. Hazen S. Pingree, the reforming governor of Michigan, made some biting comments in his inaugural speech. He said that at every session sound measures were killed:

The means used to compass their death are the paid lobbyists who infest our halls. If the members of the legislature are not intelligent enough to give independent thought and action to great public measures without the aid of those who wine and dine and cajole and flatter and bribe, at least some steps should be taken to modify the nuisance.[60]

Admitting that lobbyists could not be eradicated, he suggested that they should be forced to register and pay a fee "for the right to practice before the people's legislative jury." Unwittingly he had rationalized the function of the lobby, but for which legislators would have been as ignorant of the facts as a jury before the witnesses had been heard.

A small example from Ohio illustrates the way in which the case for any bill had to be presented on the spot.[61] A man named Charles Whittlesey

---

[58] *Ibid.*, 42.
[59] *American Commonwealth*, 3rd ed., I, 543n. His information probably came from C. F. Adams Jr.
[60] Michigan *Senate Journal* (1895), 40.
[61] Whittlesey to Brinkerhoff, Jan. 18, 1878, R. Brinkerhoff Papers, Ohio Historical Society, Columbus; E. J. B. Andrews to Brinkerhoff, Apr. 13, 1872, *ibid.* Another example from the

was interested in getting an appropriation for an official report on the relics and antiquities of the state. In January 1878 he wrote to Roland Brinkerhoff, a friend and prominent public man, asking whether any member of the legislature would make it "a subject of personal effort." Was there anyone "ready to lobby the measure at Columbus"? He believed that without this help any hope of an appropriation would be vain, but even if a start were made "everything hinges . . . upon some person or persons to persistently hound the members and the proper committee." The bill ran into difficulty in the Senate; on April 13 there was still hope, but "a little outside help might be needed." He asked if Brinkerhoff, who had influence with the legislature, would come to Columbus for a day or two. However the bill failed to pass in that session.

An example of a state board engaging in lobbying comes from Wisconsin. In 1877 the Board of Health had two bills to promote: one for an increased appropriation to print more copies of its report, and the other for compulsory registration of births and deaths.[62] The secretary, Dr J. T. Reeve, first committed them to the care of Dr W. A. Andrews of Madison, who had many friends in the legislature. The president of the Board, Dr E. L. Griffen, also wrote letters to friends and then went himself to Madison. He reported that a prominent senator would look after the appropriation but was hesitant about the registration bill. James Bintliff, a member of the board, also visited Madison but had an unpleasant reception from the appropriations committee: "I saw the Committee – not one of its members knows anything and cares less about the subject of preventative medicine – in fact they bluntly told me that they regarded the Board of Health as a humbug & would be glad to see it abolished." A senator promised to rescue the appropriation bill but could not promise success unless a member of the board remained in Madison and canvassed both sides of the Senate. A breakthrough came in February when a friendly senator with a medical degree told the secretary that he had had the bill referred to a select committee consisting of himself. This ensured a favorable report and eventually the passage of the bill, but the registration bill got nowhere and the president of the board advised that it should be allowed to die. Let other states try the experiment, he said, "while we lie

same papers refers to a bill for prison reform. It had been referred to a committee and "all the outside influence that can be used must be done to get an early and favorable report" (R. R. McLerory to Brinkerhoff. Jan. 20, 1880).
[62] Correspondence in Cornelius A. Harper Papers, Wisconsin State Historical Society, Madison, Wisc.

quiet and attend to the noble and beneficent work to which we are legitimately committed."

Lobbying had to be done, and to do it properly required careful preparation. In 1876 Sanborn advised that no legislation concerning public charity should be attempted "which does not rest upon the basis of statistics carefully collected."[63] Fred H. Wines, who had an unusually successful record in getting measures proposed by the State Board of Public Charities adopted by the Illinois legislature, described how it was done. If, for instance, he wanted approval and an appropriation for a new building, he first got an architect to make detailed plans and prepare an estimate of cost. He would get photographic copies of the plans made and approach the appropriate committee of the legislature with a good chance of success; also "a sure basis was laid for future applications from time to time to complete the building."[64] In 1891 the Commissioner of Labor Statistics in Minnesota, having seen three factory safety and sanitation bills fail, resolved that his next effort would be preceded by a thorough investigation and a report which would list every example of unsafe machinery, every unguarded mine shaft, and every filthy water closet. It was often necessary to seek publicity for reports such as this in order to generate public interest and convince legislators that action would be favourably received; but this hard work could be rewarding, for legislators normally responded favorably if they thought that a measure would be popular.[65]

The need for careful preparation and for positive action to convince legislators had salutary effects. Whatever doubts one might have about the survival of the fittest, the principle worked in state legislation; the men who ventured into the jungle of the lobbies had to have well-matured schemes that would stand up to criticism. This in itself was an inbuilt check upon the "hasty legislation" so much deplored by critics. If a measure was likely to arouse opposition its promoters had to be prepared to fight it through to the end. Godkin explained to Bryce that because committee work attracted little attention, and because debates were infrequent, it was comparatively

[63] *Proceedings of the Conference of Boards of Public Charities, 1876* (New York, 1876), 162.
[64] *Ibid.*, 122.
[65] *Proceedings of the Eighth National Convention of the Officers of Bureaus of Labor Statistics* (Philadelphia, Pa 1891). Remarks by L. G. Powers of Minnesota. Bryce noted the way in which "a small minority of zealous men, backed by a few newspapers," could carry schemes of reform. He instanced examples from "bodies so depraved as the legislatures of New York and Pennsylvania" of acts for reform of city government, secret ballot, appointments to office, and charities. "Thus, as the Bible tells us that the wrath of man shall praise God, the faults of politicians are turned to work for righteousness" (*American Commonwealth*, 3rd ed., I, 547).

easy to get a bill through the lower house, but by the time it reached the upper it was "pretty sure to have come to the notice of people interested in it." They would take steps to get a hearing before the appropriate committee, employ lawyers to present their case, and take advantage of the fact that debates in the smaller upper houses had no time limit placed upon them. An astute agency might therefore deem it better to have its bill presented first in the upper house and hope that once approved there it would be carried through the lower in the rush of business; but if an appropriation was required most state constitutions required that the bill must originate in the lower house.[66]

However skillful an agency, it seldom got all that it wanted. The first check was in the planning stage when the amount of innovation that the legislature and public would accept had to be carefully measured. Legislatures were always suspicious of any measure that required intrusion on privacy, and bills proposing new agencies often refrained from asking for all the inquisitorial powers that efficient operation demanded. If they did ask for too much they might find all their bills lost or emasculated. In a typical example, the State Board of Health of Pennsylvania found that it had made a mistake in 1886 in asking for bills that would remunerate county registration officers for making returns to the board, appoint health officers as registrars of births, deaths, and diseases, and employ additional clerical help to deal with these statistics. In 1887 it reported that while the legislature appreciated the advantages of this plan it "evidently considered that public sentiment was not yet sufficiently advanced to sustain it in the creation of so large a number of salaried officers for an object which to many would appear purely theoretical." A more ambitious bill to prevent the pollution of rivers was not even discussed.[67]

Most agencies had to fight battles, extending over several sessions, to secure the rights to subpoena witnesses to attend their hearings, take evidence on oath, and compel the production of accounts and papers. Sometimes this power was granted, but with the proviso that no man could be compelled to reveal information about his private affairs; but in the long run most agencies charged with investigating objects of public interest won the necessary powers. Much the same kind of issue, with similar results, was

---

[66] Godkin to Bryce, Oct. 17, 1884, Godkin Papers, Houghton Library, Harvard University.
[67] Pennsylvania B. of P. H., 3rd R. (1887), 10. A particularly cruel example of legislation lost by accident is reported by E.C. Wines, *State of Prisons*, 168. In Indiana a movement for prison reform was finally successful in getting a bill through the legislature; but a delay in engrossing the bill meant that it reached the Governor too late for signature. "It was like losing a prize after winning it and having it in your hand."

raised by the right of agents or inspectors to enter private premises. These matters were intimately related to the larger question of enforcing the law. It was often too easy for a legislature to win approval of interested parties by endorsing a principle, while avoiding the unpopularity that might follow its enforcement. In 1886 Arthur T. Hadley, later to be president of Yale but then commissioner of labor statistics, wrote in his report: "The enforcement of a law is not a thing that takes care of itself; it must be vigorously supported by hard work on the part of all who are interested . . . To make a law worth anything at all, somebody must be willing to incur the hardship and odium, and, if need be, actual danger, in order that its provisions may be carried out."[68] Americans were slow to realize that a law did not enforce itself, as the unhappy experiment of national prohibition was later to show, but by the close of the nineteenth century many agencies in a majority of states had won the right to investigate thoroughly, the power to prosecute offenders, and the assurance that state law officers would assist as and when necessary.

Legislatures were invariably parsimonious with money. The ordinary members of the public knew of no surer way to test the honesty and good intent of government than by watching the tax bills. A railroad commission which attracted much popular support might find itself adequately funded, but a board of public health might have to fight for every penny – unless there was real threat of an epidemic when appropriation bills were being drawn up – and a board of state charities had to press at every session for money to maintain even those services to which the State was already committed. Many illustrations will be found in the chapters on these state agencies, but one bizarre example may be cited here. In 1877 Tennessee established a board of public health but without any appropriation; in 1878 yellow fever in a virulent form struck Memphis and the public-spirited doctors on the board had to sit idly by for lack of money to spend on countermeasures. The Ohio Board of State Charities had more to complain of than most, in a state where every consideration was likely to be sacrificed to partisan advantage, but its bitter complaint of 1890 was but an extreme example of a general failure:

The persistently inadequate sums which the legislature has hitherto appropriated to the maintenance of the work of this Board . . . force us to believe that in the heat of political struggle over questions more purely partisan than economic, administrative, or humanitarian, both the public and its executive and legislative representat-

[68] Connecticut Bureau of Labor Statistics, 2nd R. (1886), xxi.

ives have given the grave questions and interests committed to the general care of the Board of State Charities less thought than they were and are entitled to.[69]

Even in Ohio persistence paid; in the 1890s more generous appropriations were made for state charities, and over the whole range of activities paid for by the states there was a steep rise in expenditure from 1870 to 1900. Figures which may not be comprehensive show that the increase was accelerated in the last decade of the century.[70] Between 1890 and 1902 the total expenditure by the states, excluding debt retirement, rose from $72 million to $182 million. Debts increased from $211 million to $235. Expenditure by local governments, much of it under powers delegated by the states, rose from $488 million to $888 million during the same twelve-year period while their debts rose from $926 million to $1,680 million. These figures are a remarkable comment upon government intervention in a period when each new extension of public responsibility had to be fought for against parochialism, apathy, and political customs geared to the leisurely processes of an earlier age.

How did it come about that the constraints of the federal and state constitutions permitted this expansion? What of the belief that the fourteenth amendment was used by the courts to impose new curbs on state power? How do these facts fit in with the argument that the Supreme Court, responding to pressure from the state courts and to advice from well-known law writers, was becoming increasingly "conservative" at the turn of the century? And what did state courts, which had to settle a vast number of questions under state constitutions, make of this great extension of public agencies and activities? These questions deserve separate consideration and the next chapter is devoted to them.

[69] Ohio B. of St. Ch., 15th R. (1890), 4–5.
[70] Bureau of the Census, *Historical Review of State and Local Government Finances*, State and Local Government Special Study No. 25 (1948). The figures from this source are given in the 1949 edition of *Historical Statistics of the United States, 1789–1845*, but not in the current edition.

3

PUBLIC RESPONSIBILITY AND THE LAW*

The principle that private property could be regulated when this was demanded by the public interest, or expropriated when it was required for public use, had deep roots in Anglo-American law. From time out of mind markets had been controlled, obligations had been imposed on common carriers, entry into some occupations had been restricted, while others required applicants to obtain licenses, individuals might be excluded from some trade because exclusive privileges had been given by law to corporations, and when health or safety was at risk summary action without prior application to the courts was justified. Anything that threatened health, imposed unreasonable inconvenience upon others, or was simply noxious could be declared a "nuisance" and its removal ordered. Equally drastic remedies might be applied to any activity which had immoral consequences. It was generally assumed that public responsibility for roads, bridges, and navigable water existed and could be exercised in numerous ways. In American law this great reserve of power was usually known as the "police power"; and, except on federal property, its exercise was the exclusive responsibility of the states. There was also the right of eminent domain, which gave state legislatures the right to take private property for public use, provided that fair compensation was given.

A classic statement of these principles is found in Chancellor Kent's

---

* *References to cases*
The normal practice is followed in citing cases by the volume, the name of the reports, and the page at which the case begins.
U.S. = Reports of the United States Supreme Court.
N.E. = Northeastern Reporter.
N.W. = Northwestern Reporter.
At. = Atlantic Reporter.
Other volumes of collected state reports are Southern, Southeastern, Southwestern, and Pacific. Leading state cases to 1885 are collected in *The American reports*.
   For observations on treatment of legal history during this period see the essay on sources and the bibliography at the end of this volume.

Commentaries on American Law, and a new edition, edited by Oliver Wendell Holmes Jr, was published in 1873. Kent wrote that there were many occasions on which the rights of property were "made subservient to the public welfare." As examples he noted the destruction of property to prevent the spread of fire, the construction of roads across private land, and the presumption that paths bordering canals were for public use: "The maxim of the law is that a private mischief is to be endured rather than a public inconvenience." While the rights of property should always be respected the lawgiver could "prescribe the mode and manner of using it, so far as it may be necessary to prevent its abuse, to the injury or annoyance of others, or of the public." Resting upon these foundations were numerous laws regulating unwholesome or offensive occupations in populous places, and it was a recognized principle that "every person ought so to use his property as not to injure his neighbors, and . . . private interest may be made subservient to the general interests of the community." The editor added a note that these powers were normally described by the general designation "police power" and added a warning that its exercise "must be clearly necessary to the safety, comfort, or well-being of society, or . . . imperatively required by the public necessity." Even this limitation left a wide field in which the police power might legitimately operate.[1]

Private property taken for public use might come under the control of a corporation performing a public service. Did this imply that it was held only on the condition that this service was performed satisfactorily? If this was so the legal basis for continued government supervision of railroads and canals was firmly laid. But were grants of power contained in charters of incorporation sacrosanct so long as the original conditions were complied with? Did the constitutional prohibition against impairing the obligations of contract, as interpreted in the Dartmouth College case, protect a corporation against new obligations imposed by law? This was to be the field for a battle which the defenders of corporate immunity ultimately lost.

If there was little difficulty in finding historic precedents for the right to regulate, the problem lay in deciding how old principles should be applied in changed circumstances. Were principles enunciated for the control of trade in country markets applicable to large commercial undertakings?

---

[1] James Kent, *Commentaries on American Law*, 12th ed., ed. O. W. Holmes Jr, 4 vols (Boston, 1873), II, 338–40.

Could the traditional obligations of common carriers be translated into requirements imposed upon large railroad corporations? Could the trade of a great port be brought to a standstill because the threat of an epidemic caused health boards to set up quarantine? Could the sale and manufacture of liquor be prohibited when vast amounts of capital were invested in the business and the livelihood of thousands was threatened? Could old laws requiring that certain trades should be licensed be adapted to insist upon professional standards in medicine? Was compulsory education justified? The questions could be multiplied and the enlarged scale of operations and the increasing complexity of society demanded answers.

If the case for increased power were granted, where could a line be drawn? Judges had frequently in mind the dictum of Lemuel Shaw, sometime chief justice of Massachusetts, that "any person is at liberty to pursue any lawful calling, and to do this in his own way, not encroaching upon others."[2] This general right could not be taken away, but the principle allowed legislatures to decide what was lawful and what encroached upon the rights of others. Moreover there must be exceptions when an individual, who did not harm anyone, was restrained by a general law designed to prevent others from acting unreasonably or in a manner contrary to the public interest. An employer might be compelled to install safety appliances where, in his judgment, there was no danger. An individual might be required to submit to medical examination or remove his clothes for disinfection because others with whom he was not associated and over whom he had no control had introduced disease. A common carrier might be required to accept payments which yielded little or no profit because others were judged to have levied extortionate charges. Even in primitive society there was no clear-cut division between private right and public obligation; in a more advanced society the problems of demarcation defied analysis though thousands of lawyers were paid to plead as though it were the simplest matter in the world.

---

[2] *Commonwealth* v. *Alger*, 7 Cush 53. Some statements on the police power in Indiana state supreme courts may also be cited. "There is a reserved and at the same time well-organized power, affecting their domestic concerns, remaining in all the states" (*Hockett* v. *the State* (1886), 5 N.E. 178). "The police power of a state is very broad and comprehensive . . . It is that inherent and plenary power in the state which enables it to prohibit all things hurtful to the comfort and welfare of society" (*Eastman* v. *the State* (1887), 10 N.E. 97). On a law requiring dentists to be licensed: "as the legislature has plenary power over the whole subject, it alone must be the judge of what is wise and expedient" (*Wilkins* v. *the State* (1888), 16 N.E. 192). In 1891 the Wisconsin Supreme Court said: "All courts agree that the police power of the state extends to all regulations affecting the lives, limbs, health, comfort, good order, morals, peace, and safety of society" (*The State* v. *Heinemann*, 49 N.W. 818).

There were several grounds on which state action under the police power or eminent domain might be challenged. It might be claimed that the use was not public or that the compensation was unjust. A regulation under the police power might be attacked as unreasonable, unconstitutional in serving a purpose unjustified by health, safety, morals, or public good, or ostensibly constitutional but in fact intended to achieve an unconstitutional result. The fourteenth amendment, with its guarantees of equal protection and due process, might be brought into play, and for a time much legal talent was employed in trying to erect this barrier against state action. Yet another plea was that legislation was local or special. It was a sound principle of law (written into most state constitutions) that an act which purported to be of general application should not confer privileges or impose restraints only on one locality, city, group, association, or individual. Deriving from this, and reinforced by "equal protection," a good deal was heard in the later nineteenth century of "class legislation," meaning a law picking out any occupational group for penalties or protection. Finally a state statute might interfere with interstate commerce.

Given the variety of grounds on which state legislation could be attacked the wonder is not that the courts found some acts void, but that so many were upheld. The states advanced into new ground with the regulation of railroads, inspection of factories and mines, and a host of laws on pure food, liquor, and sanitation. Old powers were greatly extended and new agencies came into being. Judges sometimes expressed fears, but time and time again they came back to the principle that only the law-making body could judge what means best served the public good.

Railroad and warehouse legislation were brought to the test in the leading case of *Munn* v. *Illinois* in 1877.[3] This was appropriate since unprecedented economic power called forth unprecedented exercise of state power. The legislatures in several western states had regulated the rates charged by railroads and grain elevators; and several of these laws were challenged in the courts. The Supreme Court chose *Munn* v. *Illinois* to settle the issue, as the case which raised fewest collateral questions. The State had fixed by law the maximum charges at Chicago grain elevators, and the law was challenged on the ground that it burdened interstate commerce, contravened the fourteenth amendment by depriving the warehouse owner of property without due process of law, and exercised

---

[3] 94 U.S. 113. The court also decided in favor of laws fixing maximum railroad rates in Iowa, Wisconsin, and Minnesota (*Chicago, Burlington & Quincy* v. *Iowa*; *Park* v. *Chicago & Northwestern*; *Chicago & St Paul* v. *Ackley*; *Winona & St Paul* v. *Blake*.

arbitrary and unprecedented authority. Chief Justice Waite, speaking for the 8–1 majority of the court, disposed quickly of the argument drawn from the fourteenth amendment. He quoted the earlier dictum by Taney that the police power was "nothing more or less than the powers of government in every sovereignty," and added that it has never been "supposed that statutes regulating the use of property necessarily deprived an owner of his property without due process of law." The fourteenth amendment had not been intended to introduce new principles of law or discard old ones, but to prevent states from performing acts contrary to natural justice. Toward the close of his argument Waite also dismissed the claim that the Illinois law should be invalidated for interfering with interstate commerce. A law of this kind might "incidentally . . . become connected with interstate commerce but not necessarily so." A law should not be made void because of indirect effects upon interstate commerce, because this would render invalid almost all attempts to regulate a state's own commerce. As for the police power, many precedents covered its use to regulate the charges of common carriers or of businesses which, from geographical location and the nature of their trade, were monopolies.

Having reached this point Waite could have closed his judgment, but he then adopted a more positive line, and proceeded to examine the principles which underlay the police power, introducing the famous argument that "when . . . one devotes his property to a use in which the public has an interest, he, in effect, grants to the public an interest in that use, and must submit to be controlled by the public for the common good." In any future case, presenting similar issues, it would therefore be necessary to do no more than establish that the public had an interest in order to justify regulation.

Was Waite, by implication, creating a new category of business which was *not* affected with the public interest and was thus immune from regulation? This seems improbable. He was enlarging former categories – enumerated as "ferries, common carriers, hackmen, bakers, millers, wharfingers, innkeepers, &c" – which had been subject to regulations "from time immemorial" – to embrace railroads and warehouses accepting goods for deposit. He added the possible new factor of virtual monopoly as a justification for treating warehouses as affected with the public interest and subject to regulation. He did not refer to, and had no cause to consider, the numerous instances in which businesses might be lawfully conducted as purely private concerns and yet become subject to health or sanitary laws. Nor did he have occasion to refer to other examples – such as the prohibition of child labor – in which the public interest was made manifest not in the business itself, but in its effects upon upbringing, education, and morals. He would have had before him the earlier judgment of Chief Justice Breese on the same case in the Illinois Supreme Court, where it was said:

Every sovereign power possesses inherently unlimited legislative power when the organic law imposes no restraint. The power to legislate on all subjects affecting the interests of a whole community must be conceded to exist, and it will not cease to exist until civil government shall be resolved into its original elements.[4]

Waite's definition of the public interest clearly echoed and endorsed the phrase "affecting the interests of the whole community" in the earlier opinion, while his reminder that this was "the very essence of government" takes up the earlier point that the power to legislate under these circumstances must exist "until civil government shall be resolved into its original elements." It is therefore safe to assume that Waite did not intend to narrow the very broad definition of legislative authority given in the State Supreme Court; if he had so intended it would have been necessary to say so since the earlier judgment was already on record.

Toward the end of his judgment Waite argued that it was for the legislature not the courts to decide what was reasonable when exercising the right to regulate. "We know that this is a power which may be abused; but that is no argument against its existence. For protection against abuses by legislatures the people must resort to the polls and not to the courts." This was to be the most controversial part of the judgment. Did it mean that a party could not appeal to the courts against the decision of a railroad commission? What had been at issue in the case was a law not an order made by a commission, and, while there could be no appeal against a law, surely an official might be called upon to explain why he had reached a particular decision.

As two subsequent railroad decisions by the Supreme Court have bearing upon the whole question of police power, it is as well to mention them here before looking at the way in which state courts handled other problems. In the *Wabash Railroad Co.* v. *Illinois* in 1886 it was held that a state had no right to regulate charges for interstate journeys which originated within its own borders.[5] Mr Justice Miller, who had been with the majority in *Munn* v. *Illinois*, held that, while a law was not invalid because it had indirect effects upon interstate commerce, a statute which

---

[4] Quoted in Illinois Railroad and Warehouse Commission, 4th R. (1974), 102.
[5] 118 U.S. 557.

aimed directly at fixing rates charged for interstate journeys must be unconstitutional. Abandoning the difficult task of assigning exact boundaries between the two, he argued that it was contrary to natural justice to deprive a citizen of the right to make the best bargain that he could for sending freight to New York. Should he be required to pay 25 cents a mile when he could get as much for 15 cents? This was a salutary reminder that there were always three parties in these situations, and that shippers as well as commissions and companies had rights. The attempt to outlaw special rates to the Atlantic ports commended itself to the merchants of Chicago but not necessarily to shippers in Springfield or Peoria. Nevertheless Mr Justice Bradley, joined by the Chief Justice and Justice Gray, made a vigorous dissent against this curtailment of state regulatory power, and argued that a state ought not to be deprived of the right to regulate its own railroads merely because the freight was destined for a point outside its boundaries.

In *Chicago, Milwaukee and St Paul Railroad Co.* v. *Minnesota*, decided in 1890, the point at issue was the right to challenge the ruling of a railroad commission in the courts with evidence that the rate ordered was unreasonable.[6] The Minnesota law made the commission's decision final both as to fact and as to the reasonableness of a rate ordered. The majority of the court decided that this was a denial of due process and therefore barred by the fourteenth amendment. A commission was not a court of law and was not bound by rules of evidence or procedure, while a decision of this kind was "eminently a question for judicial investigation, requiring due process of law for its determination." Mr Justice Miller concurred "with some hesitation," in a separate opinion, arguing that companies could always start proceedings in equity against the unreasonable application of a law, and that it was therefore perverse to shut them off from a remedy in common law. Justice Bradley made a strong and much quoted dissent in which he said that the decision "practically overruled *Munn* v. *Illinois*." Then it had been decided that the regulation of rates was a legislative not a judicial prerogative, but this new decision made "the judiciary, and not the legislature the final arbiter."

The reasoning behind Bradley's dissent was dubious. The legislature might be supreme but this did not mean that it could place the actions of its agents beyond challenge. In 1892, in *Budd* v. *New York* Mr Justice Blatchford went out of his way to deny that *Munn* v. *Illinois* had been

---

6   134 U.S. 418.

overruled.[7] It was one thing to declare that the decision of a commission was subject to appeal, and quite another to substitute judicial wisdom for legislative discretion. In the *Budd* case the court upheld a New York law fixing rates charge by warehouses, even though its reasonableness might have been open to question. The significance of the decision was emphasized by the first Supreme Court dissent, in which "paternalism" was identified as a danger. In the words of Mr Justice Brewer: "The paternal theory of government is to me odious. The utmost possible liberty to the individual, and the fullest possible protection to his property, is both the limitation and duty of government."

In the event there was no rush by the railroad companies to the courts. Litigation could be enormously expensive, all evidence might be reviewed in open court, and after unwelcome publicity the decision might still go against them. Discretion normally suggested private intercession with the commission, and the downward trend of rates after 1890 usually made a compromise possible. Disputes could still find their way into the courts, and one such was *Smyth* v. *Ames*, decided in 1898 in circumstances which were slightly unusual.[8] By this time it was generally recognized that deciding a reasonable rate was a complicated business, requiring knowledge of capitalization, operating costs and quality of service, as well as simple comparisons between the rates per mile charged for different journeys; yet Nebraska had set up a commission consisting of state officials with other duties to perform and no expertise in railroad questions. The appointed secretary was, in effect, the commission. Judgment was delivered by Justice Harlan who normally took a liberal view of legislative discretion.

What the company is entitled to ask is a fair return upon the value of that which it employs for the public convenience . . . What the public is entitled to demand is that no more be exacted from it for the use of a public highway than the services rendered by it are reasonably worth.

As "the basis of all calculation as to reasonableness of rates . . . must be the fair value of the property" it followed that the procedure for ascertaining that value must be open, thorough, and inspire confidence. In 1894 Justice Brewer had attempted to maintain that the sole criterion was whether a company could make a profit and pay its creditors at the rates fixed; for this *Smyth* v. *Ames* substituted value, expertly determined. It gave

[7] 143 U.S. 517. [8] 169 U.S. 466.

railroads the right to be investigated, not the right to make a profit irrespective of efficient operation or honest capitalization.

Finally the principle of *Munn* v. *Illinois* was affirmed once more in *Brass* v. *North Dakota* in 1898.[9] Rates fixed for grain elevators were challenged as unreasonable because they made no allowance for varying costs of operation in different parts of the state. In a brief opinion Justice Shiras said the court had no right to question the expediency or wisdom of a law and could not impute "an improper exercise of discretion to the legislature of North Dakota." In a further dissent Brewer showed his exasperation: "I can only say that it seems to me that the country is rapidly traveling the road which leads to that point where all freedom of contract and conduct will be lost."

Most state railroad laws prohibited charges which discriminated by giving lower rates to favored shippers, or lowered the rates at some points to meet competition, while holding or raising them where the railroad had a monopoly. These laws gave rise to a great deal of complaint and litigation. Was it fair to demand that railroads should not compete? Was it reasonable to demand that all rates should be reduced to the level to which they were forced by competition? In 1885 the Ohio Supreme Court ruled that all rates need not be the same provided that all were reasonable.[10] One kind of discrimination would always be unlawful, for "when the reduced rate is either intended or has a tendency to injure the plaintiff in his business and destroy his trade . . . he has a right to insist that rates be made the same under like circumstances"; but, the phrase "has a tendency to injure" was full of difficulty. The right of a state to forbid discriminatory rates was sustained, but there might be ground for contending that the law did not apply in a particular case as the rate charged injured no one.

States legislated for railroads on a great many questions besides rates, and in most instances these laws came squarely within the obligation of common carriers to provide services that were safe and convenient. In 1885 the Supreme Court of New York held that there could be no appeal against the finding of a commission on a question of fact, reached after a hearing and a visit of inspection.[11] In 1886 the Supreme Court of Illinois found that "it is now settled law that railroad corporations are within the operation of all reasonable police regulations. Otherwise there would be no security for the life or property of citizens residing in the vicinity."[12]

---

[9] 153 U.S. 391.   [10] *Scofield et al.* v. *Lake Shore Railway Co.*, 3 N.E. 907.
[11] *Lake Erie & Western Co.* v. *New York, Lehigh & Western Railroad Co.*, 2 N.E. 35.
[12] *Illinois Central* v. *Willenborg*, 7 N.E. 698.

An interesting example of the extension of old principles to new circumstances was the Indiana case of *Hockett* v. *the State* in 1886 which dealt with a maximum charge of $3 a month for telephone services.[13] The court went over familiar ground in stating that there was "a reserved and at the same time well-recognized power, affecting their domestic concerns, remaining in all the states" which was usually "though not perhaps always accurately" called the police power. A telephone might not come within any of the activities so far listed as subject to this power but must come logically into the same category.

Distinctions between commerce within a state and between states were not always easy to determine. In Massachusetts G. F. Hoar argued for the state that the *Wabash* decision had not deprived a state of the right to fix charges on that part of an interstate journey that fell within its borders, but the State Supreme Court decided that as the purpose of the challenged law was to control rates to points in Connecticut it was unconstitutional.[14] In Indiana it was ruled in 1888 that a sleeping car operator, under contract to interstate lines, could not be required to report his gross receipts to the state auditor; the information was required for levying a tax and "no tax in any form or for any purpose" could be levied for interstate commerce.[15] In two Pennsylvania cases in 1888 it was decided first that a corporation chartered in New York could be taxed only on business done in Pennsylvania, and then that a Pennsylvania company serving two points in the state but with part of the journey in another could be taxed on its full receipts. The United States Supreme Court invalidated a California tax on agents selling tickets for out-of-state railroads.[16] In other cases it was decided that a state could make conditions under which a "foreign corporation" might operate in its territories, could require a license fee for an office used by such a corporation, but could not discriminate between corporations which did and those which did not invest money in the state. But other decisions permitted states to require railroad engineers to be licensed even though they operated on interstate trains, and might prohibit color-blind drivers.[17]

---

[13]   5 N.E. 178.
[14]   *Commonwealth* v. *Housatonic R.R. Co.* 9 N.E. 547 (1887).
[15]   *The State* v. *Woodruff*, 15 N.E. 814.
[16]   *Delaware & Hudson Canal Co.* v. *Commonwealth*, 17 At. 175; and *Commonwealth* v. *Lehigh R. R. Co.*, 17 At. 179; *McCall* v. *California*, 136 U.S. 104.
[17]   In the case of the color-blind railroad employees Mr Justice Field said that Congress had plenary power to legislate for interstate commerce, but until Congress had acted "it is clearly within the competency of the States to provide against accidents on trains within their limits" (*Nashville, Chattanooga & St Louis R. R.* v. *Alabama*, 123 U.S. 96). But in *Minnesota* v. *Barber*, 136 U.S. 313, a law which required inspection in the state of cattle

In 1885 the general application of the police power was considered by the Supreme Court in the leading case of *Barbier* v. *Connolly*.[18] Did the fourteenth amendment prevent a state from selecting some trades for regulation? Mr Justice Field gave the decision of a unanimous court:

Neither the amendment, broad and comprehensive as it is, nor any other amendment, was designed to interfere with the power of a State, sometimes termed its "police power," to prescribe regulations to promote the health, peace, morals, education, and good order of the people, and to legislate so as to increase the industries of the State, develop its resources, and add to its wealth and prosperity.

Inevitably, he said, some regulations would "press with more or less weight upon one than upon another," but if intended "to promote with as little inconvenience as possible the general good" they were not prohibited by the fourteenth amendment. The test was not whether some individuals or occupations were affected more than others, but whether the law applied equally to all in the same situation.

Barbier v. *Connolly* was occasioned by regulations for the inspection of San Francisco laundries. In another case, in which a law prohibiting laundries from working during night hours and on Sundays was challenged, the court declared that a person's right to pursue a lawful occupation was always to be exercised "subject to such rules as are adopted by society for the common welfare."[19] However another case gave the court an opportunity to demonstrate that it did not condone the harassment of Chinese launderers when it found proof of racial discrimination in administering what might otherwise have been valid regulations. The appellant in *Yick Wo* v. *Hopkins* was able to show that he had complied with all regulations yet had been refused a license; moreover 150 other Chinese had been arrested for operating illegally, though men of other races continued to operate unmolested under the same conditions, and supervisors administering the rules were not required to state reasons for refusal of a license. This, said Justice Matthews, was "naked and arbitrary power" and a denial of both equal protection and due process. This decision made use of the fourteenth amendment in precisely the way that its framers had intended.[20]

The judge who spoke for the court in *Barbier* v. *Connolly* was Stephen J. Field, who has gone down in history as the man who did most to write laissez faire into the constitution, and a glance at some of his other

before slaughtering was held invalid because in excluding from the state all meat slaughtered in other states it constituted an interference with interstate commerce.
[18] 113 U.S. 27.   [19] *Soon Hing* v. *Crowley*, 113 U.S. 103.   [20] 118 U.S. 356.

decisions may be instructive. In *Munn* v. *Illinois* his dissent had described the statute as "nothing less than a bold assertion of absolute power by the state to control at its discretion the property and business of a citizen." Yet in *Dent* v. *West Virginia* he had no hesitation in upholding a law requiring a physician to obtain a license and to produce evidence of his qualifications before it was granted. "The power of the State to provide for the general welfare of its people" should not be impaired, and the law deprived no one of lawful rights. In 1890 he again spoke for the court in sanctioning a New York tax on insurance companies, arguing that their incorporation was a privilege and might be subject to any conditions. The fourteenth amendment did not bar special laws appropriate to certain trades or professions, and taxation of property might be selective provided that all in the same category were treated equally. Finally Field did not dissent when his colleague Bradley declared that a state might tax some trades or professions, exempt others, and tax real and personal property in different ways. Only if there were "clear and hostile discrimination" could the fourteenth amendment restrain state action.[21]

A life-long Democrat, Field was reluctant to see any fresh encroachment on state rights by federal authority. Shortly after *Munn* v. *Illinois* he deliberately seized an opportunity to deliver a concurring opinion upholding a police regulation, in order to make the point that over a very wide range the states had discretion and could not be restrained by the courts. In a public address in 1890 he emphasized the variety that must be expected when each state "may pursue the policy best suited to its people and resources, though unlike that of any other state." He did fear encroachment upon individual rights but, unlike other "conservatives," saw the danger not in majority rule but in the increasing power of wealth and its ability to dominate legislatures and to secure misuse of the state authority to "encroach upon the rights or crush out the business of individuals of small means." For Field the rights protected by the fourteenth amendment had nothing to do with unrestricted power for large corporations.[22]

When the Supreme Court gave such unequivocal support to use of the police power, state courts were unlikely to lag far behind. When the plea

[21] *Dent* v. *Virginia*, 129 U.S. 114; *Home Insurance Co.* v. *New York*, 134 U.S. 594; *Balls Gap R.R.* v. *Pennsylvania*, 134 U.S. 232. His opinions are analyzed by Charles W. McCurdy, "Justice Field and the Jurisprudence of Government–Business Relations: some Parameters of Laissez Faire Constitutionalism," *Journal of American History*, 61 (1975), 970–1,105. Carl B. Swisher, *Stephen J. Field: Craftsman of the Law* (Washington D.C., 1930), is full and balanced.

[22] From his Address in the *Centennial Celebration of the Organization of the Federal Judiciary held in the City of New York, Feb. 4, 1890* (Washington D.C., 1890), 8, 23.

was raised that an act of the Indiana legislature encroached upon the natural rights of citizens, Mr Justice Elliott of the State Supreme Court declared that "there is no certain standard for determining what are or are not the natural rights of citizens. The legislature is just as capable of determining the question as the courts." In the Reconstruction cases, he continued, the United States Supreme Court had declared that the federal government had no police power to protect individuals, and, as such power must reside somewhere, it lay exclusively with the states. Constitutions must, moreover, be interpreted in a way that gave effect to the will of the people whenever possible: "Courts do not bend the constitution when they give it the effect that the people intended it to have."[23]

Numerous state cases extended and applied the police power in new fields. In 1887 Elliott, now chief justice of Indiana, considered the right of the state to regulate the practice of medicine and surgery.[24] This was, he said, "an exercise of the police power inherent in the state," while a county clerk, responsible by law for registering physicians, did not exercise judicial power without right of appeal since registration was automatic provided that the applicant possessed the qualifications approved by the state. In 1887 the Massachusetts Supreme Court considered a case in which the Boston Board of Health, acting upon authority delegated by the state, had ordered the disinfection of a consignment of rags and required the owner to pay the cost of getting this done.[25] The Boston board, said the court, had been given by law the power to declare certain things to be "nuisances," and exemption could not be claimed on the ground that a particular "nuisance" harmed no one.

Arguments that state acts were local or special had little success. In the Ohio case of *Marmet* v. *the State* the act challenged had ordered all trades and professions in cities over a certain size (which meant, in effect, Cleveland, and Cincinnati) to register and obtain licenses.[26] It was reasonable, said the court, to apply special rules for large cities, and the law would apply to others as they attained the stated size. In other, similar, cases the courts were surprisingly lenient, and it became quite common for states to adopt this form when enacting special laws affecting only their larger cities.

Almost any law that could be directly related to public health was likely

---

[23] *Hedderich* v. *the State*, 1 N.E. 47; *Breckbill* v. *Randall*, 1 N.E. 362.
[24] *Eastern* v. *the State*, 10 N.E. 97; also *Orr* v. *Meade*, 11 N.E. 787.
[25] *Train and others* v. *Boston Disinfecting Co.*, 11 N.E. 929.
[26] *Marmet* v. *the State*, 12 N.E. 463; also *Hill* v. *the City of Cincinnati*.

to be sanctioned. In 1887 the New Jersey Supreme Court considered a case brought against the Board of Health for having ordered the destruction of animals suspected of infectious or contagious diseases. This was, said the court, action against a specific nuisance and in no way an invasion of general property rights. Nor was there any ground for alleging that such an order should not be executed without judicial proceedings.

Such a doctrine . . . would interpose an almost absolute barrier to the praiseworthy efforts everywhere made to prevent preventible diseases . . . and would render much of the health legislation of today of no avail.[27]

The most striking affirmation of state power in matters of health was in the case of the *Health Department of the City of New York* v. *the Rector of Trinity Church* in 1895. The judgment was even more remarkable in that it was delivered by Mr Justice Peckham who attempted so hard to make freedom of contract a basic right protected by the fourteenth amendment.[28] An act required the owners of all tenements to supply running water on each floor; this was contested on the ground that it imposed unreasonable expense on the owner, worked retrospective injustice as the law had not been in force when the property was acquired, offered no compensation, and denied the right of appeal against an enforcement order. Peckham disposed of all these points. A police-power law must "tend in a degree that is perceptible and clear toward the preservation of the lives, the health, the morals, or the welfare of the community"; the law in question satisfied these criteria. A general law might legitimately be framed to prevent individuals from obstructing it and, if the facts had been correctly ascertained by fair investigation, the right of appeal against an order might be denied. If unreasonable expenditure was required the courts might intervene, but the law in question imposed a duty equally on all owners of tenements and there was no ground for exemption because implementation cost one more than another. The law was indeed enacted after purchase of the property, but anyone buying tenements in a city knew that they were subject to public law and might be regulated further as time went by.

In a noteworthy part of *The Rector of Trinity Church* judgment Peckham took note of the fact that the law must recognize rising expectations. There might be no precedent for this law, but "the supply of water to the general public in a city has become not only a luxury, but an absolute necessity for the maintenance of the public health and safety." The need to recognize

[27] *Newark and S.O.H.R.R. Co.* v. *Hunt*, 12 At. 697.   [28] 39 N.E. 833.

social change was also emphasized in *Ohio* v. *the City of Toledo* in 1891 when the issue was whether a tax could be raised to pay a private company for supplying natural gas to the city.[29] If judged to be taxation for private benefit it would have been contrary to the state constitution. The state Supreme Court decided that, though only a minority might derive immediate benefit from the work, others would do so in the future, and that "it would be wrong to leave out of view the progress of society, the change in manners and custom, and the development and growth of new wants, rational and artificial, which may from time to time call for a new exercise of legislative power."

It often happens that dissents measure best the distance traveled by judicial opinion, and two examples from New York are worthy of citation. In *People* v. *Walsh* in 1889, when a law fixing maximum charges for grain warehouses was upheld, Mr Justice Peckham said that "the legislation under consideration is not only vicious in its nature, and communistic in its tendency . . . but is an illegal effort to interfere with the lawful privilege of the individual to seek and obtain such compensation as he can for the use of his own property."[30] Six years later it was Peckham's opinion in *The Rector of Trinity Church* that provoked an agonized dissent on the part of his colleague, Judge Bartlett:

A sound public policy certainly dictates at this time, when the rights of property and the liberty of the citizen are sought to be invaded by every form of subtle and dangerous legislation, that the courts should see to it that those benign principles of common law which are the shield of personal liberty and private property should suffer no impairment.[31]

Both opinions might well be taken out of context, as representative of judicial hostility to social and economic legislation; yet both were dissents.

Laws prohibiting or regulating the manufacture and sale of oleo-margarine were frequently contested. Their origin in pressure from farmers and dairymen made them suspect, and one can sympathize with Justice Field's dissent in *Powell* v. *Pennsylvania* (1887), when he asked whether it could possibly be right to drive from the market a cheap and wholesome food simply because it reduced the sale of a more expensive article. Nevertheless the Pennsylvania Supreme Court had declared that to deny the authority of legislature in this matter was "to attack all that is vital in the police power." A majority in the Supreme Court of the United States agreed.[32]

[29] 26 N.E. 1061.   [30] 22 N.E. 682.   [31] 39 N.E. 833 (at 840).
[32] 127 U.S. 678, 7 At. 913.

Prohibition of the manufacture or sale of liquor stretched state authority to its limits. It made hitherto lawful business unlawful, property valueless, and prevented the disposal of what had been honestly acquired. It created new criminal acts and might interfere with interstate commerce. Nevertheless in 1887, in the leading case of *Mugler* v. *Kansas*, the prohibitionists won a complete victory.[33] When it was claimed that men engaged in a once legitimate business had been deprived of the equal protection of the law, and that the condemnation of their property was a denial of due process, a majority of the United States Supreme Court said that the fourteenth amendment did not alter the principle "that all property in this country is held under the implied obligation that the owner's use of it shall not be injurious to the community." It was within the power of a legislature to decide what was injurious, and no one could claim compensation because he was deprived of the capacity "by a noxious use of property, to inflict injury upon the community." Justice Field dissented from that part of the judgment which denied the right to compensation, but agreed with the general proposition that a state could prohibit the manufacture and sale of liquor.

Having upheld the right of a state to restrict personal liberty in the interests of temperance, the Supreme Court took a less permissive view when it interfered with interstate commerce; but 6–3 divisions in two leading cases indicated the difficulty in drawing the line between state and federal power. In *Bowman* v. *Chicago and Northwestern Railroad Co.* the railroad had refused to accept a shipment of beer destined for Iowa because its importation was forbidden in that state. For the majority Mr Justice Matthews said that state regulation could begin only after the termination of an interstate journey. In *Leisy* v. *Hardin* a company incorporated in Illinois sought to recover a consignment of beer which had been seized by the Iowa authorities. In the view of the court majority, the crucial fact was that the beer had never been drawn off from sealed barrels and had not "mingled with the common mass of property in Iowa." The interstate journey terminated only when the goods were delivered to a purchaser in unbroken packages. This overruled the Iowa decision which had found such sales unlawful, and in this roundabout way the package store entered the American social scene.[34]

Liquor laws might fall short of prohibition but still have many implications for personal liberty. In Pennsylvania a seller of liquor had to

[33] 123 U.S. 623.
[34] 125 U.S. 465 (1888); 135 U.S. 100 (1890). *Collins* v. *Hill*, 41 N.W. 571 (1889).

be licensed, and by a law of 1889 even a licensed seller was forbidden to supply liquor to an intoxicated person. In one case a man had allowed people to assemble in his barn and supplied them with liquor, and had not desisted when some became intoxicated. The state Supreme Court held that the law could not interfere with an individual's private consumption, but as soon as others were involved he forfeited "the protection to which a citizen is entitled, and his acts became a subject of police interest and control." In the case before the court the actions complained of had rightly become "a subject of investigation and punishment."[35]

In Maryland a liquor seller had to produce evidence of good character and a certificate signed by ten respectable persons before being issued with a license. An applicant claimed that having sold liquor for years without causing offense, he should be allowed to continue under a former and less stringent law.[36] The court went over familiar ground in upholding the right of the state to legislate under the police power and to treat liquor selling as a privilege that could be revoked or modified at any time. The interests of the community must be paramount over the rights of an individual, and, in a striking phrase, Judge Bryan of the state Supreme Court added that "without the power to protect and preserve these interests, civilized government could not exist."

The New York case of *People* v. *Cipperley*, decided in 1886, dealt with a law prohibiting the sale of adulterated milk.[37] The state Supreme Court refused to consider the allegations that the law was unwise and unnecessary:

Courts cannot say that the legislature has the constitutional power to pass a judicious law to regulate the sale of articles of food, but has no constitutional power to pass an injudicious law on that subject.

The law in question was intended to safeguard health and courts must leave the choice of means to the lawmakers. Nor was it relevant to argue that the article was wholesome; it had been proved to contain more than the permitted quantity of water and that was sufficient to condemn its sale. *Barbier* v. *Connolly* was cited to support this refusal to look behind the record when dealing with cases arising from health laws. Still more doubt might attach to laws designed to restrict the sale of butter substitutes, but in 1887 in *People* v. *Arenberg* the New York court had no difficulty in upholding a law which forbade making "butterine" look like butter.[38] This

---

[35] *Altenberg* v. *Commonwealth*, 17 At. 799 (1889).
[36] *Tregeser* v. *Gray*, 20 At. 905 (1890).   [37] 4 N.E. 107.   [38] 11 N.E. 277.

case had important repercussions for the whole question of fair description and honest labeling of articles offered for sale. It was, said the court, in accord with natural justice to require sellers to describe goods truthfully, nor was anyone "entitled to benefit from any additional market value which might be impaired to it by resorting to artificial means to make [butterine] resemble dairy butter in appearance."

Another case of similar import was decided by the Minnesota Supreme Court in 1890.[39] A law made it illegal to sell baking powder which contained alum unless this was recorded on the label. The court said that it was a "common right of the people" to be informed about the contents of substances offered for sale if they contained harmful matter, or matter that they believed to be harmful, and which "they would not knowingly purchase or use." Following these precedents the Iowa Supreme Court had little difficulty in 1891 in upholding a law which required all lard not made from the pure fat of healthy swine to be labeled "compound lard" and carry a statement of its ingredients and their proportions. The law did not prohibit and restrict the sale of any article but merely required it to be sold for what it was.[40]

These decisions did not prevent the courts from voiding laws when their purposes were in doubt. A much cited case was *People* v. *Marx*, decided by the New York Supreme Court in 1885.[41] It was proved in evidence that a butter substitute was wholesome and that there had been no concealment of its true nature. For the court Mr Justice Rapallo said that while it was reasonable to lay down conditions for sale there was no ground for making the manufacture of any article a criminal act, since "no proposition is now more firmly settled than that it is one of the fundamental rights and privileges of every American citizen to adopt and follow such lawful industrial pursuit, not injurious to the community, as he may see fit." He added that measures such as these were dangerous even to their promoters; for, acting on this precedent, the makers of oleo-margarine might acquire influence with the legislature to forbid the making of butter.

In 1888 the New York court voided another law which forbade sellers to offer any gifts, prizes, rewards, or premiums as inducements to buy their products.[42] This was, said Mr Justice Peckham, one more example of the kind of law, "so frequent of late," in which an interest or class sought protection by law against competition which defeated them in the market. The police power had never been "fully described, nor its extent plainly

[39] *Stolz* v. *Thompson*, 46 N.W. 410 (1890).   [40] *State* v. *Snow*, 47 N.W. 77.
[41] 2 N.E. 29.   [42] *The People* v. *Gilson*, 17 N.E. 343.

limited . . . but it cannot be above the constitution." The action prohibited was outside any which had previously come within the orbit of the police power; it was not a lottery, not a threat to health, not a dangerous occupation, and not a fraud. Limits to the police power might be indeterminate but the limit had been reached and passed. Few would doubt the soundness of this judgment, but it reinforces an interesting point arising from *People* v. *Marx*. The principle that a court must allow a legislature to make its own mistakes prevented judges from considering the wisdom of a law, and drove those who wished to challenge the reasonableness of a statute to base their case on constitutional limitations. The decisions based on "freedoms" which the fourteenth amendment or the state constitution was believed to guarantee were to have unhappy consequences in later cases concerning labor laws which a majority believed to be reasonable.

There were a number of cases in which laws were invalidated as "local" or "special." Most of these were of minor importance and concerned the kind of law – granting privileges or immunities to groups of localities – that the conventional limitations were intended to prevent. A few cases had wider implications for legislative attempts to deal with abuses. A Pennsylvania act made it illegal to establish a cemetery within one mile of a city of the first class on ground that drained into a stream supplying it with water. This seemed reasonable, but examination proved that it could apply only to a strip of land outside Philadelphia and was aimed at the operations of one cemetery company. "It would be difficult," said the state Supreme Court, "to imagine a better example of a law both local and special than this."[43] It would however be equally difficult to see any ground on which the court could have objected to a law empowering a board of health to declare any cemetery which drained into a stream supplying drinking water to be a "nuisance." In effect the legislature was condemned for exercising too little power, not too much. What was required was a reasonable sanitary code, not niggling laws dealing with isolated instances.

Special privileges were regarded with justifiable suspicion by the courts. In 1896 in Indiana law was voided because it authorized the establishment of drainage districts on a petition from a majority of landowners and gave them authority to make binding orders with the consent of two-thirds and to assess for taxes those who had not consented.[44] Again precedent would have favored direct action by the State or by one of its agencies, but not the delegation of judicial, legislative, and executive power to a private body. In

---

[43] *City of Philadelphia* v. *Westminster Cemetery Co.* (1894), 29 At. 349.
[44] *Gifford Drainage District* v. *Shroer*, 44 N.E. 636.

Illinois in 1896 an act prohibiting barbers from working on Sundays was voided. The state constitution forbade employment on Sundays which disturbed the peace or good order of society, but cutting hair, said the state Supreme Court, did neither.[45] Some observations on this comparatively trivial case are worth recording as they show the Illinois court reaching out for general principles by which legislative acts could be judged, and become significant when set beside the labor law cases decided at the same period by the same court and discussed below.

What is understood by the term "due process of law" is not an open question. "Due process of law" is synonymous with "law of the land" and "law of the land" is general public law, binding upon all the members of the community, under all circumstances; and not partial or private laws, affecting the rights of private individuals or classes of individuals.

A New Jersey decision voided a law which allowed the Hatters' Union to affix a distinctive label to products made with union labor and made its imitation or improper use a misdemeanor.[46] This, said the court, was a privilege created by law, and would be constitutional only if available to all "whose conditions and acts render such legislation equally necessary or appropriate to them as a class." The act under review conferred a privilege from which non-members of the union were deliberately excluded; it was "class legislation," denied equal protection, and was therefore contrary to the fourteenth amendment. The decision could not have taken this line if no penalties had been attached to improper use of the labels, since the right to give a truthful description of a product could not be impaired.

The judicial limitations on the police power which have been so far considered can be justified on many grounds. Given the incoherence of much legislation and the dubious influence of lobbies it was salutary to have courts ready to scrutinize laws to ensure that their ostensible purpose was also their real one, that supposed benefits for all were not designed to confer privileges upon a few, or that a reasonable concern for health or fair trading was not pushed to the point at which harmless activities were forbidden. The laws rejected on these principles were few compared with the great number that were upheld as proper uses of the police power. Nor should one condemn the judges for seeking some general and uniform limits to legislative authority, even if this meant reading into the fourteenth amendment more than its original promoters had intended.

The argument that from 1890 onwards the state courts were massing

---

[45] *Eden* v. *the People*, 43 N.E. 1108.   [46] *Schmalz* v. *Wooley*, 39 At. 539.

their forces against the police power and embarking upon a campaign of increasing restraint is untenable. The truth is that by this time the judicial interpretation of the police power was so broad and clear in its essentials that it was pointless for individuals to test it once again; and if they chose to do so definitive judgments would be given in the lower courts. *Barbier* v. *Connolly*, reinforced by numerous state decisions, stood firmly in the way of any attempt to stem the tide of legislation whenever laws were firmly anchored to the protection of health, safety, and morals or even, more vaguely, to promotion of the general welfare. Thus fewer cases reached the higher courts in which police-power laws were challenged and upheld; the only actions worth pursuing were those in which the laws departed significantly from the sanctioned form, and when attempts were made they might fail. In *The Rector of Trinity Church* the judgment not only rejected the plea but also made it extremely difficult for any owner of city property to contest future regulations made by a Board of Health. The record of cases can thus give an erroneous impression: the few challenges to the police powers are seen out of context because they cannot be weighed against the large number of occasions in which precedents prevented legal proceedings against state laws.

It follows from this analysis that the only cases likely to reach the higher courts were those which presented for decision some issue not already settled. These were few; but unfortunately those that attracted most publicity were decided on dubious grounds and affected the duties of employers, the rights of labor, and attempts to regulate the hours and conditions of work. These cases should be set in perspective. By 1890 there were a great many state laws prohibiting or regulating child labor, providing for safety and health in places of work, laying down conditions for dangerous trades, and providing for inspection to enforce the law. In some instances enforcement might be lax, but everywhere the principle was accepted even though the need might be contested. State courts had, again and again, accepted not only laws that extended old powers but also others which adopted novel remedies for new problems. Considerable advances had been made in modifying old laws of master and servant in favor of new principles of employer liability. Several states had officially sponsored schemes for voluntary arbitration in labor disputes. Bureaus of Labor Statistics existed in many states with full power to investigate and report upon all questions affecting the lives and work of wage earners. It can be seen that judges hostile to "class legislation" were trying to stem a tide, not stamping out the first feeble breaches of the defenses of laissez faire.

Moreover the debatable decisions came from three states, and those most likely to be condemned by modern opinion from two of them. Nevertheless these cases have commanded so much attention that examination of their character and influence is necessary.

The story begins in 1885 with the much-cited New York case *In re Jacobs*.[47] The law in dispute prohibited manufacture of cigars in tenement houses in cities with a population of over 500,000 (in effect in Brooklyn and New York city). A tenement was defined as a house containing three or more families and the prohibition applied when living quarters and workshops were on the same floor. Mr Justice Earl said that it could not be justified as a health measure, did not protect the residents of tenements in any way, and prohibited an occupation in one place that was legal in another: "Under the mere guise of police regulations, personal rights and private property cannot be arbitrarily invaded." Nor was this a case in which legislative discretion should be respected, for if the State could prohibit one lawful trade it could prohibit all. The effect of this decision was that if a law regulated the conditions of work it was incumbent upon the State to prove that it was genuinely determined by needs of health or safety.

A frequent grievance, particularly in mines and isolated factories, was payment in vouchers redeemable only at company stores and the habit of holding up payments for weeks or even months with credit available only at the same store. Pennsylvania tried to remedy this by a law making it mandatory to pay regularly in lawful money, but this was voided in *Godcharles and others* v. *Wigeman* (1886).[48] Speaking for the state Supreme Court Mr Justice Gordon branded parts of this well-intentioned law as "utterly unconstitutional and void." It attempted "to do what in this country cannot be done" – to prevent people from entering freely into contracts. It infringed the rights of employers and employees, and was "an insulting attempt to put the laborer under a legislative tutelage."

The reasoning in *Godcharles* was not universally accepted. In Indiana a law requiring payment of miners at least once in two weeks and always in legal currency was upheld.[49] In the case before the court a miner sued for wages in cash despite the fact that he had made a written contract to take payment in goods. Judge Elliott said that either the law or the contract must be void and, as to the former:

---

[47] 98 N.Y. 98 (also in 50 *American Reports*).　　[48] 6 At. 354.
[49] *Hancock et al.* v. *Yaden* (1890), 23 N.E. 253.

We cannot conceive a case in which the assertion of the legislative power to regulate contracts has a sounder foundation than it has in this instance . . . The regulation consists in prohibiting men from contracting in advance to accept payment, in something other than the lawful money of the country, for wages they may earn in the future.

It was, he said, a vital national interest to protect money, which set the standard of value, and the law should be equated with others giving weights and measures universal validity. If the act benefited laborers, this was no ground for contesting its validity.

The total rejection of the Pennsylvania doctrine must have been deliberate, but in 1893, in *Braceville Coal Co.* v. *the People*, Illinois supported the earlier decision by voiding the law which required weekly payments and forbade contracts to accept payments at other times.[50] It is unfortunate that no such case reached the Supreme Court, where it seems likely that a majority would have preferred the Indiana rule and refused its *imprimatur* to the doctrine of free contract as an inalienable right which could not be regulated even when one party clearly lacked freedom of choice.

In 1895 the Pennsylvania court struck another blow for freedom when it considered a law requiring mineowners to employ foremen who had been certified as competent by the Secretary of State.[51] There were plenty of precedents for requiring evidence of proficiency in trades or professions on which the lives of others depended, but for the Pennsylvania court it was more important to establish the principle that "no man should be required to answer for the acts and engagements of strangers over whom he has no control." It also deplored "the tendency towards class legislation for the protection of particular sorts of labor." Its statement that several recent statutes "could not be sustained under the provision of the bill of rights" was virtually an invitation to employers to test all labor, mine, or factory laws and ensure that they reached the state Supreme Court.

The fame or notoriety of the Illinois Supreme Court depended upon its efforts to erect constitutional barriers to all such legislation. In *Frorer* v. *the People* (1892) it struck down an act which made it a punishable offense for anyone owning or operating a mine or factory to keep a store or otherwise furnish supplies to his employees.[52] The act was perhaps badly drafted, and might have fallen on technical grounds, but the Illinois court seized this

---

[50]   35 N.E. 62. Also *Ramsey* v. *the People* (1892), 32 N.E. 364, in which the same court voided a law regulating the method of weighing coal when weight was the basis for calculating wages.
[51]   *Durkin* v. *Kingston Coal Co.*, 33 At. 237.   [52]   31 N.E. 395.

opportunity to denounce "class legislation." Keeping a store had nothing to do with health or safety. The law prohibited one class of men from doing something which was lawful for all others. The ability to supply employees had been a bargaining counter for employers, and, if one party to a contract was restrained while the other was not, it followed that he was deprived of liberty and control over his own property. This curious reasoning was made more curious still when property was interpreted to mean not only possession of physical things but also "the right of dominion, possession, and power of disposition which may be acquired over it." In other words an employer was entitled to use every advantage which wealth and control over the livelihood of employees gave to him, and any legislative attempts to redress the balance deprived him of rights guaranteed by the constitution.

The heights of Illinois judicial logic were scaled in *Ritchie* v. *the People* (1895), when a law forbidding the employment of women in factories or workshops for more than eight hours a day or forty-eight hours a week was invalidated.[53] Speaking for the court Mr Justice Magruder said that it imposed a "purely arbitrary restriction upon the fundamental rights of the citizen to control his or her own time and faculties." There was no ground for treating women as though they were less capable than men of making contracts.

It is ironic that these cases often included eloquent rhetoric about the rights of labor and of women. In *Godcharles* the Pennsylvania court found an act which ostensibly protected the laborer was "not only degrading to his manhood, but subversive of his rights as a citizen of the United States." In the *Braceville* case the Illinois court said that labor was the primary foundation of all wealth, and that the property of every man in his own labor was the common heritage of free people. Judgment on the *Ritchie* case included a long discourse on the status of women, their progress toward equal rights, and their emancipation from subordination as a hallmark of civilized society.

The Illinois cases must have been in the mind of Associate Justice Billings Brown when he delivered the judgment of the United States Supreme Court in 1893 on *Holden* v. *Hardy*.[54] At issue was a Utah statute limiting the

[53] 40 N.E. 454.
[54] 169 U.S. 366. Justice Billings Brown has left little impact upon history apart from his opinion in this case. Like many other judges he had been an attorney for large corporations, and was thought to be somewhat conservative. It may not be too great a stretch of imagination to suspect the influence of Mr Justice Harlan, a consistent upholder of the police power when used in defense of working people or ethnic minorities, on Brown's opinion.

hours of work in mines, smelters, and ore refineries to eight hours. It was challenged as an infringement of the fourteenth amendment, and employed arguments similar to those which had prevailed in *Ritchie* v. *the People*. Justice Brown began by recalling several cases in which appeals to the fourteenth amendment had failed to convince the court. He went on to argue that while fundamental principles must remain unchanged, law must "adapt itself to new conditions of society, and particularly to the new relations between employers and employees, as they arise." The Constitution of the United States did not "deprive the States of the power to so amend their laws as to make them conform to the wishes of citizens as they may deem best for the public welfare." The laws of the states had increased with their responsibilities, and the judgment mentioned a wide range of examples – quarantine, insane asylums, public hospitals, measures to counter disease, and limitations on the hours of work of women and children – which made the Utah law in no way exceptional. It did not attempt to control hours worked by all, but only by those in admittedly dangerous and unhealthy occupations; the Utah legislature had decided that limitation was an appropriate way of mitigating their ill effects; there were reasonable grounds for accepting this view, and its decision could not be "reviewed by federal courts."

As if this were not enough Mr Justice Brown went on to attack the doctrine of free contract: "The proprietors lay down the rules and the laborers are practically constrained to obey them. In such cases self-interest is often an unsafe guide, and the legislature may promptly interpose its authority." If this did not dispose of the argument that free contract was guaranteed by the Constitution, it did mean that it could be countered by evidence of health threatened or of men constrained to enter into contracts against their own best interests. Moreover the majority of seven votes to two was convincing.

In its final report, issued in 1902, the Industrial Commission commented on the implications of *Holden* v. *Hardy*:

This decision of the Supreme Court of the United States makes it plain that State legislatures are competent, so far as the Constitution of the United States goes, to regulate the hours of labor in any occupation, or for any class of employees, where it can be shown that the occupation is injurious to health, and that the proposed reduction of hours is not excessive or unreasonable.[55]

[55] *Industrial Commission*, XIX, 786. There was one Colorado case in which a law restricting hours worked in mines was voided on the ground that it conflicted with the *state* constitution. *Ritchie* v. *the People* had also relied on the State constitution, not the fourteenth amendment.

This may have been a slight overstatement, but only prejudice, or perhaps ignorance, has deprived *Holden* v. *Hardy* of a place in constitutional history on a par with *Munn* v. *Illinois*.

In 1913 Charles Warren, reacting against Progressive attacks on the Supreme Court, pointed out that it had given over 560 decisions involving the fourteenth amendment, and invalidated state statutes concerning economic or social questions in only two of them (of which one was of minor importance). Every state labor statute, with one exception, had been upheld; likewise every law relating to pure food, liquor, licensing, and safety. In twenty-five years only thirty-four state laws had been invalidated, and of them twenty were tax cases voided largely on technical grounds:

The actual record of the Court . . . shows how little chance a litigant has of inducing the Court to restrict the police power of a State or to overthrow State laws under the "due process" clause; in other words it shows the Court to be a bulwark to the State police power, not a destroyer.[56]

On Warren's count the Supreme Court had dealt with 158 cases involving the obligations of contract, found 137 state statutes constitutional and only 27 unconstitutional, of which 16 were concerned with the rights of creditors and debtors and only 11 with social and economic questions. Of course the small number of laws invalidated might be offset if they were of critical importance, but the record gave Warren the best of the argument with progressive critics of the court and does not support the view that under pressure from the state courts the Supreme Court gradually incorporated into the Constitution the doctrine that freedom of contract was a fundamental right.[57] *Holden* v. *Hardy* had effectively disposed of the argument that contract could be free when one party held all the cards.

The counterargument depends upon *Lochner* v. *New York* decided by a majority of five to four in 1905.[58] It was common knowledge that one justice changed his vote at the last moment. If he had stuck to his original

---

[56] Charles Warren, "The Progressivism of the United States Supreme Court," and "A Bulwark to the Police Power – the United States Supreme Court," *Columbia Law Review*, 13 (1915), 244–313, 667–95. The remark by Louis Filler that "Warren was an undisguised conservative and wished to discount libertarian tendencies on the Court" is misleading. It occurs in his essay on John M. Harlan in Leon Friedman and Fred L. Israel (eds.), *The Justices of the United States Supreme Court, 1789–1969*, 5 vols (New York, 1969), II, 1,293.

[57] This view is advanced in Clyde E. Jacobs, *Law Writers and the Courts: the Influence of Thomas M. Cooley, Christopher G. Tiedman, and John F. Dillon upon American Constitutional Law* (Berkeley, Calif., 1954). This work has many other merits but is mistaken in this argument.

[58] 198 U.S. 45. As Warren pointed out, *Lochner* v. *New York* is normally the *only* case cited to demonstrate the "conservatism" of the Supreme Court during the Progressive period.

opinion the case would have been seen as the logical consequence of *Holden* v. *Hardy* and another milestone on the interventionist road. Justice Harlan's dissent would have been the opinion of the court and Justice Peckham's opinion a dissent. Justice Holmes would have been content with silent concurrence in a majority of five to four; and it was the late change that brought forth his brief but celebrated dissent. Holmes' observation that the fourteenth amendment did not enact Herbert Spencer's *Social Statics* has been taken as a rejection of prevalent doctrine, but it came after a short but effective summary of state restriction upon individual freedom. The maxim that an individual could do what he liked so long as he did not interfere with the liberty of others was, he said, refuted every time a man submitted to school laws or paid taxes regardless of whether he approved of the way in which they were spent. The famous phrase repudiating *Social Statics* was intended to describe existing practice.

The law limited the hours worked in bakeries to ten a day or sixty a week. It differed from *Holden* v. *Hardy* in that the State brought no evidence to show that health was imperilled by longer hours or that the public might suffer. Nevertheless the act had been upheld by the New York Supreme Court as a legitimate use of the police power, and Peckham may have derived satisfaction from overruling his former colleagues, with whom he had differed on so many occasions. He began with a reference to the recognition by the court of "the exercise of the police powers of the States in many cases which might fairly be considered as border ones." *Holden* v. *Hardy* differed in one important respect because the Utah law had provided for emergencies in which the law would not apply, thus permitting overtime by agreement, while the New York statute allowed no discretionary power. This seems to be a weak distinction, but the heart of his decision came in the assertion that there must be some limit to the police power, otherwise state legislatures would have absolute authority and need assert only that an act had some relation to health, safety, or morals in order to justify it: "The claim of the police power would be a mere pretext – become another and delusive name for the supreme sovereignty of the State to be exercised free from constitutional restraint."

In *Holden* v. *Hardy* Justice Billings Brown had left open one line of attack upon exercise of the police power, when he said that in each case the question was whether the legislature had exercised "reasonable discretion" or whether its action amounted to "unjust discrimination, or the oppression, or spoliation of a particular class." This looked back to *Yick Wo*, but it also meant that a court could decide whether any act which came before it was reasonable. Peckham took advantage of this to ignore the grounds on which New York had acted: the conditions of bakeries, the nature of the employment, and the expected consequences of limiting hours. He asserted that it was not "within any fair meaning of the term a health law" but "an illegal interference with the rights of individuals, both employers and employees, to make contracts regarding labor."

The argument that the whole community had an interest in the health of all its members, adopted in *Holden* v. *Hardy*, was brushed aside, and the conditions of work in any occupation were treated as though they were of interest only to the two principal parties. In other cases the court had adopted the view that, if the effects upon the public were not clear, the decision of a legislature that they were harmful must be respected. As Harlan said in his dissent, the burden of proof lay upon those who asserted that a statute was unconstitutional; it was no business of the judges to introduce theoretical reasons of their own.

The majority decision in *Lochner* v. *New York* was not a logical culmination of "conservative" trends in judicial opinion, but a temporary departure from lines that had been charted for a quarter century. Moreover it curbed the power of the states in social legislation at one point alone: the police power could not be used to limit the hours worked by adult males when there was no clear proof that health or safety were adversely affected. It did not cut down the very wide range of other activities regulated by the states.

Even in the field of labor law the effect of *Lochner* v. *New York* was limited. In *Muller* v. *Oregon*, decided in 1908, a ten-hour law for women in laundries, mechanical establishments, and factories was upheld; so far as the United States Supreme Court was concerned, this laid forever the ghost of *Ritchie* v. *the People of Illinois*.[59] Justice Brewer, nephew of Field and supporter of Peckham, delivered the opinion of the court. There was no dissent. Louis Brandeis, for the State, had submitted voluminous evidence about the effect of long hours and cited many precedents for limiting hours worked by women. This enabled Brewer to distinguish the case from *Lochner* v. *New York*, and declare that the limitations placed upon the freedom of a woman to contract were "not imposed solely for her benefit, but also largely for the benefit of all." Finally in 1917 in *Bunting* v. *Oregon* a majority effectively overruled *Lochner* by accepting the argument that a

[59] 208 U.S. 412.

ten-hour rule for all employees in factories was a reasonable exercise of the police power.[60]

This review of opinion in state and federal courts suggests that far too much prominence has been given to the few cases in which state statutes were invalidated, and far too little to the widening stream of judicial approval for more and more advances in the regulation of social and economic life. The extent of the new responsibilities which evolved will be reviewed in the following chapters, and here it is necessary to state only some general conclusions.

With few and unimportant exceptions, the enormous development in public health legislation encountered no judicial obstacles. The difficulties experienced in railroad regulation arose largely from the division of responsibility between states and nation. The courts insisted that railroad companies should retain the right of appeal against the findings of commissioners, but they did not object to state laws throwing the burden of proof upon those who complained and preventing delays in the implementation of rates fixed by commissions. Judges had clung to the right to decide what was reasonable when a rate was challenged, but the enormous cost and unwelcome publicity had perhaps stemmed a rush by companies to the courts. Laws governing safety on railroads gave rise to an enormous amount of litigation, but what was usually at issue was conflict of evidence and interpretation of the law; the laws themselves were seldom if ever challenged. The same can be said of laws governing safety in mines and factories, sanitary laws, liquor laws, and laws requiring various trades or professions to be licensed.

Public responsibility therefore presents a record of continuous growth, occasionally but not permanently curbed by judicial decision. Taking a broad view one finds the courts were more fertile in finding reasons for facilitating than for checking this growth. Comparing 1900 with 1870, one

[60]   243 U.S. 426. In 1910, in a second case involving the Ritchie company (*Ritchie & Co.* v. *Wayman*), the Supreme Court of Illinois upheld a law limiting the hours worked by women in "any mechanical establishment, factory or laundry" to ten in any period of twenty-four hours. Subsequent legislation extended the scope of the act, and its additional provisions were upheld by the courts. For the significance of these decisions and the arguments employed see Earl R. Beckner, *A History of Labor Legislation in Illinois* (Chicago, Ill., 1929), Chapter 9, *passim*. The law was challenged as a breach of the Illinois constitution of 1870, which provided that "no person shall be deprived of life, liberty or property without due process of law," and as special or class legislation. Louis Brandeis prepared a 600-page brief covering the history of legislation restricting the hours of work of women, the medical effects of excessive hours, and the economic and social benefits of restriction.

finds that in every field the states did more, spent more, and employed far more people. Judicial attempts to introduce a universal law of free contract into labor relations were short-lived exceptions, not the rule. The general conclusion is that where the political will existed the legal way could be found.

4

THE CHARITIES OF THE STATE

Public responsibility for the afflicted without means of support had deep roots in English and American traditions, but normally as the last resort after personal savings, family support, and private charity had been exhausted. Modern times have seen a shift of responsibility from the community to the center, and from private to state institutions. In this transition the boards of state charities, which came into existence in so many states, played a crucial part.[1]

The Civil War left its legacy of domestic misery among widows, orphans, and maimed veterans, and almost before this problem had receded Americans became aware of a rising tide of pauperism. A pauper was a person wholly dependent upon public support; he or she might have reached this condition because of old age, chronic illness, feeble-mindedness, or physical incapacity. Or the cause might be drunkenness, incurable idleness, or a record of crime which made the pauper unemployable. Finally there might be temporary paupers – persons thrown out of work by slack trade or by changes in technology – who might be expected to return soon to independence. Soon after 1870, and with increasing frequency during the depression of 1873, Americans became aware of large numbers of paupers who fitted readily into none of these categories. They were able-bodied, willing to work, but could find no employment.

Whatever the causes of pauperism, nineteenth-century Americans were convinced that it was a monstrous evil that would debilitate society if allowed to grow unchecked. "Pauperism," said the Illinois Board of Public Charities in 1877, "is an evil too great, too widespread in its extent, too far

---

[1] Various titles were used: e.g., Board of State Charities, Board of Public Charities, Board of Charity and Correction, Board of Charitable and Reformatory Institutions, and State Board of Charities. For convenience the most common designation – "Board of State Charities" – will be used except in references to the board of a particular state.

reaching in its consequences, too minute in its ramifications, to be left to the haphazard of individual caprice."[2] Relief was not merely humanitarian, for the mass of paupers supplied recruits for what were coming to be known as "the dangerous classes" – thieves, prostitutes, tramps, and violent criminals.

How far should the state go in helping those who could not help themselves? The young who were blind, deaf, or mute deserved education. Treatment for the insane and feeble-minded should measure up to standards set by humane reformers in this difficult field. Should steps be taken to arrest drunkenness and check the spread of venereal disease (both, by general consent, accepted as major causes of pauperism)? What of those who were desperately poor, and trembling on the brink of pauperism? Proper treatment in reformatories might ensure that young delinquents became good citizens. Above all conscience might be aroused by the plight of abandoned or neglected children, and of those forced into early association with elders of vicious habits. "Child saving" was a noble and necessary task that the State must assist if it did not control.

These problems might have been easier to solve if local institutions had been efficiently and humanely conducted. Yet the jails, poorhouses, and infirmaries of counties and cities were wretched places, and investigation confirmed the worst suspicions. "In our jail system," said the Ohio Board of State Charities in 1868, "lingers more barbarism than in all our other state institutions together." Two years later the same Board declared that "our jails and station houses . . . have become the *speediest* . . . as they are the *surest* route to ruin in our civilization." State inspection was essential if these institutions were to improve, and the Ohio board added that it was the duty of the State "to see that no prisoner is made morally worse." Reports on poorhouses gave plenty of reasons for the horror with which they were regarded by the destitute poor, and even a child, consigned to a poorhouse, might carry the stigma to the end of his days.[3]

So far from looking to local institutions to carry increased responsibilities, anyone who looked into their condition added his voice to the demand for state inspection, supervision, and reform – for regulation where there was hope of improvement or for replacement by state

---

[2] Illinois B. of P. Ch., 4th Annual R. (1877), 202. The author of the report was the Reverend F. H. Wines, of whom more anon.
[3] Ohio B. of St. Ch., 2nd Annual R. (1868), 10 (the probable author was the Reverend A. G. Byers, who will also deserve further notice); 2nd R. (New Series) (1878), 88; Illinois B. of St. Ch., 4th R. (1877), 119; Ohio B. of St. Ch., 4th R. (1879), 5.

institutions when this was improbable. The inadequacy of local government therefore provided arguments for centralization, and once some responsibilities of the state were recognized others emerged. Were the causes of pauperism to be sought primarily in hereditary or in environmental factors; if the former, what could be done to prevent others from acquiring the defects of character that might be transmitted to their descendants; if the latter, was it the duty of the state to guard against poor housing, bad sanitation, and unhealthy conditions? These were large problems that could be tackled only by investigation backed by the authority of the State.

The nineteenth-century faith in scientific investigation gave hope that, once inquiries had been undertaken systematically, the answers would be found. "One of the most marked instances of the scientific spirit in this age is the increased control of reason over the management of charities," declared *The Nation* editorially in 1869. There was springing up "a science of charity."[4] In 1873 the Illinois Board of State Charities was confident that "the operation of causes of misfortune is, upon any extended scale of operation, uniform and constant." It went on to lay down the principle that "the laws which govern the unfolding of our social life are as immutable as the laws which determine the growth of a plant or of an animal or which control the movement of the stars and the succession of the seasons."[5] In 1884 Josephine Shaw Lowell, with many years of experience in New York, could declare that "the task of dealing with the poor and degraded has become science."[6] Thus the movement for state supervision of charities, though inspired primarily by humanitarian concern for the weak, was sustained by a belief that proper investigation and scientific analysis could lead to efficient administration, and thus benefit the whole society.

The case for state action might be clear to those who believed in a science of society, but was less apparent to state legislators. Paupers, delinquents, criminals, and children had no votes; nor could legislation on their behalf yield partisan advantage. Indeed the threat to set professional standards for the administration of local institutions might cut into the political patronage upon which the parties relied. The reports of the state boards repeat, year after year, complaints that recommendations have been ignored or lost amid the pressure of other business, or that they have succumbed to hostile attack. No complaint was more frequent than lack of money to do the job, as legislators resorted to the familiar expedient of enacting a law but refusing the money to make it effective. These difficulties

4 *The Nation*, June 10, 1869.   5 Illinois B. of St. Ch., 2nd R. (1873), 11.
6 Josephine Shaw Lowell, *Public Relief and Private Charity* (New York, 1884), Preface.

produced compensating advantages – at least for the social historian – as the various boards sought to win support by reporting their findings with an eye to the public. Shocking conditions were often described in language calculated to shock. Only by touching the conscience and giving the newspapers startling revelations could they hope to break through ignorance, apathy, and petty obstruction at the Capitol. In addition it was usually essential to win support from the Governor, who was more likely to be moved by the exposure of scandal than by scientific abstractions. All this makes the reports of the boards of state charities lively reading, especially in the early days when they were still struggling for recognition and financial support.

When boards were first set up, they seldom had executive authority. Their function, as defined by the New York board in 1872, was to be "the moral eye of the State and its adviser in relation to the management of all its eleemosynary institutions." Most boards advanced little beyond this point, though some acquired responsibility for the management of selected institutions. Others could issue orders for the movement of paupers or the insane from one institution to another, and if a state ordered the removal of children from poorhouses the state board might be the enforcement agency.[7] A board entrusted with unusually wide powers was that of Wisconsin in 1878. Its aim was "to secure the just, humane, and economical administration of public charity and correction," and to this end it was "to regulate and supervise" all institutions supported or aided by the State, to investigate poorhouses, and to report on the causes of the increase or diminution of pauperism. Within this broadly defined framework it could "make . . . bylaws, rules, and regulations not incompatible with the law."[8] Most boards had more limited powers, and some preferred to keep the tasks of investigation and enforcement entirely separate. Whatever the limits of their power, the boards of state charities were pioneers in a new field of state responsibility. For the first time official bodies, clothed with authority from the sovereign legislature, were required to look into the dark places of American society.

The first Board of State Charities was that of Massachusetts established in

[7] New York B. of P. Ch., 5th R. (1872), 2. Frederick J. Bruno sees a sharp difference between the older boards and the boards of control set up in western states (*Trends in Social Work 1784–1956* (New York, 1957), 38–9). He writes: "In fact the authors of the state boards of charities were seeking something quite different from what was desired by the initiators of boards of control." I find some difference in emphasis between eastern and western boards but not a marked distinction.

[8] Wisconsin St. B. of Ch., 8th R. (1878): "The Revised Law of 1878."

1863. The chairman was Samuel Gridley Howe, whose achievements ranged from an early and romantic involvement in the struggle for Greek independence to notable pioneer work in educating the blind. The secretary was Franklin Benjamin Sanborn, friend of Emerson and former abolitionist, whose work as secretary of the American Social Science Association has already been described. For many years, as secretary and later as chairman, Sanborn would dominate the board. The composition of the Massachusetts board provided a model that was widely imitated. It had five unpaid members who met at regular intervals, were responsible for general policy, and might conduct individual investigations and visitations. The secretary and a general administrator were salaried officials. The Massachusetts law was unusual in giving the governor rather than the board the right to appoint the secretary, who was *ex officio* a member; he was thus a servant of the board but entitled to vote upon his own instructions.

The Massachusetts Board had authority to investigate and supervise "the whole system of the public charitable and correctional institutions" and to recommend changes in the law. In practice the board was reluctant to employ its latent authority, and, in its second report, said that "government should seek to call forth and increase the charitable feelings of the people, but should not assume their duties or actions without strong necessity." It might seek publicity but leave changes and their implementation to others. It was reluctant to criticize private trustees or to encroach upon city, township, or county authorities.[9] Relief of the afflicted was "the Christian duty of individuals," and an official body was ill-advised to assume responsibility. To do so would "divorce love from duty." It was enough to point out what ought to be done, and private charity would respond so that "the poor should not suffer." This emphasis upon the need to communicate with an enlightened and humane public continued for several years. In 1867 "the causes of social evils" were set forth in the report "not simply for consideration of the legislature, but for discussion and application by the people." Even where control could be exercised, the board aimed at "throwing off from the State the charge and responsibility for as many establishments as could be properly assumed by municipalities, societies, and individuals."[10]

This optimistic estimate of what would be done by private initiative was gradually eroded, while public regulation picked up momentum. In 1868

---

9 Massachusetts B. of St. Ch., 2nd R. (1866), xi. The early reports are dated in January of each year; the report for 1866 therefore refers to work of the board in 1865.

10 *Idem*, 5th R. (1869), xx–xxi; 3rd R. (1867), xxvi; 7th R. (1871), xxiii.

Sanborn included "unjust and unwise laws, and the custom of society" among the causes of pauperism, and recommended that private charities should be required to report to the state board.[11] In 1870 a new official, the Visiting Agent, was appointed, to supervise children removed from poorhouses and placed in private homes. In the same year the board launched the first of its attacks upon county jails, recommended their transfer to the State, and asserted that "local prisons ought always to be subjected to frequent and close inspection by some general authority, which is not hampered by any local interests, and is disconnected from any local corps of officers."[12] In 1871 the board complained of insufficient funds, which hampered extension of its work. By 1874 it argued that "the vast means expended by the State for charitable and correctional purposes" could never be wisely applied "until some central board shall be clothed with power to co-ordinate the existing forces, and make them work harmoniously to a common end." The board as constituted had insufficient power, and what it had was "more in name and appearance than in fact." Thus within a decade the board had moved from admonition to a demand for authority to correct evils.[13]

The result was seen in new officials and new responsibilities. A commissioner of prisons was appointed in 1871. A second visiting agent – for the sick – followed, and in 1875 it was claimed that the work of the two agents was greater than that of the whole board in earlier years.[14] Several laws had resulted from the board's recommendations, and when the legislature had failed to act the board had discreetly used its regulatory powers to initiate change. The first report of the commissioner of prisons had found the Boston lock-up "a wretched place and a disgrace to the State and county"; another local prison was even worse – "a disgrace to civilization." In 1873 the board was clear that the whole prison system needed thorough reformation, but change was thwarted by local interests and the State must act.[15]

Another move by the Massachusetts Board of State Charities brought it into the field of environmental improvement. By 1878 it had appointed a sanitary committee to investigate sewerage, pure air, water, and food. Nevertheless the board wished to go further and complained that, though charged with the supervision of public institutions, it could not influence

[11] *Idem*, 4th R. (1868), 132, 144.   [12] *Idem*, 7th R. (1870), 81, 101–2.
[13] *Idem*, 8th R. (1871), xxii; 10th R. (1873), xxxv.
[14] *Idem*, 11th R. (1875), xx–xxv.
[15] *Idem*, 9th R. (1872), 141; 10th R. (1873), 89–90.

appropriations, appoint officials, or control new buildings.[16] As a compromise between these demands on the one hand and opposition to increased expenditure on the other the legislature amalgamated the boards of state charities and public health, and gave the new board stronger regulatory powers. The union was happier for charities than for public health and many of the formal meetings were monopolized by detailed consideration of complaints, proposals, and orders relating to public institutions. By 1885 the State was spending over $550,000 annually on state charities and reformations, and much detailed examination of expenditure and accounts was necessary.[17]

The pressure of routine business assumed by the joint board, and returned to state charities after the two separated once more in 1886, excluded the more speculative inquiries of earlier years. The board had found an accepted place as an influential state agency, but lost the eager optimism of early years which assumed that evils had only to be identified for public-spirited citizenry to find a remedy. An epoch came to an end in 1888 when Sanborn was dismissed from the post he then held as Inspector of Charities. The specific cause of his dismissal was that he had experimented, without authorization, in the removal of harmless insane from asylums. The underlying reason was that the board was concerned with the efficient working of a large administrative agency, and did not welcome officials who complicated matters by independent innovation.[18] The transition from a weak but enthusiastic to an accepted, well-recognized, but less adventurous agency was to be familiar in the history of the boards of state charities, though few rivalled that of a Massachusetts in authority.

The Pennsylvania Board of Public Charities began work in 1870. Private charities had proliferated in the state, but state institutions were poorly organized and a strong tradition of local autonomy resisted the enlargement of state power. The board's first investigatory efforts yielded a poor harvest, as few replies were received, and many that were displayed "such ignorance of the subject and such want of appreciation of all recorded information" that the inevitable conclusion was that city and county

[16] *Idem*, 14th R. (1878), xxi; 15th R. (1879), x.
[17] The minutes of the first Board of Health, Lunacy, and Charity are in the Massachusetts State Archives.
[18] Board of Lunacy and Charity Minutes, Oct. 6, 1888, Massachusetts State Archives, Boston. Sanborn questioned the legality of his dismissal. He wrote to F. W. Bird that he was not making frequent visits to his office so that his clerks would not be embarrassed, but continued to visit establishments and issue orders (Oct. 27, 1888, Bird Papers, Houghton Library, Harvard University).

officials were either incompetent or lacking interest in their work. The board's first request was for a law to make it mandatory to comply with authorized requests for information.[19]

Between 1871 and 1875 the board pressed, with little success, for laws on compulsory education, special schools for "friendless and destitute children," a constitutional amendment that would enable the State to aid private charities, and a complete reform of the prison system. It condemned the system of solitary confinement (which earlier generations had praised as the State's distinctive contribution to penal reform), and preferred work in groups, reform by "moral influences instead of physical force," and prison officers trained for the job. It will be observed that the Pennsylvania board was valiantly trying to seek out the root causes of pauperism in poorly run institutions and a defective prison system that produced unemployable people who, in turn, sought relief from the State. In 1875 its criticism was both penetrating and comprehensive: "The effects of ignorance, vice and extravagance, the necessary consequences of errors in our social life and system, are written in the records of shame and crime, from the smallest larceny to the highest grade of offences." The evidence for appalling conditions could not be ignored, and the board concluded that a very heavy responsibility was "resting upon the Commonwealth."[20]

The Pennsylvania Board was not merely complaining from the side lines. The first president, George L. Harrison "sacrificed valuable time, anxious thought, intelligent study, personal comfort and convenience, and a degree of earnest energy that overtaxed brain and body, for the sake of those helpless classes in whose behalf the Board was organized."[21] The year 1875, in which Harrison retired, was one of great activity, with visits to institutions in all parts of the state, and though there still existed much apathy and hostility there was also "an increasing appreciation of the work of the Board and a greater earnestness in the adoption of measures for bettering the condition of the various classes over whom the State is exercising its beneficent care." The board was also able to conclude that "the benefits arising from a State commission, invested with supervisory power over all the charitable and correctional institutions of the State, are too obvious to require explanation."[22]

Thus the Pennsylvania board acted in its early years as a pressure group

---

[19] Pennsylvania B. of P. Ch., 2nd Ann. R. (1871), xxi.

[20] *Idem*, 5th Ann. R. (1876), 9, 10: 2nd Ann. R. (1871), cv; 5th Ann. R. (1876), 10; 4th Ann. R. (1873), lxix; 3rd Ann. R. (1873), *passim*.

[21] *Idem*, 6th Ann. R. (1875), 23. [22] *Ibid.*, 17, 20.

rather than as an administrative agency. The pressure was exerted against the legislature, recalcitrant local officials, and the public. It could count upon the traditionally charitable attitudes of Quakers and other religious denominations, but had to do battle against a political leadership that was normally insensitive to all but party demands. Nevertheless, after only five years of existence, it could claim some success. If its legislative recommendations were usually ignored, investigation and publicity began to work changes at the grass roots. Though the board was severely critical of political attitudes at the top, it must also be emphasized that nothing at all could have been achieved without authority from the State to inquire, supervise, report and recommend. It was as an agency of the State that the Pennsylvania board gradually advanced from weakness to strength.

, It often happened that a state agency, in its formative period, was strongly identified with the work of one man. This was certainly true of the Ohio Board of State Charities. The Reverend A. G. Byers was secretary from its establishment in 1867 to his death in 1890. In a formal tribute the Ohio board recorded that

In every children's home, prison, and reformatory, asylum, infirmary or jail in the State, are traces of his work, and of the single-hearted, determined devotion with which he consecrated himself to the cause of the helpless, the infirm, the unfortunate or fallen. In jails, prisons, and infirmaries especially his work was prominent, and the results of it can be properly appreciated only by those who can make the comparison from their own knowledge, or from official reports, of the condition of those institutions when he began that work in 1867, with their condition now.[23]

Byers' private papers and diary enable one to judge what "single-hearted, determined devotion" meant when translated into day-to-day work.[24] On New Year's Day 1871 he visited one infirmary and found "much disorder." For a good deal of the time he was kept busy with the directors of the institution, though it had been difficult to procure their attendance; but there was time for a tour of inspection which revealed a choked night soil pipe, a frozen drain, and an "intolerable" madhouse. He preached in the evening from Luke 19.10 on "the lost classes of society and the duties of Christians concerning them." On the following day another infirmary was visited. Here the house was filthy, the superintendent made an excuse for absence, a poorly informed subordinate was sent to accompany Byers, and

---

[23] Ohio B. of St. Ch., 15th R. (New Series) (1890), 46. There was a gap of four years (1872–6) when the legislature made no appropriation for the board. This caused some confusion in numbering the reports. For convenience the reports of the new board, starting in 1876, are called "New Series."

[24] The diaries are with the Byers Papers in the Ohio Historical Society, Columbus.

the insane wing was overcrowded and full "of bad odors"; indeed there was a "sickening stench pervading the building, accounted for by need of nature; there were forty-seven children in this terrible place." A week later he recorded a day spent around the Capitol, including a visit to the state printer, an interview with a representative about jails in his county, and an arrangement with a senator to visit an asylum in Toledo. On the following day he was again at the Capitol, saw several senators and representatives, and wrote a letter about an orphanage.

A year later it seemed that all this hard work was going to be lost. On February 15, 1872 he wrote in his diary: "Closed my office – Board of State Charities repealed." His wife later added a note: "From here we have no heart or time for diaries. Period of 4 years and 2 months on his own." During this period Byers continued the visits, though without salary or official backing. For instance in September 1875 he was at an infirmary in Noble County where there were 167 children, "more pipes than would fill a smoking car," a girl of fourteen chewing tobacco, "everything filthy, and many things indecent." The matron was dead and had not been replaced, the superintendent was hard-working but incompetent, and the whole institution was "a pauper propagating establishment." In Legare County the infirmary had no cistern or well, and all water had to be carried a hundred yards, but the interior was cozy, clean, and quite comfortable. An infirmary at Wilmington also seemed to be well run, but inmates comprised an unhappy mixture of insane, feeble-minded, epileptic, and senile, as well as thirteen children. Happier times were promised in 1876 when the state board was restored, but nothing was going to be easy in the state of Ohio.

County jails were as bad as ever, containing "all the essential ingredients of degradation that can be conceived of," while suggestions for improvement, often repeated, were "generally regarded with indifference."[25] Much of the trouble stemmed however not from county administration, but from the political character of Ohio. The state was intensely partisan; it was normal for control of the Assembly to change hands almost every two years; and every change meant a purge of officials belonging to the other party, from principal officers down to the minor functionaries in the counties. Everything possible was dragged into the patronage net. Even the unpaid trustees of state institutions had become political appointments because they controlled a handful of small jobs. Infirmary directors were elected, and there was "a more or less continuous squabble for the place in the interest of local parties." Experience, training, a willingness to learn

[25] Ohio B. of St. Ch., 2nd R. (New Series) (1878), 82, 88.

were irrelevant, and following each electoral victory an "eager and importunate lobby" demanded places for their adherents.[26]

In 1880 a new act made the Board of State Charities bipartisan, with the governor a member and president ex officio. State and county officials were required to furnish the board with all information requested; the board would send for persons and papers, and take evidence on oath. Byers believed that the governor genuinely intended "to have all the institutions of the State brought under the eye of its Board," and the board certainly now possessed the power to investigate, inspect, and report on all prisons, jails, infirmaries, public hospitals, and asylums.[27] It was still unable to order changes, appoint or remove officials, shift inmates from one institution to another, or eliminate political patronage from the system.

By 1888 however the board felt justified in allowing a note of mild self-congratulation to appear in its report. No healthy child was to be found in an infirmary save under exceptional circumstances. More than one-third of the counties had provided children's homes, and there had been a decline in juvenile delinquency. Mentally defective children were properly cared for. The move to improve county jails was along "a path beset at every step with difficulty, and yet marked year by year with progress and reform"; although there were still too many filthy and poorly constructed jails, twenty-three had been built or altered to the board's specifications. Treatment of the insane had made great progress. Reformatories were less satisfactory, for there were still confined in them too many children who had committed no offense but for whom there was no suitable institution. Infirmaries were still in bad shape, and it was thought that outdoor relief was often distributed to the wrong persons for the wrong reasons.[28]

Despite these advances the board still struggled against the refusal of the legislature to provide enough money. In 1888–9 the appropriation was $2,977, out of which the secretary received a salary of $1,200 supplemented by members of the board out of their own pockets.[29] In 1890 some plain speaking was justified:

The persistently inadequate means which the legislature has hitherto appropriated to the maintenance of the work by this Board . . . force us to believe that in the heat of political struggle over questions more purely partisan than economic, administrative, or humanitarian, both the public and its executive and legislative

[26] *Idem*, 4th Report (New Series) (1877), 19–20, 70.
[27] Byers to R. Brinkerhoff, Apr. 24, 1880, Brinkerhoff Papers, Ohio Historical Society.
[28] Ohio B. of St. Ch., 13th R. (1888), 13–14. In 1881 a count had found 987 in infirmaries, along with 925 insane, 1,086 senile, 594 idiotic, and 2,361 indigent sick (6th R. (1881), 89).
[29] *Idem*, 14th R. (1887).

representation have given the grave questions and interests committed to the general care of the Board of State Charities less thought than they were or entitled to.

Since the revival of the board in 1876, sixty-one legislative recommendations had been made, of which seven had been adopted and ten partly adopted, twenty-nine awaited action, and fifteen had been dropped or incorporated into later recommendations. Once again partisan patronage was seen as the principal cause for this poor record: "Can there be no neutral ground . . . exempt from the raids and reprisals of the spoils principle?"[30] It would be a simple matter to make all posts in charitable and reformatory institutions non-political, but partisanship was so entrenched that many people regarded it as treason to suggest any modification.[31]

A governor came to the help of the board when in 1891 James F. Campbell commended the board's report in his annual message, and called for action on its recommendation.[32] In 1892 the courts of common pleas were charged with the appointment of boards of county visitors to inspect all public institutions, supervise the treatment of children, and to attend court when a child was threatened with committal to a reformatory. These boards were to be non-partisan and appointed for a fixed tenure. Thus, after twenty years of existence, the Ohio board was winning its way to acceptance as a permanent and useful part of state administration, but it still lacked executive authority to implement its proposals, and even as late as 1894 its future was still in doubt.[33] So far its history had exhibited in an extreme form the difficulty of advancing a non-political cause in an area of intense political partisanship. There is also a strong suspicion that Byers, for all his admirable qualities, was not adept at influencing the politicians who could alone grant power and appropriate money.

The Illinois Board of Public Charities was identified with the Reverend. Fred H. Wines, who was its secretary, with one short break, from 1869 to 1898. He inherited an interest in charitable and correctional work from his father, Enoch Wines, who won an international reputation as an authority on prisons and punishment. Fred Wines was a more intellectual man than

---

[30] *Idem*, 15th R. (1890), 4–5, 6–10, 15.
[31] *Idem*, 16th R. (1891), 11.
[32] Annual Message for 1891, Campbell Papers, Ohio Historical Society.
[33] The threat is inferred from a letter from ex-Governor Charles Foster to Joseph Byers (who succeeded his father as secretary) in which he paid tribute to the work of the board and added: "I would regard the abolishment of this Board as almost calamitous to the Charities of the State" (May 1894, Byers Papers, Ohio Historical Society).

Byers, and his writing shows the influence of early theological and philosophical training at Princeton. Passages from his early reports have already been cited as closely reasoned analyses of the problem of pauperism; he also wrote several pamphlets and a book entitled *Punishment and Reformation*, published in 1895. He was employed by the U.S. Census to compile reports on charities, crime, and prison. He gave considerable attention to the disagreeable task for lobbying and to the more congenial duty of preparing detailed plans for legislative committees. Much of the success of the Illinois board was the outcome of these skills, but Wines was also helped by the long Republican dominance in the state which gave continuity to administration. Ironically the only difficult period was during the governorship of John Peter Altgeld, normally hailed as a great reform governor; Wines himself was dismissed and the public institutions were subjected to a purge of Republican officials.

The Illinois board was launched in 1869 with authority to inspect all state institutions. City and county almshouses, poorhouses, and jails were specifically included. The board could take evidence on oath, and was bound to report on all requests for additional public assistance. It immediately took the initiative by asking for a law to prescribe the statistical records and returns to be made by institutions, and requested authority to prepare a general law for the regulation of state and county institutions. The statistical law was passed in 1871, and the general regulatory law in 1875.

The rationale for public responsibility was presented by Wines in his first report.[34] The questions to be asked and answered were: who could claim relief, on what grounds, and from whom? If relief were justified by whom should it be administered and by what method? The answers were more difficult than the casual observer might believe, because there was not one state of dependency but several.

In fact there is no absolute line of demarcation. The graduations are imperceptible. There are no abrupt transitions in nature . . . What constitutes the essential difference between congenital idiocy and that imbecility which is often the last stage of lunacy? Is pauperism the result of crime, or crime of pauperism?

It might follow that what was required was trained, experienced, and professional understanding to administer the charities of the State. All dependency, Wines argued, resulted from loss of individual power, but this might be caused by accidental, hereditary, circumstantial, social, or

---

[34] Illinois B. of P. Ch., 1st R. (1871), 15–24.

personal causes. By "constitutional" he meant defects or deformities that were not inherited, "circumstantial" might now be described as "environmental," while "social causes" were those resulting from the social and political system.

Despite the complexity of these issues, Wines asked for action. To do nothing would be to allow the evils to accumulate, and sentiment might be a better guide than rules based on theoretical principles. Investigation, assessment of evidence, and cautious experiment were the essential steps to progress. Yet this could not be left to voluntary action: "There must be interference on the part of the governing power." Moreover, if it was difficult to lay down precise rules for all cases, there was the overriding principle that "a good government with one hand holds the rapacious in check while with the other it elevates the weak."

In the second report of the Illinois board, Wines moved from general principles to their application. The board was a branch of the executive, the medium of communication between the governor and public institutions, and his source of confidential information on topics connected with them. It had power delegated by the legislature to report on matters that it would be impractical for a normal legislative committee to investigate. It was a central board of supervision, though executive power normally remained with the local trustees of institutions. Its principal duty was to visit, and its findings would be communicated to the governor and by him to the legislature and to the people. It was charged specially with providing statistical information about dependency, insanity, crime, and the causes of dependency. Finally it was to conduct correspondence and organize conferences so that information on these questions should be gathered, accumulated, and circulated.[35]

Though the Illinois board was aware of the hostility and indifference that could be displayed by local officials, it knew that success depended upon winning them over. In 1875 the board summarized its own function as the duty to acquire and report information, but this meant reliance upon local authorities and not the exercise of power that the board itself did not possess. What it did was to lay down the essential guidelines for those who had to act: the law was supreme, public officials were accountable, economy must be observed, accurate records were essential, uniformity in administrative method was desirable, and concealment or misrepresentation was self-defeating folly.[36]

[35] *Idem*, 2nd R. (1873).   [36] *Idem*, 3rd R. (1875), 48ff.

These were admirable principles, but in any nineteenth-century society implementation would have been difficult. Despite the law of 1872, record-keeping was still weak in 1877. Registers had been sent out by the board, but in many counties not a single entry had been made in them. The board itself had no means of checking accuracy or supplying omissions, because its entire office staff was one clerk. The unpaid board members could not afford the time for personal visits, and the harassed secretary could not do everything that was required.[37]

Similar difficulties beset all the boards of state charities, though in Illinois they were more likely to be overcome. But nothing came without effort, for, as Wines wrote in 1895, "without continual and persistent agitation of [these] questions . . . there is danger that what has been gained . . . will be lost. Eternal vigilance is the price, not only of liberty, but of everything else worth having or preserving."[38] Not least among the tasks was close attention to the legislature and its committees, and to members in a position to influence the outcome of bills or the fate of proposals submitted by the board.[39]

The New York Board of State Charities was closely associated with influential voluntary organizations, and its members made distinguished contributions to the literature on poverty and child saving. The best-known private charity was the Children's Aid Society founded by Charles Loring Brace in 1853, which gathered destitute or delinquent children from the streets of New York city, placed them temporarily in special homes, and then sent them west to be placed with farming families. As time went on it was realized that some at least should be trained for industrial employment or assisted to find employment in the city, and in the late nineteenth century the society maintained twenty-one industrial schools, eighteen night schools, a farm school, and six city lodging houses for young people. Over 12,000 were enrolled in the various schools, the daily attendance was 5,000, and it was estimated that since the society's foundation 85,977 had been helped. Records kept of all children placed in private houses demonstrated that less than three per cent had turned out badly.

The Children's Aid Society helped able-bodied children who might otherwise have turned to crime. Brace was no believer in hereditary degradation; rather, he saw in each child an individual to be rescued from

---

[37] *Idem*, 4th R. (1877), 169.
[38] F. H. Wines, *Punishment and Reform* (New York, 1895); citation from 2nd Ed. (New York, 1910), 308.
[39] Conference of Boards of Public Charities, *Proceedings* (1876), 122.

an environment for which he was not responsible. In 1886 he wrote of the "absolute necessity of treating each youthful criminal as an individual, not as one of a crowd," and of "the vital importance of breaking up inherited pauperism by putting almshouse children in separate homes."[40]

Numerous other private charities were at work in New York city, and though each had its separate constituency and plan there was strong emphasis upon the environmental causes of destitution and crime. Josephine Shaw Lowell, who played a prominent part in both state and private charity, wrote in 1895 of the terrible conditions in New York poorhouses years earlier. There were insane men and women chained naked in the outhouses, while the sick, the feeble-minded, adult paupers, destitute women and children were all crammed into a building without plan or regulation. "The whole thing was frightful."[41] William P. Letchworth, for many years a prominent member of the State Board of Charities, wrote in 1876 that vast numbers of children were herded together in poorhouses, and recalled the disgust of the English philanthropist Mary Carpenter at the sight of "degraded women and incapable men" placed in charge of children. Letchworth discovered one New York county poorhouse where a virulent eye infection had flourished for several years and children had been infected and become blind. It was a shocking comment on an opulent society that it tolerated an evil "that permits the light of day to be shut out forever from the eyes of orphan children."[42]

The state board was founded in 1867, after the way had been paved by a powerful argument in the Constitutional Convention for State action. A committee on charities reported that so long as lives were worth saving, morals worth preserving, and crime and other evils worth preventing, the State was "bound to interpose its power and means." When personal, local, and religious efforts were exhausted there remained a "vast work" for the State to undertake. Private charities merited aid, but must also submit to "revision, supervision, and regulation."[43] The new board aimed to harness voluntary effort rather than supplement it. In 1872 a Charities Aid Association was founded by Louisa Lee Schuyler to set up committees in each county to visit public institutions, press for needed improvements, and keep a watching brief on legislative action or reaction. In 1882 a Charity

[40] *The Life of Charles Loring Brace*, 432.
[41] William R. Stewart, *The Philanthropic Work of Josephine Shaw Lowell* (New York, 1911), 78. The author was himself chairman of the Board of State Charities for many years.
[42] William P. Letchworth, *Supplementary Report of the Board of State Charities on New York County* (Albany, N.Y., 1876), 17, 21–2.
[43] *Documents of the Constitution of the State of New York* (1867–8), IV, Doc. 106.

Organization Society, suggested by the State Board and inspired by Josephine Shaw Lowell, was established. Mrs Lowell was a member of both the state and the voluntary bodies, and hoped to co-ordinate the efforts of private charities and, where necessary, press for their improvement.

Members of the State Board carried out personal investigations and submitted reports that were adopted by the official agency. In 1875 *Outdoor Relief* by M. S. Anderson appeared as a supplement to the board's report, and in 1876 the report included *Homes of Homeless Children*, a massive study of orphanages and other institutions caring for children by Letchworth. In the following year the secretary of the board, Charles P. Hoyt, published a 200-page essay on the causes of pauperism as part of the board's tenth report. Finally Josephine Shaw Lowell's *Public Relief and Private Charity* drew upon her experience as a board member, though it was not an official publication.

The influence of individual members and the support of voluntary associations won for the New York board an enviable legislative record. In 1872–3 its duties were extended and defined, and a law regulating the treatment of paupers was passed. In 1875 a law forbade the keeping of children in poorhouses; it has been described as "a milestone in child welfare history." In 1881 the board was authorized to order the arrest of persons suspected of cruelty to children. In 1884 the laws relating to destitute children were consolidated, and contract labor by children in reformatories was forbidden. But it was by inspection and publicity rather than by legislation that the conditions in poorhouses and insane asylums were ameliorated. Unlike other boards of state charities the New York board never sought power over county jails.

Despite the influence that it wielded, the New York board had weaknesses. It tended to concentrate on certain problems and pay less attention to others. In a very large state it did not develop the administrative machinery for regular inspection, relying rather upon its voluntary associates. In February 1880 the *New York Times* asserted that there was "an almost universal belief that enormous abuses prevailed in the administration of charities in the city." If the allegations were substantiated the charity commissioners should "enforce a reform or resign a place they are unable to fill." In the same year Governor Alonzo Cornell declared that the conditions of many indignant insane persons was "pitiable in the extreme" and that some jails were "a disgrace to our civilization." He recommended that the board should be given power to inspect jails, but the legislature failed to act. Two years later Cornell said that though primary responsibility lay with local officials the State was "responsible for the well-being of its citizens" and should intervene to protect the weak. In 1883 there was an outcry over maltreatment of delinquent boys in a reformatory. Governor Grover Cleveland assumed that the Board of Charities knew nothing of this but claimed that ignorance was proof of its incompetence. He recommended the board's abolition and its replacement by a single full-time commissioner "vested with the supervision and control" of all state institutions. Again the legislature failed to act and the Board of State Charities continued as before.[44]

In 1894, when the state constitution was revised, the New York Board of State Charities won a position of unusual strength. It was given a place in the new constitution beyond the reach of legislative or executive hostility, and with greatly enlarged power. It could veto the establishment of new charitable institutions, resolve the discretionary powers given to those that already existed, transfer inmates from one institution to another, and, except in reformatories, discharge them. Its consent was necessary for any appropriation for charitable or correctional establishments. All this meant that a wide range of supervisory powers could be executed without seeking legislative authorization or approval by the governor. A critical issue was power to regulate private and denominational charities that received state aid. The proposers of the new articles in the constitutional convention argued successfully that they must be regulated by a responsible body and that "the State Board of Charities, subject to general laws to be passed by the legislature," should exercise the necessary supervision. In the outcome the board controlled seven reformatories, eight institutions for the deaf, two for the blind, one for epileptics, three for the feeble-minded, one for Indian children, one for soldiers and sailors, fifty-eight county poorhouses, one hundred and fifty-one orphanages and homes for the friendless, one hundred and twelve hospitals, forty-five dispensaries, and a total of over 62,000 inmates. In addition it supervised a large number of private charities receiving state aid. No other State Board of Charities had so many responsibilities, so great an authority, or so much autonomy.[45]

Two other states – California and Michigan – may be mentioned at this stage to illustrate the diversity of public responsibility for the destitute and handicapped. California did not have a state board until 1903, despite efforts to establish one from 1880 onwards, but a number of separate lesser agencies were developed. The constitution of 1879 contained express

[44] *Messages of the Governors of New York*, 11 vols (Albany, N.Y., 1909), 431.
[45] *Revised Record of the Constitutional Convention of New York* (1894), IV, 801.

authority to aid charities caring for children, and state aid also went to a number of hospitals and homes for old people, and to a San Francisco home for inebriates. The state government also grappled with special problems created by a surplus of males in the population, and a large influx of seasonally unemployed from the interiors of the cities. By 1895 an unusually large number of aged were being supported in almshouses, though in that year aid was ended on grounds of economy and the whole burden thrown on private charity and local authorities. Efforts to set up a controlling board were opposed by some of the ad hoc agencies set up in early years, especially the State Board of Health, which had acquired an interest in the supervision of hospitals and almshouses. In 1897 a State Commission in Lunacy was established and added its voice to those opposing central control. Thus the absence of a Board of State Charities did not mean that the afflicted were ignored, but made for administrative confusion and rivalry between the various agencies.[46]

Michigan was slow to establish a state board, and when it did its authority was limited to some specific tasks. As early as 1871 Governor Henry Baldwin attacked county jails, and suggested that the whole system was bad, ought to be thoroughly reformed, and should be brought under the control of the State. Nothing was done at this stage, though the publicity may have prompted some voluntary improvement. The State was however active in protecting the interests of children: their employment in objectionable or demoralizing occupations was forbidden, and, in an unusual display of state paternalism, children could be removed from parents who were criminals, habitually drunk, or engaged in prostitution. In 1885 the procedure was established by which an abandoned or neglected child could be committed to special schools or homes. It was in line with these trends that the state agency, when established in 1891, was a board of control; but its function was to manage the state institutions and not to undertake roving inquiries into the causes of pauperism.[47]

---

[46] Frances T. Cahn and Barry Valesku, *Welfare Activities of Federal, State, and Local Governments in California, 1850–1934* (Berkeley, Calif., 1936), *passim*. Enoch Wines paid a tribute to California's prison system; it was "in the forefront of all States on the North American continent in the matter of prison reform" (*State of Prisons*, 184–5). He was particularly impressed by the Board of Prison Directors, set up by the constitution of 1879, which had comprehensive power to direct the whole state prison system and power to bring county and city prisons under its control.

[47] *Senate Journal of the State of Michigan*, Governor Baldwin's Annual message, Jan. 6, 1871; Michigan State Board of Control, 1st R. (1890–2), 8, 89, 93, Appendix. The prison system of Michigan was also praised by Enoch Wines. The state was "most actively and intelligently reaching out in the direction of social progress" (161).

The leading institution placed under the new board's management was the State Public School which provided training and a temporary home until children could be placed with families. It claimed that nearly ninety per cent turned out to be "dutiful children" and grew up to become "useful and respected citizens." This was a less striking record of success than might appear, because children who were mentally deficient or physically deformed were not accepted in the first place, while those who proved to be incurable or exercised a pernicious influence upon others were returned to their counties. In other words the State expended its best efforts in training and placing those who promised well, and placed upon counties responsibility for those who seemed destined to become dependent or criminal. However the state board did control schools for the blind and deaf which were excellent institutions by the standards of the day.

So far this chapter has described in outline the legislative and administrative history of the Boards of State Charities in selected states. It is now appropriate to examine the assumptions which guided them, and the advances made in the treatment of social problems. One misconception must be rejected at the outset. No one ever suggested that it was a crime to be poor. When discussing pauperism crime was usually listed as one of its causes, but the normal approach was to stress the defects in character from which both crime and dependency were derived. Nor was it suggested that affluence was a sign of virtue, though it was accepted that riches gave men more opportunity to be virtuous if so minded. It was agreed that poverty made men susceptible to all kinds of pressure and temptation, but it was not argued that the poor inevitably succumbed. Remarks which appear to reveal a perverse social theory should always be looked at in context, but one difficulty is that vocabulary, then as now, was inadequate to explain the gradations that existed between the destitute and the poor but independent.[48]

Most men who were experienced in social inquiry drew a line between being poor and being dependent: "Although poverty must always exist," wrote Sanborn, "pauperism need not." Charles Loring Brace told a gathering of teachers in industrial schools that the first great difficulty in

---

[48] In its report for 1892 the Ohio Board of State Charities emphasized this difficulty: "The term *poor* has many and varied meanings. When used of persons with a reference to the possession of property, it is often applied to those who are not destitute of property but who are not rich. The legal definition of the term, however, is "so destitute of property as to be entitled to maintenance from the public," and it differs very little from the ordinary definition of "pauper" which is "a poor person, one so indigent as to depend upon the parish or town for maintenance."

social work lay in "drawing the delicate line between the necessary alleviation of poverty, and the encouragement of pauperism and dependency." Help should be given to the destitute "in such a way as to raise them above the need for help."[49] The belief that indiscriminate charity might lead the poor into pauperism comes up in almost all discussions of the problem, and this meant that a good deal of argument was directed against unregulated aid. In 1870 the Boston Overseers of the Poor had no doubt that indiscriminate almsgiving was the most prolific source of vagrancy and of the petty forms of vice. A generation later their successors lamented that, following the depression of 1893 the number of applications for relief "rose at a bound to extraordinary figures," and that charitable but unwise response had accustomed too many to dependence on public aid. In this situation they saw great merits in organized paid labor even if the products were of little use, and managed to divert the funds of some private charities for this purpose.[50]

Charles S. Hoyt, secretary of the New York board, asserted that many paupers "had been trained and educated for the poorhouse by outdoor relief administered by law or private charity."[51] Mrs Lowell, whom no one could accuse of indifference to suffering, approved the comments of one superintendent of the poor, who said that people often recommended for relief families "composed in part of bright, intelligent children," but failed to realize that what they asked was "almost sure to ruin those bright children and educate them for paupers or criminals."[52]

Though aid unwisely given could have this disastrous consequence, it was believed that for most paupers the fundamental cause lay in their own character. By far the greater number in poorhouses had been brought to that condition, said Hoyt, "by idleness, improvidence, or some form of vicious indulgence."[53] Yet there were hereditary influences against which the individual might contend in vain. Fred Wines argued that "when we contemplate the pauper, we must reflect that he is the product of a long succession of causes, of parental influences that have been at work for generations."[54] The Massachusetts board (probably reflecting the views of

---

[49] Massachusetts B. of St. Ch., 2nd R. (1865), 213; C. L. Brace, *Address on Industrial Schools* (New York, 1868), 9.
[50] Overseers of the Poor of the City of Boston, Report for 1870–1, 5; *idem*, Report for 1893–4, 9.
[51] Charles S. Hoyt, "The Causes of Pauperism" in New York St. B. of Ch., 10th Ann. R. (1877), 197.
[52] Josephine Shaw Lowell, *Public Relief and Private Charity* (New York, 1884), 55–6.
[53] Hoyt, *op. cit.*, 195, 196.   [54] Illinois B. of St. Ch., 4th R. (1877), 193.

Sanborn) argued that the primary cause of pauperism was "poor stock," characterized by "lack of vital force," vicious habits, and drunkenness. But a distinction was made between "inherent and permanent paupers" and those who still retained enough vigor to help themselves under favorable circumstances. A man or woman might inherit the weakness of character that would lead to dependence, but this weakness might be counteracted by appropriate action. This opened a wide door for charitable and remedial measures, and suggested the need for fine adjustment between aid that would precipitate a person into pauperism and what would arrest the debilitating process before too late.[55]

The most influential statement of the hereditary explanation was *The Jukes* by R. L. Dugdale. This account of a real New Hampshire family traced a record of petty crime, prostitution, and pauperism in every generation back to a progenitor who had contracted syphilis in 1812. Force was added to the example by showing that another branch of the same family, uncontaminated by the fatal disease, had remained hard-working and respectable New England farmers. But Dugdale was too good an observer to resort to a simple explanation that the sins of the father were visited upon the children. Once a family had won a bad reputation it was difficult to find marriage partners except among cousins or people of similar behaviour; the inherited tendencies were thus reinforced in each generation, and children bred in such an environment would find it almost impossible to escape. In other words the inherited weaknesses were augmented at every stage, while other people drawn by accident or misfortune into the same circle would increase the number exposed to the same demoralizing influences. If there was an inherited weakness that could not be eradicated its effect should be mitigated and contacts saved from contamination. It was among the very young that intervention was most likely to succeed.

The elder Wines, in his work on prisons, wrote that orphans and the children of criminal parents presented a challenge to society. Here were recruits for "the great army of crime." Born for it and brought up for it, "all this little world is borne along by a current that rushes ever towards the deep sea." It must be drawn to the shore. "We must gather, shelter, and elevate these little ones." Letchworth saw pauperism as the result of a gradual "letting down," sometimes extending over two or more generations before reaching the final point of degradation. It should be treated,

---

[55] Massachusetts B. of St. Ch., 2nd R. (1866), xxii; see also 4th R. (1868), 132.

he thought, "as a moral disease." Like any disease there was a chance of arresting it, and one should "spare no exertion to restore to society in a healthy condition such as may be curable, among whom may be classed the children." As a first step Letchworth believed that there should be a law compelling authorities "to place all destitute children in suitable homes, and to prohibit their committal to poorhouses." It has already been noticed that the New York Board of State Charities persuaded the legislature to pass such a law in 1879.[56]

Should prevention be carried further? Was it enough to remove children from corrupting associations, when society itself had failed to adopt the laws and customs that would prevent them from entering this environment in the first place? The Pennsylvania board strongly advocated compulsory education, and realized that the law alone was not enough if social conventions operated against the poor. "Respectable" parents demanded standards of cleanliness and dress "which effectively excluded the ragged, filthy hordes" from school. Poorly nourished children could hardly stand the pace of educational competition, and steps were necessary to see that they were given plentiful and wholesome food in the school itself. As it was unlikely that well-to-do parents would readily accept the necessary changes, special schools might be necessary. This may seem a weak retreat in the face of class prejudice, but it was realistic and identified a gap in social policy. The board concluded that "the State should interpose, and take the care and maintenance of the children into its hands."[57]

The Massachusetts board turned its attention from destitution to the environment of poverty. In 1879 its report examined implications of the fact that physical disease was a major cause of pauperism. Sanitation, water supply, ventilation, and impure food all had their bearing upon the problem, and there must be regulations in the interests of decency and health. It was hardly the province of a board of state charities to take these reforms in hand, but the Massachusetts board had recognized that social policy had to be seen as a whole.[58] This need for a comprehensive approach had been foreseen by Dr R. T. Davis of New York in 1874 when he told the Conference of Public Charities that pauperism could be reduced only by the supervision and co-ordination of all charities, the strict enforcement of compulsory education, the removal of poor children from degrading

---

[56] Enoch Wines, *State of Prisons*: W. P. Letchworth, "Pauper and Destitute Children" (Appendix to *Homes of Homeless Children* (Albany, N.Y. 1876)).
[57] Pennsylvania B. of P. Ch., 2nd R. (1871), cv; 5th R. (1876), 10, 41.
[58] Massachusetts B. of St. Ch., 15th R. (1879).

associations, the encouragement of migration from urban to rural areas and the reduction of relief to the able-bodied, accompanied by the provision of employment for those who could work.[59] F. C. Wines almost anticipated Keynesian economics when he argued that poverty could be relieved by natural operation of economic laws if the rich spent more freely. Distress generated "the cry of retrenchment, economy, and the husbandry of resources," but if no capital were employed, labor would be un-employed. "A restoration of confidence, and the unlocking of the vaults in which the money of this country is locked up" would be the surest remedy for distress and its unhappy consequences.[60]

These precepts might not always help those who had immediate responsibility for alleviating distress. Charles Hoyt believed that "the whole policy of the State should move in the direction of caring for the really unfortunate and worthy sick poor in hospitals while a vigorous system of labor should be organized and administered for the vicious and unworthy."[61] But what, in practice, was to be done when men and women who were neither sick, nor vicious, nor unworthy were rendered destitute by hard times? There was a recurrent argument that "outdoor relief" should never be given save in rare cases of acute distress. Josephine Shaw Lowell persistently maintained that even in hard times the able-bodied should either find work or rely on private charity; and if private funds were inadequate this would at least cut down on "indiscriminate" giving which enticed men into permanent pauperism. Yet what of the family that might be broken up if the father was forced to choose between the poorhouse or traveling far afield in search of work? What of the destitute mother who saw her children removed to a home when small sums might have enabled her to support them? And what of the situation in which there was no work for the most willing worker?

These and similar questions caused the authorities to give outdoor relief much more readily than writers on the subject recommended. The Boston Overseers of the Poor were fully aware of the difficulties that might arise in a large city if destitute persons crowded in hoping for food and shelter; but in the winter of 1876–7 they felt obliged to give outdoor relief to almost seven thousand families. They included "some weak ones who never had and never will have any vital force to keep them above the condition in which they were born," but also sick, aged, widows with dependent children, and a large number "deprived of their living because of hard

[59] Conference of Boards of Public Charities, *Proceedings* (1874).
[60] Illinois B. of P. Ch., 4th R. (1877), 201.   [61] Hoyt, 196.

times."[62] At the Conference of Boards of Charities in 1877, M. S. Anderson insisted that relief was necessary outside the poorhouse when pestilence, crop failures, or mechanical innovation threw men out of work; but this should be accompanied by systematic efforts by the State to find them employment. Sanborn summed up briefly when he said that while care and experience were essential in the administration of outdoor relief, it was abundantly clear that there were many occasions on which it could avert pauperism. Critics might find cases of maladministration but there was "absolutely greater abuse practised in indoor relief."[63]

The need for outdoor relief might also be inferred from the numerous complaints from state boards about the condition of county institutions. In county jails could be observed the actual process by which men and women who were guilty of minor offences or awaiting trial were turned into criminals or joined the ranks of paupers. At least some of these unfortunates had been forced into petty crime by destitution. In 1868 the Ohio board quoted Dorothea Dix that if it had been the deliberate intention to create a criminal class "no better way could have been devised than county jails." Eleven years later the same board found that "one of the most revolting and abominable places on earth is a jail in a large city." In 1875 the jail of Erie county in Pennsylvania, built for twenty-five, housed forty-one, of whom thirty-seven were awaiting trial: "Always crowded beyond its capacity, proper cleanliness and order could hardly be expected." Bedding was straw, changed not more than once in six months, and drainpipes were too small, "from which unpleasant consequences occur." The Cumbria county jail was new and contained only twenty-nine persons, of whom most were awaiting trial; one woman, accused of a minor offense against the liquor licensing law, had had to bring two young children with her; four prisoners were insane. The Alleghany county jail had been built for fifty, but in 1875 171 were "stowed away" in it – four or more to a cell; efforts to keep the place clean were futile, while "to dissipate the foul exhalation from the throats and bellies of nearly two hundred vagabonds, shut in a prison such as this, was simply impossible." Yet in this prison juvenile delinquents were mixed with old offenders, and acquired their habits.[64]

Poorhouses and infirmaries were less obnoxious than the jails, but most

[62] Overseers of the Poor, R. for 1885–6, 5.
[63] Conference of Boards of Public Charities, *Proceedings* (1877).
[64] Ohio B. of St. Ch., 2nd R. (1868), 11; 4th R. (New Series) (1879), 6; Pennsylvania B. of P. Ch., 6th Ann. R. (1875), 103, 111.

were sad places where the senile and chronically sick, the unemployed and unemployable, the feeble-minded, together with abandoned children, dragged out pointless lives. There was no need to insist that poorhouses should deter the able-bodied from seeking their shelter when the poor and elderly dreaded the day when authority would insist upon removal to those places, from which few escaped. Jane Addams, describing the struggles of an old woman to remain independent, wrote of the "gripping fear of the poorhouse in her eyes" and thought that this horror was general among the aged poor.[65] Hardened wrongdoers and confirmed vagrants might welcome a night of shelter in conditions to which they had grown impervious, but everyone agreed that the thought of healthy young people growing up in this environment was shocking. It is no surprise that humane Boards of State Charities and city authorities preferred to run the risk of demoralizing the poor and provided outdoor relief. Moreover once an individual was confined to a poorhouse society might be deprived forever of his labor. The Massachusetts board welcomed any law which would preserve the family, keep children in public schools, and retain "that productive power which is dissipated and lost by commitment to pauper institutions."[66]

By 1884 the Boston Overseers of the Poor maintained a Wayfarer Lodge for men seeking employment and took payment in labor performed. Though still suspicious of those who claimed a *right* to relief, the Overseers normally preferred to help families "rather than that they should be forced to become inmates of public institutions."[67] The prejudice against relieving able-bodied men and women did not entirely abate. In 1892 the Ohio board found that the number receiving outdoor relief was startling, and suspected "such corruption, imposture and favoritism, that many students of social service and many practical workers in its field favor the entire abolishment of this form of relief in large cities." If recipients were not sick they should take their chances with private charities.[68] There was obvious inconsistency in this suggestion as the Ohio Board, in common with most others, had frequently accused private charities of unwise benevolence; so if the state authority refused to assist it might well be breeding paupers for the next generation.

[65] Jane Addams, *Twenty Years at Hull House*, Chapter 8.
[66] Massachusetts B. of St. Ch., *Report of General Agent* (1875), civ. A new law of settlement made a town responsible for destitute persons who had resided for five years and paid taxes for three, and for women who had resided for five years without receiving relief. Before this enactment they would have been classed as persons without settled residence and become a charge upon the State.
[67] Overseers of the Poor, R. for 1885–6.   [68] Ohio B. of St. Ch., R. for 1892.

Despite both doubts and confident assertions to the contrary, the State Boards of Charities were edging towards a general system of public relief, but American society was still loosely organized, and systematic administration in this difficult field could not be achieved. The problems were made manifest in the wake of the 1873 depression when tramps were abroad in unprecedented numbers. Even when allowances had been made for men traveling in search of work, said the Pennsylvania board in 1876, there remained "no way of escaping from the conviction that the number of genuine tramps has largely increased within three years." They presented, said the Illinois board, "the most perplexing problem in the treatment of pauperism," and in 1878 the Wisconsin board lamented that "from a small beginning, as a few honest and worthy men seek employment which could not be given, the class has become an army, and gradually criminal in character." It was no trivial problem in county districts and small towns where tramps could terrorize the neighborhood. In Pennsylvania every county road swarmed with them, and the people regarded them as unavoidable afflictions. "Refuse them food, and your hen roost pays the penalty. Deny them a bed in the barn, and they set it on fire. They travel in gangs and disperse to forage, levying contributions right and left." Their number had been estimated at 30,000 or 35,000 in 1874, and it probably increased by a third in the next twelve months. Even allowing for exaggeration the numbers were disturbing.[69] In Illinois gangs of one hundred or more were reported, terrorizing communities, boarding trains, and traveling without paying fares. In Springfield a man, apparently educated and calling himself "King of the Tramps," made a public speech in which he spoke of "a secret organization . . . among them with signs, grips, passwords, and regulations."[70]

Not only was the number of tramps unprecedented, but their behavior challenged conventional wisdom about paupers. Depraved and criminally inclined they might be, but they were not physically degenerate or lacking in initiative. Indeed they seemed to be remarkably adept in helping themselves. It was idle to assert that no one had a right to relief, when gangs would disturb the public peace unless they got it. Some local authorities found that the easiest way of solving the problem was to pay their railroad fare into another county or state.

In Boston and elsewhere a work test was attempted. If tramps would do a

---

[69] Pennsylvania B. of P. Ch., 4th R. (1877–8); 6th R. (1875); Illinois B. of St. Ch., 4th R. (1877), 98; Wisconsin St. B. of Ch. & Reform, 8th R. (1878), 55.
[70] Illinois B. of St. Ch., 4th R. (1877), 206–7.

day's work on the roads or in a woodyard, they were given food and lodging. Was this an implicit recognition of the "right to work"? The overseers denied emphatically any sympathy "with that spirit of communism predicated upon the theory that government is bound to furnish labor to the unemployed." They claimed to relieve only those who convinced them of real need. In practice the "work tests" had a limited effect. So long as it was left to local authorities tramps could always move from one which was strict to another that was lax.[71]

Less was heard of tramps as times improved, but they had demonstrated the inability of social institutions to cope with mass unemployment. It was however the good fortune of America that economic expansion ensured that in normal times demand would soak up surplus labor. Though unable to devise remedies for what was an exceptional problem, the boards of state charities had nevertheless explored many of the paths that would lead to modern notions of public responsibility for remedying the defects of the social system. Policy might still be fragmentary and poorly coordinated, but significant principles had been accepted. Wherever the boards of state charities had been created it would be impossible to return to the earlier condition in which incapacity and destitution were left to local authorities and private remedies. The discussions which occupy the pages of so many reports laid the foundations of knowledge which could be applied in future. If some of the problems remain unsolved today, after a century of experience and controversy, they had been identified and a start made in their analysis. Thus the boards of state charities mark the beginning of a new era in which government would accept responsibility for the treatment of ills that had formerly been regarded as inevitable, incurable, and decreed by an inscrutable Deity.

[71] Overseers of the Poor, R. for 1878, 6.

5

THE BOARDS OF PUBLIC HEALTH

The advance of public responsibility for health is one of the most significant though least noticed phenomena of modern times. Prime movers were the growth in knowledge, fear of disease, and middle-class revulsion at appalling conditions in growing cities. Rapid advances in medical knowledge and an incentive to speculate about the prevention or cure of conditions that had hitherto been regarded as unavoidable and incurable, excited individuals and inspired them to press for action. In 1873 it was possible to say, for official consumption, that almost every village or hamlet contained medical men who were "versed in sanitary science" and who "demanded from local authorities that all efforts be made to preserve public health."[1] Collectively this meant that in every state there were active doctors, often dominating the State Medical Society, who pressed for more drastic and authoritarian measures in defense of health. The rise of the germ theory meant that impure water, dirty streets, and the noxious smells from heaps of refuse became major enemies in the battle for health. "Nuisances" which had been meekly tolerated became objects of fear, while streams, water pipes and sewers carried mysterious killers into public places and private homes.

Disease had always been feared, but now the cause of much infection had been revealed and confidence born that, given time, the ancient plagues of mankind would be mastered. Under these circumstances fear acquired a new dimension. Something was to blame if disease took hold, and someone could find a remedy. Smallpox was preventable if only vaccination became general. Typhoid could be contained if human and animal excrement did not contaminate the water supply. Cholera need not spread if infected districts were isolated, and rigorous cleansing were carried out. Still perplexing was the transmission of malarial diseases and yellow fever, but

---

[1] Ely McClellan, M.D., Assistant Surgeon of the United States, "The Cholera Epidemic in 1873," *Executive Document No. 95*, 43rd Congress, 2nd session, 2.

though the carrier was not identified until after the century there was hope that quarantine or disinfection would defeat these scourges, and their association with swampy water fostered the belief that something could be done.

Fear of disease was classless. Though typhoid and cholera spread most often in congested city streets, they might easily spread into good residential areas. Yellow fever was no respecter of class or race. Indeed, it was an established fact that in any epidemic fewer blacks than whites contracted the disease and fewer died.

Fear of the consequences strengthened revulsion at the atrocious conditions in the poor parts of many cities, where filth, dilapidation and neglect were visible only a short distance from fashionable streets. New York, because of its size, overcrowding, and the constant arrival of new immigrants was, perhaps, the worst afflicted; but it was no more than a concentration of the evils that could be found in every large city. In the spring of 1873, in the Five Points district of New York city, the side streets were covered with frozen snow, which was in turn covered with the winter's accumulation of filth; garbage boxes overflowed, refuse was piled in heaps, while pale children played in the mud. In 1874 the rivers were described as gigantic sewers, the wharves were "black and rotten with filth of the most horrible kind," and unfashionable streets were deep in the accumulated dirt of years. In 1875, with the wind in the wrong quarter, city dwellers gasped for fresh air amidst effluvia emanating from gasworks, oil factories, sluggish sewers, and excrement decomposing in vaults. Alleys and courts were worse than the streets, and the interiors of tenements were often indescribable. The inhabitants themselves spoke of "tenant-house rot" to describe the steady physical deterioration which resulted. The price was paid in high mortality rates, especially among infants.[2]

Conditions in Boston were little better than in New York. A medical commission of 1875 reported an exceptionally high death rate especially in 1872 and 1873. The general cause was believed to be bad sanitation, though it was thought that a flood of immigrants from Ireland had introduced fresh disease. Polluted water was identified as a major cause of disease. The law was too weak and imprecise to prevent the discharge of sewage into sources of drinking water, and even if the public supply was avoided infection might be passed on in adulterated milk.[3]

[2] *New York Times*, Mar. 29, 1873; Nov. 9, 1874; Jan. 3, 1875; Stephen Smith, *The City That Was* (New York, 1911), 65–6, 100–5; New York Times, Aug. 6, 1878.
[3] *The Fiftieth Anniversary of the Founding of the State Board of Health of Massachusetts* (Boston, Mass., 1919), 227, 272, 275.

As the sphere of investigation was extended the consequences of neglect and malpractice became more and more apparent. Slaughterhouses were often abominable, and the attendant industries of bone boiling, fat rendering, and tanning filled the atmosphere with nauseating smells. Food was widely adulterated and often with harmful effects. Vendors of patent medicine might sell at best nostrums that were harmless but useless, at worst poisons; cosmetics might contain poison and corrosives; no one could trust the label on a package or a bottle. Many doctors in practice had no qualifications or possessed worthless degrees from colleges that sold them as a commercial venture. Medical education was unimpressive, with hosts of inferior colleges lowering standards, contracting the length of courses, and examining in a perfunctory way.

Not all of this was realized before the dawn of investigation and inspection, and thousands of American citizens shared the delusion that they lived in a healthy country; but enough was known to stimulate a demand for improvement, to build up pressure to extend investigations, and stimulate the demand for more coercive power. Improved knowledge and more plain speaking meant that revulsion against present conditions and fear of future consequences created a climate in which public responsibility was first accepted and then steadily enlarged.

There had been local boards of health in towns, counties, and cities throughout the country, but in practice they did little except in epidemics (and then acted independently to create greater confusion) or when "nuisances" became intolerable. Membership seldom included medical men, and there was no requirement to appoint and pay health officers. In contrast an ideal state board of health had a membership of six or seven, a majority of whom were medical men, a salaried full-time secretary, and, as time went on, health inspectors, sanitary engineers, inspectors to enforce food and drug laws, analysts, chemists, and biologists. They also disseminated an enormous amount of literature on the prevention of disease and preservation of health. A brief survey of the history of four such boards will illustrate the opportunities, obstacles, and progress.

The Massachusetts board was founded in 1869 with a highly respected Bostonian, Dr H. I. Bowditch, as chairman. The law sketched its responsibilities in broad terms. It was to "take cognizance of the interests of the life and health of the citizens of this Commonwealth," undertake sanitary investigations, inquire into the causes of disease, and advise the state government on health matters. As Bowditch said, in his first address, it was "capable of doing good to the citizens in all future time," or might prove to be "a perfect abortion." The latter outcome was, perhaps, more likely as the legislature had failed to appropriate any money for the performance of these many duties.[4]

The Massachusetts board survived, received an appropriation, and in 1871 was required to enforce the state laws regulating slaughterhouses. Hearings on complaints against slaughterhouses would occupy much time in subsequent years.[5] In 1875 the board investigated the sanitation of Boston, made a highly critical report, and obtained the appointment of a state sanitary engineer and the passage of a law forbidding the discharge of offensive matter into streams supplying drinking water. It also fired the opening shots in a campaign to make local boards, with medical advisers, mandatory. This introduces a notable feature in the development of public health administration. Whereas the boards of state charities found local authorities antiquated, inefficient, and obstructive, and often sought to superimpose upon them the authority of the State, the boards of public health pressed consistently for the creation or reinforcement of local health boards. Many powers conferred upon state boards were delegated to local boards, giving doctors who were active and well informed a local sphere of influence while providing an additional source of strength for the state boards.

One reason for this development was that in emergencies it was normally the local boards that had to implement policies. They were also in the best position to keep an eye on local "nuisances," offensive trades, sanitation, and water supply. If active and competent they could carry out many duties of investigation and inspection which would otherwise have been forced upon an overloaded state inspectorate. Another reason for boosting the authority of local boards was to obtain comprehensive, prompt, and accurate vital statistics and reports on disease. The Massachusetts board had early cause to complain of inadequate information and to stress the difficulty of deciding policy when so little was known with certainty about the causes of death and the incidence of disease; emphasis upon the need for

---

[4] Board of Health Minutes, Massachusetts State Archives, Boston. A printed copy of the address is in the minute book.
[5] A particularly burdensome case arose out of a complaint against J. S. Squire & Co. of Cambridge received in 1873. Hearings were held on fourteen days in December 1873. The company was represented by counsel. The site was visited in January, and after some consultation with the State Judiciary Committee it was decided to suspend judgment. Further petitions were presented, and in October 1875 the board appointed a committee to investigate, which reported in December that the business was now well conducted and "need not be the source of nuisances," though some neighboring small fat melting establishments were condemned.

ample vital statistics became a feature in the reports of every state board.[6]

In 1879 the Massachusetts board was merged with that of State Charities to form the Board of Health, Lunacy, and Charity. Health duties were assigned to a standing committee, with a salaried health officer, but charities and asylums took up most of the time at formal meetings of the board.[7] The major health work continued to be the investigation of polluted water, and this laid the foundations for a service which would eventually be recognized as the foremost authority on water supply, drainage, and sewerage in the country. In other respects it was difficult to extend work until public health became once more independent in 1886. In 1888 the board obtained the right to review, accept or reject new sewerage plans. It also enforced a Food and Drug Act in 1882 (the first in the country), and from this there soon developed a laboratory with permanent analysts and biologists. The board also inspected dairies, slaughterhouses, and cold storage depots. In 1889 it investigated complaints against an establishment making Paris Green, and after elaborate tests of the effects on soil, vegetation, and employees, ordered and obtained extensive modifications. Another duty was the inspection of ice, much of which was found to come from polluted ponds.

By 1900 the Massachusetts Board of Health was a powerful agency. Despite complaints of inadequate funds, the organization had grown steadily. In 1902 the central office staff consisted of the secretary, an assistant secretary, and eleven others; a Department of Water Supply and Sewerage had a chief engineer, an assistant, and twenty-six others; a Department of food and drug inspection had a chief inspector, five inspectors, and three other persons. The board also maintained a laboratory for testing food and water, and another, set up in 1894, for the production of diphtheria antitoxin. From early years it had also made a practice of employing engineers and academic scientists on short-term contracts.[8]

The success of the Massachusetts board owed much to the efficiency of its leading members. The first secretary, George Derby, held office only for five years, but was responsible for the early reports which determined lines

[6] Massachusetts St. B. of H., 7th R. (1876), 12, 16.
[7] The minutes of the board are in the Massachusetts State Archives, Boston.
[8] William T. Sedgwick headed the department of Biology and Public Health at M.I.T. In 1888 he became Consulting Biologist to the State Board of Health. This post gave special focus to the work of his department – bacteriology, sanitary biology, water supply and drainage – and also enabled him to employ young scientific workers at critical stages in their careers.

of policy for the future and won widespread support for the principle of health administration. Samuel Abbott became health officer of the combined board in 1882 and then, for eight years, secretary of the separate board. Hiram F. Mills joined the board in 1886, as its engineering member, served for twenty-eight years, and built up an unrivalled knowledge of all aspects of sanitary engineering. Above all, Dr Henry Walcott joined the combined board in 1880 as health officer, then served as a board member, and in 1886 became chairman of the separate Board of Health until 1914. Thus there was no period in its first half century when the Massachusetts board lacked strong and experienced leadership.

The history of this successful Board of Health may be contrasted with that of another founded in the same year in distant California. Its duties were similar to those of the Massachusetts board, and in its first report, issued in 1871, it sought to allay fears of authoritarian action. Fears had been expressed "lest in this land of liberty the sanitary measures sought might press too heavily on the individual and lessen too much the freedom of personal action." The board disclaimed any intention to interfere too frequently; its duties were advisory and not executive. Nevertheless, there might be occasions when it would become necessary "to compel obedience to the rules of hygiene." Few individuals could control the purity of the air they breathed or the water they drank, and here, "as in many other emergencies that may arise, the State must step in for the protection of its citizens and enact rules which shall be binding on all."[9]

The expectation of hostility was better founded than the hope for coercive powers, and the record of the California board was to be filled with failure and frustration. In its third report the board complained that it could not compile vital statistics because its clerical staff was too small. It had investigated safety in mines, and found that existing laws were ignored; but no legislation followed. A recommendation of 1877 that adulteration of milk should be prohibited was equally unsuccessful. In 1877 the legislature did agree to make mandatory the establishment of local health boards, but many localities failed to comply and three years later the board stated that those in existence failed to supply the information requested. By 1886 only nineteen out of sixty cities and towns had local boards, and the board sadly reported that California was far behind many sister states "in failing to have upon her statute books many needed sanitary laws." There was no quarantine law, no health code, and though there was a state analyst

---

[9] California B. of P. H., 1st R. (1870–1), 18.

there was no money to pay him for duties performed. Vital statistics were rudimentary, and thanks to the absence or inertia of local boards information on health matters was not widely circulated. For all their reputation as self-reliant individuals Californians were unable to cope with epidemics, catastrophic disease, or the normal hazards of impure food and water.[10]

It is lamentably true that in such a calamity, the iniquities of the constitutional authorities are generally laid at the door of the Almighty. He is blamed when the blame belongs to the people themselves, who will not see the dangers that daily threaten their health, until the enemy storms the citadel and slays its hundreds.[11]

Apathy among the people was reflected by obstruction and ignorance in the legislature. A law requiring the notification of death before burial was lost, as was a bill to make the registration of death compulsory. The same fate awaited a bill to enforce the existing law requiring the appointment of local health officers. A bill requiring compulsory vaccination for children in public schools was lost through the opposition of one senator, "a political wire puller, with great influence." Reviewing the record in 1888 the board concluded: "This has been the history of our attempts at improving the health laws . . . Upon every occasion we were ignominiously defeated, through the ignorance or design of those who were elected by the people to serve their interests." Ironically there was no difficulty in securing the passage of laws to preserve animals from infectious disease.[12]

This plain speaking made the secretary, Dr G. Tyrrell, "one of the best-hated officials in the State," but produced some results. A compulsory vaccination law, a more stringent local health board law, and a law requiring deaths to be reported were passed. It was made a misdemeanor to violate a health law, but the offense had to be willful which was usually impossible to prove. A new law regulated sanitation in factories, but without an appropriation for enforcement. Meanwhile the secretary remained the only salaried official of the board and no inspectorate was created. Weakness did not avert hostility, and in 1891 membership of the board was completely changed.[13]

The new secretary, J. R. Laine, included in his first report a long essay on the "police power" which took the argument back to the point at which it

[10] *Idem*, 2nd R. (1871–2), 141 (mines); 3rd R. (1874–5), 8 (milk); 4th R. (1876–7), 3 (local boards); 6th R. (1878–80), 8 (registration); 9th R. (1884–6), 27 (local boards); *ibid.*, 5 (backwardness in health legislation).   [12] *Idem*, 10th R. (1886–8), 35–41.
[11] *Idem*, 9th R. (1884–6), 53.
[13] *Idem*, 11th R. (1888–90), 47–8, 223.

had started over twenty years before.[14] This long period had not been entirely barren; some improvements could be attributed to growing awareness amongst the people of health matters, but they still had much to learn. In 1888 the state analyst submitted a dismal report on adulterated food and drink, and concluded that no real improvement could be expected without support from the law "by an intelligent and hearty public sentiment."

Faced with apathy and ignorance the board had failed to accomplish its objectives, but some fault must also be attributed to individuals who tried to do too much too quickly and ended by doing very little. Resistance to the board did not spring from principled objection to state intervention. During the same period there were created Commissions for Banking and Insurance, a Board of Forestry, a Fish Commission, and Bureaus for Dairies and Mining. The vicissitudes of the Railboard Commission will be dealt with in another chapter, but from 1877 onwards there was never any doubt about the right of the State to regulate.[15] Some part of the Board of Health's poor record may therefore be attributed to mistaken tactics and insufficient attention to the art of lobbying.

The experience of two other state boards – Michigan and Maryland – illustrates further the importance of careful planning in the campaign for public health. The Michigan board was organized in 1873, largely as a consequence of pressure from Dr Ira H. Bartholomew, who won election to the legislature to promote these objectives. His cause was aided by public alarm over the sale of unregulated and impure illuminating oil which had caused several explosions and fires. In the new board the moving spirit was its president, Dr H. O. Hitchcock, whose second annual address presented an extended view of the problem. Looking first at the hereditary causes of disease he argued that almost every person inherited some strain of weakness – physical or mental – and that unwise conduct or poor sanitation would bring it to the fore. Trouble began in the home. Even parents in comfortable circumstances subjected their children to poor ventilation, unsuitable food, impure milk, or bad sanitation. Hazards to health could be made worse by the attractive productions of commerce. "The walls of the bedrooms of children were covered with bright and showy wallpaper, pleasant to the eye, but which loads the air with fine dust of arsenic and slowly poisons the innocent sleepers." The neighborhood contributed its

[14] *Idem,* 12th R. (1890–2), 31.
[15] Gerald D. Nash, *Government and Economic Development in California* (Berkeley, Calif., 1964), provides a full account of these agencies and their work.

toll of cesspools, unclean stables, pigsties, slaughterhouses, establishments for bone boiling, fat rendering, glue making, and soap making – all "fruitful sources of preventable sickness and avoidable death."[16]

This recital of evils involved attack upon a vast array of enemies: builders of houses, vendors of food and milk, manufacturers of wallpaper, a host of trades which were regarded as unpleasant but necessary, and the private disposal of human excrement. Wisely Hitchcock realized that the first essential was to educate the public and train physicians. This was to be a major theme of the Michigan board. Then there must be vigilance and vigor among men experienced in sanitary matters, which implied professional local boards armed with power to act. Michigan already had a large number of local boards, but many were inactive and a large majority had not appointed health officers. The legal power to deal with nuisances and campaign against disease already existed; the problem was to persuade people of the need to use them. This emphasis upon information, local organization, and use of existing laws gave the board a tactical advantage.

In 1890 the state board still considered information and co-ordination its major functions. It received special reports on dangerous diseases, routine weekly reports, and full annual reports from local health officers. It kept a register of medical practitioners and health officers. It published a large number of pamphlets, leaflets, and health bulletins. Large portions of its annual reports were taken up with weighty essays on a variety of medical and sanitary topics. A list of subjects covered in state board publications, from 1873 to 1898, included 1,837 separate headings, many of which had references in several reports, revised editions, and supplementary pamphlets.[17]

The strategy of the Michigan board was explained in 1890 by the secretary, Henry Baker:

I believe very strongly in local self-government, and we do not wish to have power, or be called upon to perform duties which should be done by local officers, and this results in permanent sanitary progress. We are gradually able to improve the laws . . . through experience, legislators paying more attention to the demands of their constituents than to State Executive officers, for the improvement of laws governing localities.[18]

[16] Michigan St. B. of H., 2nd R. (1875).
[17] Thomas S. Ainge, *A Quarter Century of Public Health Literature in Michigan* (Lansing, Mich., 1898).
[18] Michigan St. B. of H., 16th R. (1890), 50 (Baker to Prosecuting Officer of Kent County, Apr. 1890).

It was often necessary to give guidance to local boards on how to deal with specific problems, and this occupied most of the secretary's time. Sometimes general guidance was given, as, for instance, in 1889 when the correct procedure for dealing with nuisances was outlined. The order to remove must be issued by the local board and not by the health officer. If the nuisance were on private property the order must be in writing. If there was any doubt whether a nuisance was a "nuisance" – in a technical or legal sense – application should be made to a circuit court for an order to abate it. If legal difficulties had to be overcome, a circuit judge had power in equity to grant an injunction to prevent or abate a nuisance. There were some actions which were legally defined as nuisances (e.g., siting a slaughterhouse close to a public highway), and in these cases an immediate order could be issued by the local board. Finally the council of every village had the legal right to assign places where offensive trades could be carried on and to forbid them elsewhere. An order could be issued immediately if these rules were ignored.[19]

Doubtless many dark and dirty corners remained in Michigan, while many local boards remained sluggish or incompetent. Nor did the state board have to meet the challenge of any major epidemic to test its efficiency. Yet in pursuing the plan of campaign sketched at the outset the Michigan board was remarkably successful. In 1891 it came under attack from Governor Edwin B. Winans who said that it was concerned "mainly with statistics" which could be as well collected by the Secretary of State. Perhaps because of its policy of generating pressure from below, the State Board of Health survived this ill-informed criticism, and was not included in an attempted reorganization and reduction of state agencies. The next governor, John T. Rich, took a very different view, and emphasized the importance of retaining the services of unpaid but experienced and painstaking board members.[20]

The Maryland Board of Health encountered problems which were not unique but appeared in exaggerated form. There was one large and growing city, a western hinterland that was a geographical oddity, an eastern shore that remained a haven of old southern customs, swamps and inlets in great numbers, and a legislature which met biennially for short sessions in a small town. It was therefore extremely difficult to serve the interests of all parts of the state, to evolve a coherent policy, or to get action on legislative recommendations. The State Board of Health was established in 1874 with

[19] *Idem*, 15th R. (1889).   [20] Michigan, Journal of the Senate (1897), 40.

purely advisory powers. Ten years later its duties were enumerated as supervision of all matters affecting health, sanitary investigations, inspection of public hospitals, prisons and asylums, collection, classification and publication of vital statistics, and preparation of a biennial report. As might be expected these manifold duties were to be performed with a miniscule staff and miserly appropriations which had to be fought for at each session. The establishment of local boards was therefore essential if any progress was to be made, though Maryland society apart from Baltimore was hardly conducive to enlightened action.[21]

The board obtained an act in 1886 making local boards mandatory, but in 1890 reported that this law was not being obeyed. Only a few counties had health officers, of whom many were so poorly paid that they had to spend most of their time on private practice. Recommendations to the legislature in 1890 obtained an act which gave the board power "to make such rules and regulations respecting nuisances, sources of filth and causes of sickness as it shall judge necessary for the public health." If the rules were not obeyed, the board could issue a further order, and then prosecute. "This power," said the board, "may seem, at first view, to interfere with the enjoyment of private rights; but it belongs to that class of police regulations to which individual rights are subject, and is indispensable to the well-being of the body politic."[22]

Wisely the Maryland board decided to concentrate its energies upon the problems which most obviously affected the public interest: water, food, and milk. It also pressed forward with educational literature to persuade taxpayers to reject "the sordid idea that pestilence is better than a depleted treasury." An analyst was appointed and within a short time had evidence of adulteration in milk, coffee, tea, wine, and whiskey. The connection between impure milk and infant mortality was demonstrated from experience in New York and Boston. The water from Lake Roland, supplying water to Baltimore, was shown to be heavily polluted by drainage from pigpens, stables, and private houses. Perhaps the legislators were impressed most by the revelation that all samples of whiskey tested were found to be adulterated; it was no longer possible to assume that the liquor was distilled from grain and matured with age when it invariably contained chemical compounds, blenders, and other so-called "improvers."[23]

The Maryland board had other complaints. An act of 1888 made a

<hr>

[21] A brief history and survey of work is given in Maryland State Board of Health, 9th R. (1892), 24ff.   [22] *Ibid.*, 26.   [23] *Ibid.*, 44ff.

diploma from a reputable college, verified by the board, a requisite for medical practice; but this was ineffective because there was no way of knowing what training a diploma implied. Stronger measures were proposed unsuccessfully in 1891, with a comment from the board that "it must be a source of regret to every honest person that some measure cannot be adopted to stop the depredation of human life by quacks and impostors." Nor was an act of 1890 requiring reports on all deaths from contagious diseases complied with.[24]

Nevertheless the board's report for 1892 ran to 368 pages, and provides evidence of steady progress in several fields. An act of 1890 had consolidated the board's position and powers; its scientific work derived great benefit from association with the new Johns Hopkins University and hospital; and even when power to enforce seemed inadequate the threat of publicity had produced results. The first year of milk inspection in Baltimore saw the closure of several dairies which dared not face exposure, while the standards of others improved significantly. But perhaps a major contribution by the board to the cause of public health was the huge number of pamphlets and circulars which were widely distributed and dealt with hundreds of different diseases and health hazards.

This brief survey of four boards of health illustrates common problems, difficulties, and opportunities. Even the least successful had survived early difficulties and won acceptance as permanent agencies. The State had accepted new responsibilities; however grudgingly their legislatures made appropriations or acted upon recommendations, the commitment was there to stay. Success bred success as medical men, sanitary engineers, and informed members of the public added their weight to demands for new laws. In addition to active members of local boards, the state boards could count on their own inspectors, engineers, and scientists to act as cohesive pressure groups, while the advance of medical knowledge added conviction to the claim that disease could be defeated or at least mitigated, and that poisons in the air, water, or food need not be endured. The record was one of steady progress, but this is not to deny that there were setbacks as well as triumphs in many fields. Examination of some specific problems will illustrate this generalization.

All boards of health agreed upon the fundamental importance of vital statistics. In this they reflected the nineteenth-century conviction that facts were the keys to unlock truth; but vital statistics were also essential for day-

24 *Ibid.*, 43, 203.

to-day decisions. Was the death rate rising or falling; what was the mortality in the different age, ethnic, and occupational groups? What were the causes of death and how should they be classified? What was the frequency and distribution of disease? What conditions seemed conducive to which diseases? How effective were measures to combat them?

The exciting possibility of what could be done with this information sometimes obscured the difficulty of collecting it. Regular, prompt, and accurate information was required from a great many people who were not accustomed to give it and did not see why it was required. It meant that in every locality someone must be responsible for keeping a record, and forwarding it at stated intervals to the state board. Amongst those called upon to do the work it required a clear understanding of the purpose and determination to carry it through; individual enthusiasm was the best prescription for success, but a firm law to compel the unwilling to act was also necessary. On the part of a Board of Health clear directions and systematic handling of the data at all levels were required. Thus the apparently straightforward collection of vital statistics meant both a revolution in individual attitudes to government and the development of efficient administration; and though it appeared in almost all laws establishing boards of health, it was one of the last tasks to be perfected. Indeed the short-lived Georgia Board of Health found the task so formidable that it declined to continue. The attempt brought the board "into conflict with the medical profession of the state," and, though agreeing that statistics should be collected, recommended that someone else should shoulder the burden.[25] As late as 1890 the Ohio board complained "that a large amount of money and much time has been wasted in this work, for Ohio's vital statistics are next to worthless."[26] Some states made quicker progress, but by the close of the century there were few in which accuracy could be guaranteed.

All state boards adopted the formation of local boards and the appointment of full-time health officers as primary aims. This proved to be easier in the western states than in the older states; in the former there was a *tabula rasa*, in the latter too many people with tradition and vested interests in maladministration. When the Connecticut state board was established in 1878, local boards already existed but they consisted of justices of the peace and selectmen – often totally without medical knowledge – and were stirred to action only by the threat of smallpox. A principal aim of the new board

[25] Georgia B. of H., 1st R. (1876).   [26] Ohio B. of P. H., 5th R. (1890), 14.

in its early years was to make compulsory the appointment of local health officers, but this was not achieved until 1887. Local boards continued to act – or more frequently failed to act – independently of the state board. Local health officers were elected, and held office for short periods, usually in conjunction with other posts. An act of 1893 lengthened the tenure of health officers, made them non-elective, and provided adequate salaries. The result was close co-operation with the state board, and for the first time it was possible to plan a uniform code of sanitary regulations; but the act of 1893 did not apply to cities and boroughs, where health officers continued to be treated as a part of political patronage.[27]

In Michigan the state Board of Health took the initiative in 1873 by describing precisely the form and function of local boards. They should contain a majority of physicians and, if possible, a lawyer and an engineer. Appointments should not be political. "The function of a board of health must be for *all the people*." The secretary should always be a qualified doctor, and be paid a salary. The board should not be merely advisory but "judicial, mandatory, and executive." It should publish its own circulars, distribute those issued by the state boards, give advice on hygiene, hear complaints of contamination, pollution, or other threats to health, and order remedies. It should issue rules and regulations for action in epidemics, supervise drainage and water supply, decide the location of gasworks, and ensure their safe operation, and inspect the sanitation of all schools and public buildings. The local board was also responsible for collecting statistics of disease and mortality, and recording meteorological and other influences on health. Finally it was to attend to requests from the state board.[28]

There was often uncertainty about the authority of local boards. In 1886 the Pennsylvania Board of Health reported that it had consolidated relations with all existing boards, secured the establishment of others, and helped them to codify and enforce health regulations. In 1884 the Indiana Board of Health exhorted local boards to "*insist* upon and *compel* householders, landlords, corporations and officials" to comply with sanitary rules designed to limit the spread of cholera. In 1885 the secretary of the Wisconsin Board told local boards that their authority "to abate or remove nuisances or cause of sickness is of the most extensive and absolute character," but in 1887, in response to numerous requests, he tried to define those powers and found the relevant laws scattered and difficult to interpret.

[27] Connecticut B. of H., 19th R. (1896), 3ff.
[28] Michigan B. of H., 2nd R. (1873), 7.

There were "numerous points that at first sight appeared to be within the jurisdiction of local boards of health, but which on examination were found to belong to the courts of the State."[29]

Several states passed laws making it mandatory to establish local boards, though compliance was not a matter of course. In 1887 the Ohio state board found that it had no power to establish local boards; their existence depended upon the whim of city councils, the members were frequently unqualified or inexperienced, and party considerations often ruled appointments. The legislature responded by passing an act which made local boards mandatory, but a year later sixty-eight out of the 500 towns had yet to take action. A year passed and forty-two had still to comply, and the state board had no power to push the matter. It was suggested that a penalty, laid down by law and enforced by the courts, should be applied. The happier side of this story is that within two years after the original recommendations over 450 towns had set up boards, and most had accepted the code suggested by the state board. As the state board itself was less than four years old this was not bad going. A similar story could be told in several other states.[30] As the failures of local boards were more likely to be noticed in state reports than their successes, silence may be prima-facie evidence that they had been established and were working satisfactorily.

It was a logical step from concern for local practice to the qualifications of doctors. Medical education in America was at a low ebb in the middle years of the nineteenth century, with competition and commercialism leading to a lowering of standards. The normal procedure for an aspiring physician was to study for three years with a preceptor – an established physician who accepted pupils – and to take two courses in a college, extending over two years. This could be easily abused. According to one account the normal practice in Cleveland, Ohio, was for the student to keep his preceptor's office tidy, answer inquiries, assist at minor operations or dressing, memorize Dalton's *Physiology* and Gray's *Anatomy*, submit to an occasional quiz, and "last but by no means least collect bills from slow-paying clients." Case Western Reserve cut the requirement to one year with a preceptor, and two college courses. There was a final examination, but few ever failed and special reasons could be found for exempting candidates even from this formality. At Worcester Medical School the requirement looked heavier – the standard was three years with a preceptor and two

[29] Pennsylvania B. of H., 2nd R. (1886), 5; Indiana B. of H., 3rd R. (1884), 60; Wisconsin B. of H., 9th R. (1886); 11th R. (1887).
[30] Ohio B. of H., 2nd R. (1887), 270; 3rd R. (1888), 101; 4th R. (1889), 12.

courses of lectures – but the second course was a repetition of the first, no alternatives were offered, and there was no grading.[31]

Colleges for eclectic or homeopathic medicine undercut even these modest standards, as many allowed both courses to be taken in a single year. Though the enthusiasm of instructors, anxious to prove their superiority to "regular" medicine, might be some compensation, students who had failed elsewhere might find it comparatively easy to graduate. As the fees of professors in all colleges depended upon the number of students enrolled, nothing save complete illiteracy disqualified a man from admission and no one wished to acquire a reputation for severity. The American Medical Association was founded in 1846 (largely to beat off attack by practitioners of "irregular" medicine) and put pressure upon states to charter only institutions approved by the association; but even where some success was achieved the regulations were easy to evade. After the Civil War there was some improvement; dissection was legally permitted, laboratory work was added to the curricula, and professors tended to become full-time. Medical schools gradually gained ascendancy over the preceptors, took over clinical instruction, and insisted upon attendance at hospitals. Nevertheless progress was slow. As late as 1885 a leading professor at Case Western Reserve admitted that he had never looked down a microscope, and two years later the university had only one instrument with a single eye-piece.[32] Away from large universities in the more advanced states, dozens of small colleges still handed out worthless diplomas.

The case for uniform action by the states in fixing standards and examining qualifications was clear, but obstacles were not likely to be overcome unless one or more large states gave a clear lead. Much of the credit for change must go to the State Board of Illinois and especially to its long-serving secretary, Dr John H. Rauch. Though qualified and teaching before the Civil War his introduction to the problems of medical administration came as medical director of the army of the Potomac and later as secretary of the Chicago Board of Health. First president of the State Board in 1877 he then served as its full-time secretary from 1879 to 1891, acquiring a national reputation as a pioneer in public health. A most important aspect of his work, begun while he was still in Chicago, was the

---

[31] William T. Corlett, *Reminiscences* (Cleveland, Ohio, 1920), 113ff.
[32] Notes and lectures by Professor F. C. Waite, Henry Dittrich Museum of the History of Medicine, Cleveland, Ohio.

promotion of legislation for licensing physicians.[33] The major law came into effect at the same time as that establishing the State Board of Health, which became also a board of medical examiners with power to grant or withhold licenses. To obtain a license an applicant had to present a diploma from a reputable college or submit to an examination. The penalty for practicing without a license might be as high as a $500 fine or a year in prison for each offense, but physicians who had practiced in the state for more than ten years were exempt.

The Illinois board therefore began its life with a clear mandate to raise medical standards, and its first report spoke scathingly of "diplomas with grand gold medals of honor for distinguished attainments" obtained by purchase without evidence of medical qualifications. Nine medical colleges were immediately refused recognition because they sold diplomas, and without false modesty the board claimed that it had already "accomplished more in breaking up this nefarious traffic than any other agency had been able to do." It warned the public not to be deceived by the impressive certificates displayed by "the advertising specialists, quacks, and abortionists that have hitherto traveled through this state from town to town, promising to cure all the ailments that flesh is heir to."[34]

The second report of the Illinois board contained a register of licensed physicians that ran to 252 pages, and the third report stated that 1,750 without recognized qualifications had left the state or given up medicine. Itinerant "doctors" had been reduced in number from seventy-three to nine and "cancer doctors" from twenty-three to four. The board hoped that, with public support, the time would soon arrive when no license would be issued without a state examination. The proliferation of self-styled medical schools made it impossible to check on all their qualifications, and state examiners could alone impose standards that were uniform and fair.[35]

By 1885 the Illinois board was taking cognizance of unprofessional conduct and medical advertisements "calculated to deceive and defraud the public." The threat to make all applicants for licenses take a state examination was not carried out, and in *Lucas Williams* v. *the People* it was declared unconstitutional to revoke licenses; but small colleges began to compete for the recognition of their degrees while publicity curbed the activities of qualified men who engaged in unethical practice.[36] In 1893 the

[33] Cf. F. Garvin Davenport, "John Henry Rauch and Public Health in Illinois, 1877–1901," *Journal of the Illinois State Historical Society* (1957), 277.
[34] Illinois B. of H., 1st R. (1878), 16–17.
[35] *Idem*, 2nd R. (Register of Physicians) (1879); 3rd R. (1880), 25, 35.
[36] *Idem*, 8th R. (1885), xxxii; Isaac D. Rawlings, *The Rise and Fall of Disease in Illinois*, 2 vols (Springfield, Ill., 1927), I, 153.

first Pan-American Medical Congress was told that the reports of the Illinois Board of Health had exerted a more powerful influence upon medical education than any other publication.[37]

As time went on the burden of examining began to tell upon a board that was anxious to extend its activities. Bills to create separate Boards of Health and of Medical Examiners were proposed but lost in 1899 and 1903. Indeed its very success in raising standards had diverted attention from other endeavours. Illinois dropped somewhat behind in establishing local boards, and despite its efforts Chicago's drinking water remained polluted. It had however performed valiant service in promoting compulsory vaccination.[38]

By 1887 there were laws regulating medical practice in thirty-four states, but there were many loopholes. In California the law was strong on paper but weak in effect; there were three separate examining boards – regular, eclectic, and homeopathic – and an applicant who failed in one might apply successfully to another. A Kansas licensing law had been found unconstitutional because examiners were appointed by an unofficial body (the State Medical Society). In Texas the examining board was bound to license a graduate of any chartered medical college without examination. There was a similar law in Wisconsin, which also forbade unqualified persons to use the titles "doctor," "physician," or "surgeon" but laid down no procedure for validating diplomas.[39] In Indiana it was left to the clerk of the circuit court of a county to decide what was a "reputable" college.[40]

In Illinois a valuable precedent was set in 1878 when the Supreme Court decided that no one had a *right* to practice medicine, with or without a diploma, and that further examination was a legitimate exercise of police power. The Illinois courts also held that members of the profession were best fitted to decide what was "unprofessional conduct."[41] By the end of the century one could say that the exception proved the rule, and that it was becoming normal for states to license doctors, recognize only colleges of good standing, examine in cases of doubt, and enforce standards of professional conduct.

States took more rapid action to regulate pharmacy. As early as 1873 a writer in the *Journal of Social Science* declared that "the pharmacist must be made responsible to the government and the law."[42] Most states took

---

[37] F. Garvin Davenport, 293.
[38] Illinois B. of H., Preliminary R. for 1903–4, 10, 23.
[39] *Proceedings of the Fourth National Conference of State Boards of Health* (1887), 39; Wisconsin B. of H., 12th R. (Compendium of Health Laws) (1889).
[40] Indiana B. of H., 4th R. (1885), 3; 6th R. (1886), 3.
[41] *Fourth National Conference*, 41.
[42] *Journal of Social Science*, 5, 126.

steps in subsequent years to regulate pharmacy, and several had Boards of Pharmacy to examine credentials, investigate complaints, and prosecute offenders. Beyond the fringe of those who sold drugs about which they were ignorant, were the purveyors of potions and pills that were positively dangerous. In 1891 the Massachusetts board found that "Madame Fale's Excelsior Complexion Bleach" and "Madame Rapport's Face Bleach" both contained harmful chemicals. It was possible to prosecute under an act of 1888 forbidding the sale of poison without a doctor's prescription, record of sale, and the word "Poison" boldly inscribed on the label. The board soon congratulated itself on the fact that all drugs and cosmetics offered for sale conformed to uniform standards.[43] Wisconsin legislated against the use of false or misleading labels as early as 1874, and in 1882 went on to lay down that pharmacists must be registered, hold a degree in pharmacy, and submit qualifications to state examiners. Several other states took steps to prevent the sale of harmful drugs without prescription, and restrained the trade in fraudulent remedies.[44]

A primary task of most boards was to improve sanitation, but all that this implied took time to realize. Dirty streets and foul sewers could not be remedied effectively without improving the disposal of refuse and excrement, and this normally meant that action had to be forced upon landlords. Polluted water led investigators back to its rural source, and the discharge from farms, houses, and factories into streams. In 1868 Massachusetts passed a Tenement Act to improve conditions in the most overcrowded towns, but two years later the Aldermen of Boston had failed to enforce it. "A large portion of the poor," wrote Dr George Derby, "are crowded into buildings whose construction sets at defiance the laws of health." The condition of yards, privies, and alleys made them "liable at any time to become centers from which pestilence may extend in every direction." There should be a Boston Health Commission free from "local and political influences."[45]

Slaughterhouses and establishments for processing their by-products – bone boiling, fat rendering, grease and glue making – were always causes for complaint; factories were unsafe and insanitary, discharged noxious waste into rivers, and poured stinking chemicals from their chimneys into the air; ancient powers to deal with nuisances existed, but it required a strong hand to enforce them. The Pennsylvania State Board of Health

[43] Massachusetts B. of H., 22nd R. (1891), 420–1.
[44] Wisconsin B. of H., 12th R. (Compendium of Health Laws) (1890–1).
[45] Minutes of the Board of Health, July and Dec. 1870, Massachusetts State Archives.

successfully prosecuted and lodged in jail an individual who was "poisoning the air of a lovely village for the sake of compelling his neighbors to buy his property."[46] But it was seldom possible to prove willful intent, and when the offensive fumes or waste had been for years accepted as normal action might be even more difficult. Appeals for more and tighter laws were a perennial theme in the Reports of the boards. The Maryland board made a comprehensive plea in 1890 for "severe penalties on those who wantonly destroy the health and lives not only of their own families but also of their neighbors . . . and who are responsible, morally, for the presence of infection and contagious diseases in their midst."[47] Logically this would carry the authority of the State into the very homes of offenders and penalize them for offenses committed in their own households.

State boards asked for power "to compel the execution of sanitary works in towns where they are neglected, to require that proper drainage should be made and pure water supplied."[48] Public acceptance of abuses was a major obstacle to improvement and fed upon ignorance. The Wisconsin board observed that the American was "relentlessly independent and logical so far as his personal experience carries him." If told that there was death in sewer gas, he would say that he had lived all his life in an atmosphere that was now said to be unhealthy.

Tell him that well water in cities is a fruitful source of disease and he will show you hundreds who have used it for years with impunity. When you ask him to go to the enormous expense of carrying away the sewage more safely, and to spend a great deal of money to obtain better water, or tear up his floors and his walls for costly plumbing, he will show a good deal of impatience, if he does not consider you altogether foolish.[49]

It followed that the most important aspect of sanitary improvement was education of the public, and it was often as necessary to shock as to inform.

The Tennessee board, faced with a legislature that was hard to convince, resorted to a sanitary examination of the Capitol Building in Nashville. It found the basement insanitary, full of decaying matter, and a source of smells. The water closets were old, and imperfect, with wooden partitions giving off "ammoniacal odors." The sewer terminal was open and near to the building, so that with the wind in the right direction legislators worked

[46] Pennsylvania B. of H., 2nd R. (1886), 3.
[47] Maryland B. of H., 8th R. (1890), 23–4.
[48] Tennessee B. of H., 2nd R. (1880–4), 32.
[49] Wisconsin B. of H., 11th R. (1887).

in an atmosphere of sewer gas. There was a choice between no ventilation or draughts. Heat came from two old furnaces which carried foul air from the basement up through dilapidated wooden ducts. Finally the water supply was drawn from an old, dirty, and corroded tank. No health record had been kept of assemblymen but their frequent complaints and absences suggested that they were more prone to sickness than the average inhabitant of Nashville.[50]

The Indiana board judged that a critical review of schoolhouses would stimulate public pressure for change. In 1883 it found that one-fifth of the schools had no water closets, and those which existed were seldom if ever cleaned or disinfected. Ten Indianapolis schools had polluted drinking water, sixteen had serious defects in water supply, and others depended on contaminated wells. Country schools were little better. The typical school was a wooden box placed on ground too poor for farming, "unfenced, undrained, and wanting in anything ornamental or tasteful to please the eye."[51]

In 1891 the Ohio board found itself overwhelmed with requests for visits of inspection, mainly to deal with sanitary questions. It found the water of the Ohio River to be polluted, and recommended that all new plans for public water supply should be first approved by the board. When no action was taken the board came back two years later with the admonition that it was high time that the State should take some action for the protection of public water supplies. On this occasion the legislature took note and gave the board the required power, and in 1894 it was reported that state supervision had been generally welcomed.[52]

Progress was nearly always slow, but the Louisiana State Board of Health was unusually dilatory. It had for years exercised tenuous authority over the sanitary state of New Orleans, but complaint was more frequent than action. Not until 1896 was the board prosecuting individuals for failure to remove garbage, for operating insanitary bakeries, or for keeping unhealthy dairies. Not until 1899 was a tax voted for sewerage and water improvements, and work was not started until 1903 on new sewers and until 1905 on the water system. Both neared completion in 1911 and New Orleans could at last drink pure water and dispose safely of sewage.[53]

[50] Tennessee B. of H., 2nd R. (1880–4), 32ff.
[51] Indiana B. of H., 2nd R. (1883), 32–3.
[52] Ohio B. of H., 6th R. (1891), 5, 9; 8th R. (1893), 10; 9th R. (1894), 9.
[53] John Duffy (ed.), *The Rudolph Matas History of Medicine in Louisiana*, 2 vols (Baton Rouge, La., 1959, 1962), II, 495; Board of Health Scrapbook for 1894–7, Rudolph Matas Library, New Orleans.

The battle for better sanitation was not won in a year or a decade; no improvement could be maintained without constant vigilance, and it was natural for its protagonists to slip into the language of war. As Dr H. Wardner told the Illinois board in 1880:

We need to remember that we have enemies to confront and dangers to avoid upon every hand . . . Every selfish property owner who is compelled to make costly improvements in his houses and tenements in the interests of public health becomes a hostile influence. Still worse, perhaps more difficult to combat, is the inertia of mere conservation. How solidly this force can stand in resistance to anything which savors of change, merely because it is change, every one of us knows, and no one can adequately tell.[54]

As well as human folly the sanitary inspectors had to struggle against the obsolescence of equipment, while the frequent identification of new threats to health meant they could never cease to learn. A sanitary inspector is not normally pictured as a heroic figure, yet there is nobility in the dedication with which this new breed of men fought to win the battle for civilized life.

The fight for pure food and milk was closely allied with sanitation. Massachusetts passed a Food and Drug Act in 1882 and made the State Board of Health, Charity, and Lunacy responsible for its enforcement. Two analysts were appointed, and, when their investigations revealed a shocking state of affairs, two more were added. Board reports spread the news of their findings and other states began to consider the need for laws to protect the consumer. These responsibilities continued and expanded when the Health Board once more became separate.

One approach was by inspection and prosecution, another was by insistence upon accurate description of goods offered for sale. In 1887 the Ohio board observed that "the true way to put down this evil, is to brand it with the mark of its own sin." It recommended a law that every package should copy a statement of its contents in comprehensible language, and false description should be treated as obtaining money under false pretenses.[55] Dr Joseph Jones of Louisiana pressed for the regulation of canned goods, which should be date-stamped, and for strict control over the use of coloring matter.[56]

In 1888 the first Pure Food Convention was held at Washington to

---

[54] H. Wardner, M.D., "State Medicine in Illinois," Illinois B. of H., 3rd R. (1880), 40–1.
[55] Ohio B. of H., 2nd R. (1887), 307. It was asserted that the proposed law would require a well-known brand of raspberry jam to be labeled "Boiled tomatoes, strained, *ad lib.*, glucose, hayseed, raspberry syrup to flavor."
[56] Joseph Jones, *Public and International Hygiene*, Address to 9th International Medical Congress (1887) (no page numbers).

discuss proposals for federal regulation. The National Board of Trade had offered a prize for the best draft of the law, which was won by Professor Wagner, president of the English Society of Analysts. He proposed a Bureau of Adulteration to create a law prohibiting importation, manufacture, or sale of impure food and drugs. The bill approved by the convention was introduced in Congress by Senator Faulkner, referred to the Committee on Agriculture and Forestry, never reported, and thereafter lost without a trace. Bills in the next Congress were equally unfortunate, despite several petitions in favor of a pure food law. It would be eighteen years before Congress passed an effective law, and in the intervening years whatever was done to set and enforce standards was done by the states.[57]

Considerable progress was made. By the end of the century substances that were positively harmful were no longer used as adulterants, as components in drugs, or in cosmetics. In many states laws on the labeling of packaged products had been passed, improved, and enforced, though this activity owed much to the anxiety of dairy farmers that oleo-margarine should not be sold as butter. The courts upheld these laws with opinions that opened the way for still further regulation.

In 1893 the Louisiana board requested a law for the compulsory inspection of dairy cattle; this failed in the legislature although the cost would have been only $6,000. In 1895 the board reported that in a sample of cows tested almost half were tubercular. Many of the dairies were "foul in the extreme" and few had taken advantage of a scheme for analysis and certification offered by the board. Photographs of dairies were included in the report to make the point. The water unofficially added to the milk was about fifty per cent urine. Revelations such as this could hardly fail to make an impression and Louisiana got its first milk law. It was difficult to test milk and dairy herds unless the livestock keepers and dairymen were prepared to co-operate, and this was unlikely until the public showed itself aware of the danger and ready to reject uncertified milk. Voluntary schemes in some cities achieved considerable success in bringing this about.[58]

Whatever else was achieved the public was likely to judge a Board of Health by its success against epidemic or persistent disease. Yellow fever was the most sudden, drastic, and mysterious of epidemics. It was known that it was introduced during the summer by ships from tropical parts where the disease was endemic, and spread rapidly until checked by the onset of

[57] Congressional Record, 50th Congress, 2nd Series, 303.
[58] *Matas History of Medicine*, II, 489–90.

cooler weather. No one realized that mosquitoes were the carriers, and lacking this essential information all kinds of preventive measures were proposed and controversy raged around their respective merits. Generally the remedies ranged from lengthy quarantine to short detention and drastic disinfection. Though yellow fever always entered the country by sea, it could be carried inland by navigable rivers, rail, or road, and news of an outbreak in the Gulf ports might therefore prompt inland local authorities to cut off communication with the infected areas. Particularly affected was the great port of New Orleans, whose inland commerce might be brought to a standstill, and one can understand the anger of merchants when rumor or faulty diagnosis produced this result. If quarantine was imposed too late there was bound to be recrimination, but if imposed on suspicion the Board of Health might be accused of needlessly endangering the trade of the city.

It was primarily to combat sea-borne epidemics that the first State Board of Health was established in Louisiana in 1855. It might therefore have deserved earlier consideration, except that it was atypical and did not set precedents for other boards. As one influential doctor observed in 1879, "Louisiana has legislated on paper a State Board of Health and Vital Statistics, but in reality we have no State, merely a city, board of health, organized under laws which nobody except politicians (and a designing or ignorant class of these) can possibly approve."[59] After the Civil War it was plagued by financial difficulties, lack of co-operation by the New Orleans city authority, and perennial disputes with the State Medical Society. In the early 1870s, its major concern was with smallpox (2,200 cases were reported in New Orleans and 1,100 deaths). It made some attempt at sanitary reform in New Orleans but little elsewhere, and this despite the belief – prevalent among board members – that disease was carried by foul air.

Meanwhile controversy developed over yellow fever quarantine, and in 1875 a majority of New Orleans physicians petitioned the legislature for a relaxation of the quarantine law which required – nominally at least – a long period of detention for all ships from affected ports. In 1876 a new law gave the Board of Health discretion to reduce the period, provided that disinfection of the ship had been carried out thoroughly, but a severe outbreak in 1878 was attributed by some to this relaxation. President Hayes set up a three-man Yellow Fever Commission and its report led to

[59] Dr Stanford E. Chaillé, "Address to Louisiana State Medical Society" (1879), quoted *Matas History of Medicine*, II, 464–5. The history of medicine in Louisiana has been unusually well covered. In addition to the *Matas History* there are: *The Louisiana State Board of Health*, by the Secretary of 1904 (New Orleans, 1904); Gordon E. Gillson, *The Louisiana State Board of Health: the Formative Years* (Baton Rouge, La., 1966).

the establishment in 1879 of a National Board of Health to gather information, co-operate with State Boards, and act if local quarantine arrangements were considered unsatisfactory. The National Board was welcomed by the Louisiana State Medical Society and by the local press, and the stage seemed set for a national quarantine system in which the Louisiana board would play a key role.

Later it would be claimed that during the short period of co-operation between the national and state boards quarantine worked efficiently. The main effort was to contain any outbreak within a small area by prohibiting movement out of it, while widespread disinfection was carried out. One suspects that its effect was to kill mosquitoes and to prevent infected persons from traveling, and that it was therefore as effective a way of dealing with yellow fever as was likely to be discovered. It had the additional advantage that there was only slight interference with commerce in other localities, though incoming ships were held for cleansing at the quarantine station. By luck or judgment the cases in 1879 were limited to forty-nine (eleven deaths) in a small area.[60]

Unfortunately disputes soon arose. The National Board was dissatisfied with the Louisiana arrangements for quarantine, and proposed that all inbound ships should be held at a federal station off the coast. There was also an outcry when a national inspector diagnosed two mild cases in Plaquemines parish and suggested that infection came from the Louisiana station. Two New Orleans doctors failed to confirm his diagnosis, and though the National Board had not proposed isolation of the area it was denounced by the State Board for exceeding its authority.

Harmonious relations might have been restored but for the new president of the Louisiana board, Dr Joseph Jones, an extremely able but tactless and insensitive man who "led the Board successfully through four years of the most strenuous existence such a body had ever known." The reports in these years made frequent reference to "enemies" and "read something like the records of a military campaign"; these were not the enemies described by other boards, but the National Board, the State Medical Society, New Orleans merchants, and railroad and shipping leaders.[61]

---

[60] From a paper by S. S. Herrick, M. D., entitled "Forgotten Sanitation," in the miscellaneous records of the Louisiana Board of Health, Rudolph Matas Library, New Orleans.

[61] *Louisiana State Board of Health*, 17–18. Dr Jones was a professor at Tulane University, and had served as a surgeon in the Confederate army; he was an honorary member of medical societies in Philadelphia, New York, and Leipzig, and president of the section on Public and International Hygiene at the International Medical Congress at Washington in 1887.

The points at issue were whether suspected areas should be reported immediately to neighboring states or await action by the Louisiana board; whether other states should be allowed to have observers in New Orleans and at the quarantine station; and whether infected vessels should be allowed to enter the Mississippi before disinfection at the federal quarantine station.[62] To sustain his side of the argument Dr Jones put on the armour of state rights, while conducting a personal feud with Dr Stanford Chaillé, a member of the National Board and formerly of the State Board, who normally had the backing of the State Medical Society. The New Orleans Auxiliary Sanitary Association also supported the National Board and endorsed the remarks of a delegate from Pensacola ("a Democrat opposed to centralization"), who argued that there must be concerted action against disease though shipping should be interrupted as little as possible. The State Board replied by recommending the suppression of the association.[63] Triumph came for Dr Jones when Congress failed to renew the appropriation for the National Board, which consequently ceased to exist.

To do Dr Joseph Jones justice he made determined efforts to improve the state quarantine system. When he took over, the Mississippi station was in a deplorable condition, while shipping companies and other merchants opposed to lengthy quarantine had obtained an injunction against the levy of fees to support it. As well as carrying out renovation and improvement at the station, he vigorously contested the legal action and won a notable victory in 1884 when the State Supreme Court upheld both the quarantine law and the fees. "After a continuous battle of four years' duration," said the Board in its report, "in which the vast maritime interests of the State, and the powers and influence of the wealthiest railroad and steamship company in the south-west, were marshaled against the legally constituted health authorities, the Board of Health . . . achieved a memorable and signal victory." Whatever the unfortunate personal disputes behind the case, it was a notable vindication of state authority. The court decided that fees charged for quarantine services were not a tax on interstate commerce, and that quarantine imposed by individual states was a legitimate use of the police power.[64]

Calmer days followed when Dr Jones was succeeded by Dr Joseph Holt, who was "enthusiastic, untiring, and possessed of strong personal magnet-

[62] *Matas History of Medicine,* II, 469ff.
[63] Report by Dr S. Chaillé, *National Board of Health Bulletin,* Supplement No. 5 (1881).
[64] New Orleans *Times Democrat,* Dec. 3, 1882 (clipping in Board of Health Miscellaneous papers, Matas Library); *Matas History of Medicine,* II, 468.

ism." He gave up a lucrative private practice, and "devoted himself to the herculean task of convincing the skeptical of New Orleans, the hostile and suspicious authorities of other States, and most important of all, the State Legislature."[65] Persuasion was necessary because he proposed a new system of quarantine that would emphasize disinfection rather than detention. Vessels from "clean" ports were inspected and sent on their way if clear of disease. Vessels with disease on board or from infected ports were quarantined, all persons were disembarked, clothing was boiled, sulphur dioxide was pumped into the hold, and the decks were treated with bichloride of mercury. The whole process took from one to three days, lengthy detention was avoided, and refinements of the system in future years led to its adoption as a model for other ports. In a formal address in 1890 the Louisiana Board of Health paid tribute to Dr Holt who had "rendered immense service to Humanity and Commerce."[66]

It is likely that the apparent success of Holt's system was due to the killing of mosquitoes on the ships by fumigation, while on land most cases were quickly reported and the area sealed off.[67] Unfortunately, so long as the real carrier was not identified, no measures could be effective for long. Yellow fever returned in 1897, and public outcry led to the resignation of the whole Board of Health. This had a fortunate outcome in that it led to a new and much improved Health Law. A new state board was given exclusive control over maritime quarantine and all infectious diseases ashore; its jurisdiction was extended to the whole state; it could make a sanitary code, appoint inspectors, and enforce its regulations; it could also maintain a public health staff including analysts and scientific officers. Dr Edmund Souchon, first president of the new board, drew up a 400-page sanitary code. The establishment of local boards was encouraged, publicity and health education were emphasized, improved inspection of food and drugs was authorized, as was preventive medicine including vaccination, and, finally, mosquito control was begun. After forty-three years in existence the Louisiana board finally had the full apparatus of modern public health administration.

Other boards in the Mississippi valley also wrestled with the problem of

[65] *Louisiana State Board of Health*, 24. In July 1884 Holt persuaded the legislature to appropriate $30,000 to inaugurate his new system.

[66] *Address of the Board of Health, State of Louisiana, to the People of the Southern States and Mississippi Valley* (New Orleans, 1890), 3.

[67] In 1883 the U.S. consul at Rio de Janeiro sent to Dr Joseph Jones a newspaper clipping about the experiments of Dr Domingo Freire proving that yellow fever was carried in the blood, and that infection resulted if blood was transferred from one individual to another. No one followed this up. (Board of Health Papers, Matas Library, New Orleans.)

yellow fever and malaria. In Mississippi a board was created in 1877 at the height of alarm over yellow fever, and an amended act of 1880 gave it wide powers to make and enforce regulations; but the secretary's salary was only $800 so it could not be more than a part-time job. The association between malarial disease and swampy ground was correctly deduced, though for the wrong reasons, and the board concentrated on drainage and removal of human habitation to healthier places. This program was unlikely to move fast or far, and as the immediate threat of yellow fever diminished after 1880 the board turned its attention to other health matters; but in spite of strong powers on paper it remained weak in action.[68]

The most frustrating yellow fever experience was that of the Tennessee board in 1878. It had been set up in 1877 "after much effort and explanation" from the State Medical Society. It had no executive power and no appropriation, and its only means of communication with the public was through the press. Its first biennial report was printed only because a private company was prepared to take the risk. In this extraordinary situation the board had to face a devastating outbreak of yellow fever in Memphis – and could do nothing:

It was powerless to do aught to stay its dreadful ravages . . . It had no powers to enforce its advice or money to pay its agents. Hence it could only look on and take counsel of despair.

Local authorities tried to improve their own quarantine against persons coming from Memphis, all commerce ceased, and in the city the threat of starvation was added to the danger of infection. The city contained 45,000 persons; in the last week of July – when alarm was first sounded – a large number left the city, leaving about 5,000 white and 10,500 black. In this reduced population 7,000 cases were reported, and over 3,000 deaths; in outlying suburbs perhaps another 1,000 died. Some of the estimated 24,000 who left the city were accommodated in camps, and because of local opposition state troops had to be employed to occupy the sites. There were 1,304 in the largest camp and 225 yellow fever cases, though deaths were cut to four per cent because medical attention was immediately available. People leaving the city carried infection with them, mainly along the railroads, and deaths were reported in every town within a radius of 300 miles. The total death toll was estimated at 12,000.[69]

---

[68] Mississippi B. of H., 1st R. (1880–1), 5–6, 8.
[69] Tennessee B. of H., 1st R. (1880–1), *passim*.

Faced with this catastrophe the legislature moved to give the Board of Health more power, and though "there were not wanting people who claimed that such powers as contemplated were subversive of liberty," the princely sum of $3,000 was appropriated. Thus armed the board was able to take action when a yellow fever case was reported in Memphis in July 1879. It immediately issued orders to inspect all trains leaving infected places, to cleanse and fumigate all cars and baggage, to transfer all passengers and baggage to new trains after five miles, to transfer all freight at a distance of not more than fifty miles, and to heat all mail bags to 250° before forwarding. All leaving the city were advised to go to upland areas. No steamboat from an infected place was allowed to dock without a certificate of inspection. All cases were to be reported immediately, and all contacts kept under observation for five days. These measures reflected the board's belief that the disease had "no power in itself, or traveling from place to place, but may be suspended in the air, and diffused by atmospheric currents," but not transmitted directly from person to person.[70]

The Tennessee board was strongly in favor of national action, expressed lack of confidence in the Louisiana State Board, and favored the system introduced by Dr Holt. Other boards in the Mississippi Valley expressed similar support for national action. For instance, in 1887 the Ohio board urged that the State's representatives in Congress should be instructed to support national quarantine. The energetic Dr Rauch of Illinois did most to promote co-operation between states. Following the 1878 epidemic he organized a Sanitary Council of the Mississippi Valley to ensure "a cordial cooperation of State with State, and of all with the General Government."[71]

A cloud of uncertainty hung over all efforts to combat yellow fever until the mosquito was identified as the carrier, but the horrific nature of the disease and the commercial consequences did as much as anything to concentrate the minds of legislators on the need to exert state authority. Naturally it was the southern states and those of the Mississippi Valley that were most affected. Texas had no State Board of Health (though one was authorized by the Constitution of 1876), but a state health officer was appointed and the governor was given wide discretionary power to impose quarantine. The Texan ports were normally closed for half of the year to all

---

[70] *Idem*, 2nd R. (1880–4), 444–5. One order forbade the ginning and baling of cotton in Memphis. A local judge issued an injunction against executing this order, but it was upheld by the acting Chancellor.
[71] *Ibid.*, 44ff; Ohio B. of H., 2nd R. (1887), 297; Illinois B. of H., 2nd R. (1879), 29.

ships from Mexico, the West Indies, and Brazil. Conditions remained unsatisfactory and were criticized by the U.S. Marine Hospital Service in 1896.[72] In Georgia public health had an unhappy history despite yellow fever in Savannah in 1876. The board was set up in 1875 with an appropriation of $1,500; two years later – despite an exhortation from the board that "public hygiene is fast becoming one of the great questions of this age . . . it must be taken hold of by the States" – no appropriation was made. Not until 1903 did Georgia have a new board of health.[73]

In spite of this patchy record the author of a carefully prepared work on public hygiene said in 1911 that the southern boards had been pioneers in many respects and controlled the most advanced research facilities. This progress must be attributed largely to the impact of malaria and yellow fever, and, paradoxically, to ignorance of the way in which these diseases were transmitted since this led to emphasis on many aspects of sanitation, cleansing, disinfection, and inspection that might otherwise have been neglected.[74]

Smallpox was a menace in most states. The way to prevent it was known, but again and again legislatures drew back from compulsory vaccination. A compromise was to make it obligatory for all children attending public schools. In 1881 the Illinois board issued such an order; certificates of vaccination – on forms provided by the board – were to be signed by a physician; no child was to be admitted without one, and the school principal was responsible for returning them to the board. In the following year the board included a long essay on vaccination in its report, with an injunction that it should be enforced rigorously, and that "if a question should arise as between private rights or interests and the interests of the health of the community, the public interest must be held paramount." Clearly this law, even if conscientiously enforced, left many open to infection, and there was no compulsory revaccination. In 1895 its effect was completely undermined when the state Supreme Court decided that the law could be enforced only when there was immediate threat of smallpox. In 1904 the board reported a marked increase in the disease since 1899. Outbreaks in 1900, 1901 and 1902 had led to widespread vaccination, but this fell away in 1903 when few cases occurred, and in 1904 smallpox returned in a particularly virulent form. The best that a board could do

[72] Gould M. Porter, "A History of the State Organization for Public Health Administration in Texas," M.A. thesis, University of Chicago, 1942.
[73] Georgia B. of H., 1st R. (1876).
[74] Thomas S. Blair, *Public Hygiene*, 2 vols (Boston, Mass., 1911), I, 209.

under these circumstances was to ensure that supplies of vaccine were available, and keep up the flow of publications on the subject. In 1894 Wisconsin also passed a school law requiring vaccination before admission both to public and private schools, but this was invalidated by the State Supreme Court as unconstitutional and unreasonable. The Indiana board tried to get a compulsory vaccination law in 1886, but it was lost in the legislature. The fight to eradicate smallpox in the United States was yet in its earliest days; for the time being and in most instances legislators and judges treated disfigurement and death as sacrifices on the altar of liberty.[75]

Disappointments clouded the records of the state boards of health, yet in retrospect progress appears profound and rapid. The small minority who had actively promoted the cause of public health had obtained state boards, steadily increased public powers and activity, and became a legion. Though many had gone through lean times, only in Georgia had a board once established been allowed to lapse. In 1894 a veteran of the campaign in Ohio had these words for his colleagues at a meeting in Columbus:

I wish we were on higher ground than we are, and yet . . . it does seem to me that we ought to be encouraged. I have been looking back . . . eight years. Some of us wanted to organize a sanitary association, and we met in this city. We had only about half a dozen. We expected that the people of Ohio would rally to the cause and thought we should have a house full, but were badly disappointed. That was eight years ago. And now, gentlemen, are you aware of the fact that there are today over 10,000 people in the State of Ohio who are officially connected with boards of health? We have between 1,700 and 1,800 boards of health, when ten years ago there were only a few, and most of them were inefficient.[76]

In its first report the Ohio board had lamented that "the knowledge of the people regarding the laws of health is less perhaps than of any other subject so nearly concerning them." Since that time the state boards of health had undertaken a great task of public education, and by 1898 the Connecticut board could record "a public sentiment no longer opposed to, but actively interested in and cooperating with, all proper efforts at sanitary progress." Often this could be attributed to the heroic efforts of individuals.[77] In 1886 Dr Thomas F. Wood, who was almost a one-man Board of Health for North Carolina, began publication of a monthly *Health Bulletin*, largely written, wrapped, and mailed by himself. It

[75] Illinois B. of H., 5th R. (1882), 515; *idem*, Preliminary Report for 1903–4; Cornelius Harper, "History of the Wisconsin Board of Health" (typescript, Wisconsin Historical Society); Indiana B. of H., 5th R. (1886), 47.
[76] Ohio B. of H., 9th R. (1886), 337.
[77] *Idem*, 1st R. (1886); Connecticut B. of H., 19th R. (1896), 13.

included reports from county superintendents which gave, for the first time, a panoramic view of health in the state, and often provided items for the newspapers. This persuaded the legislature to vote a much enlarged appropriation for 1887.[78] One indicator of the changed mood was the growing number of questions, complaints, and requests for advice or visits submitted to the board, and the reports of all state boards provided evidence of increased work and demands for the services of their officers.

Public interest came in response to government's acceptance of public responsibility. In 1885 the Indiana board found that, wherever it had been necessary to enforce the law, "the people and the public press . . . had unmistakably demonstrated their willingness to sustain the actions of the Board." The Connecticut board noted that "the immediate effect of appointing a sanitary inspector in a town, in causing a very general cleaning up of back yards, etc." was astonishing. The Tennessee board reported that as soon as a local board was established "a spirit of emulation" had been aroused, and "a disposition to enter into a general cleaning up" had taken the place of deeply rooted apathy.[79]

In the upper echelons of the medical profession the board reports and other publications provided a national forum, and exchanges of views were institutionalized in state and national public health conventions. Under the aegis of the boards had grown up new branches of scientific and technical knowledge, and professional oversight of sanitation, water supply, food and drug laws, pharmacy, and medical education. Laboratories had been built and public hygiene was winning recognition as a subject for academic investigation and training. New professions had come into being with the health inspectors, sanitary inspectors, specialists in water supply and drainage, public analysts, and their supporting technical staffs. Viewing these great changes it is possible to endorse the confident prediction of the Pennsylvania board in 1885 that its creation had marked "a new era in the history of the State."[80]

---

[78] Benjamin E. Washburn, *The First Fifty Years of Organized Public Health in North Carolina* (Raleigh, N.C., 1966), 17.
[79] Indiana B. of H., 4th R. (1885), 6–7; Connecticut B. of H., 19th R. (1896), 13; Tennessee B. of H., 1st R. (1878–80), 59.
[80] Pennsylvania B. of H., 1st R. (1885), 9.

6

THE BUREAUS OF LABOR STATISTICS

The nineteenth century was the first age of statistics in Great Britain and the United States. The new era dawned with the first federal census in 1790 and the first British census in 1801, but as first conceived the purpose of enumeration was very limited. In the United States the primary motive was to obtain exact figures on which to base the apportionment of seats in the House of Representatives; in Britain the demand for figures reflected anxiety about the burden of poor rates and controversy over whether the population was rising, declining, or merely shifting.

Once the census was instituted it became comparatively easy to add new questions to the enumeration, and to subject the figures to more sophisticated analysis. In Britain, in the 1830s, the registration of births, deaths, and marriages became compulsory, and before long the death rate was recognized as the standard by which the statutory requirement for the establishment of a local board of health could be determined. Private insurance companies had run somewhat ahead of governments in working out their own tables of life expectancy, but by 1850 there was accumulating evidence on the incidence of disease, on accidents, wages, cost of living, and poverty.

The counting of heads had been traditionally associated with some new and probably unpleasant purpose of government: taxation, the raising of armies, or the regulation of trade. In the nineteenth century it became increasingly associated with economic and social change. Reformers demanded the figures – or were told to produce them – before their proposals could be considered; once accepted the figures provided a platform on which they could stand. Private statistical societies began to appear, and though their members were often amateurs of conservative instincts they believed that their new science was the key to social betterment. Yet there remained a link with the old attitude to enumeration

148

as an instrument of government policy, since the collection of statistics was normally advocated to prepare the ground for public action. It was no accident that the rise of bureaus of labor statistics in America was closely associated with the growing power of organized labor, and with widespread anxiety about the "labor question."

By the early years of the twentieth century these bureaus existed in thirty-two states. All reported annually or biennially, and this provided an enormous volume of statistical, descriptive, and argumentative material about all aspects of labor life and work. While each bureau had its own history and evolved in its own way, all were influenced by the experience of the Massachusetts bureau, which was the first to be founded.

Massachusetts, at the close of the Civil War, was more conscious of the "labor problem" than any other part of the nation. Immigration, the rise of factories, the existence of an unusually high proportion of skilled trades, wartime inflation, and dislocation of the labor market all combined to produce agitation for labor reform. Two separate reform movements developed – the ten-hour and eight-hour men – with differences not confined to the length of the working day. The ten-hour movement drew its strength from factory workers and leadership from philanthropists and some politicians. Its aims were to protect women and children from exploitation, and, incidentally, to prevent long hours and low pay from cutting the work available for adult males. Ostensibly its aim was to raise the standards of working-class life by gradual stages. The eight-hour men, led by Ira Steward and George McNeill, drew their strength from the organized skilled workers, whose immediate aim was to protect and improve a comparatively high standard of living, and ultimately to alter the structure of industrial society. Shorter hours without a reduction of wages would make more money available for consumption, increase production, give the working class more time for education and participation in public affairs, and ultimately substitute co-operation for capitalist control. Of more immediate concern to politicians was the fact that Steward argued that poverty was creeping up the social ladder; if skilled labor felt the pressure in one decade, farmers, clerks, and small professional men would feel it in the next. The message was one which many voters would find disturbing.

The legislature responded by setting up commissions of inquiry into labor conditions in 1865, 1866, and 1867. Information was difficult to obtain, and members of the commissions had little sympathy with the eight-hour movement, though they were more responsive to the amelioration of working conditions for women and children.[1] The one positive result was the passage of a law to ensure that factory children received an adeqate education.

These first attempts to inquire into the conditions of labor were, however, of considerable importance. The commission of 1866 was appointed to investigate the "hours of labor in . . . relation to the social, educational and sanitary condition of the working classes." In the words of Carroll D. Wright, who was to become the great authority on the bureaus and their work, "This language is very significant. It is found in nearly every act creating a bureau of statistics of labor in the United States."[2] The implication was that investigation would throw open the doors upon a wider field of social problems.

The compulsory education act for factory labor in 1865 affected factory children between the ages of ten and fourteen, and in 1867 a more rigorous act forbade employment of children under ten and of children between ten and fourteen who had not attended school for at least three months in the preceding year. No child under fifteen was to be employed for more than sixty hours a week. Even more significant than these prohibitions was the appointment of a new officer (as a deputy constable of the Commonwealth) to enforce them.

The new official was Henry Kemble Oliver, sometime schoolmaster turned soldier, and then the enlightened manager of cotton mills at Lawrence. He was strongly committed to the protection of child labor, but quickly found the problem more intractable than had been anticipated. The law was evaded by parents as well as by employers, and even the children seemed to prefer work to school. Local authorities were apathetic, and employers refused to supply information. Attempted enforcement revealed the extent to which one problem was but part of a network of interconnected forces tending to depress the conditions and prospects of working men and women.

Meanwhile a surge of activity in organized labor – led by the Knights of St Crispin, a shoemakers' union – brought new pressure to bear upon the legislature. Denied statutory authority to use union funds to finance cooperative purchasing agencies, the Knights turned to politics and backed a newly formed Labor Reform Party, which won ten per cent of the votes in the state elections of 1869. It also gained powerful support from Wendell

---

[1] The first commission sent out 1,000 printed circulars asking for information and received eighty replies.

[2] Carroll D. Wright, *The Industrial Evolution of the United States* (New York, 1895), 271.

Phillips, the well-known abolitionist orator, and General Ben Butler, the controversial former Democrat turned Radical Republican, and sworn foe of the commercial, manufacturing, and professional elite of the state.[3] Faced with this political threat and impressed by the difficulty of controlling child labor, the legislature took defensive action and in June 1869, without debate or recorded vote, passed a law establishing a Bureau of Labor Statistics. Oliver was appointed as its head, and McNeill, the active unionist and campaigner on behalf of factory children, was his deputy. It was authorized "to collect, assort, systematize, and present in annual reports to the legislature, statistical details relating to all departments of labor in the commonwealth, especially in its relation to the commercial, industrial, social, educational, and sanitary condition of the laboring classes, and to the permanent prosperity of the productive industry of the commonwealth." It was to be copied in thirty-one states, and "marked the beginning of a new movement in this country."

Oliver and McNeill were not the men to chart an unobtrusive course for the new bureau. They had studied the Factory and Mines Reports produced in Britain between 1833 and 1850, and believed that the same methods of investigation would make the case for reform. When the facts were "laid before the legislature and the public, a cry of mingled surprise, shame, and indignation will arise that will demand an entire change of the method of earnings and pay."[4] Investigation must not be narrowly defined, the public as well as the legislature must be involved, and reform would be a necessary consequence of making the true facts known. The first report exemplified the spirit in which Oliver and McNeill approached their work and seemed to justify their confidence. A first-hand account of conditions in Boston tenements, presented with the names and income of their owners, had an immediate impact, stimulated a press campaign, prompted the formation of a citizens' committee, and brought about a marked improvement in conditions.[5]

---

[3] *The Nation* was alarmed by the strength of the Labor Reform Party. It commended the legislature for having refused to incorporate the St Crispins because they restricted entry to their trade: "That a perfectly just refusal on the part of a Republican legislature to allow caste to be established in a democratic society should be made the ground for such a platform out of pure spite, does not incline one to think hopefully of the future." The platform endorsed debt repudiation and "the eight-hour delusion," and seemed "not wholly averse to a general distribution of real and personal property among the laboring population." If this platform won 13,000 votes in one state, how much support, asked *The Nation*, did it "command in the country at large"? (*The Nation*, Nov. 25, 1869).

[4] James Leiby, *Carroll Wright and Labor Reform: the Origin of Labor Statistics* (Cambridge, Mass., 1960), 56; quoting from Massachusetts Bureau of Labor Statistics, 1st R. (1870), 38.   [5] *Wright and Labor Reform*, 57.

Serious technical difficulties were encountered during the bureau's second year. It attempted to determine average wages and their purchasing power, and to decide whether living standards were adequate; but it soon became apparent that averages might be meaningless. What was required was classification, minute information, and some way of measuring what would now be called "expectations." This was beyond the resources of the bureau, which instead relied mainly upon material collected for the 1870 federal census; but its own inquiries into one related topic – the belief that the large volume of deposits in savings banks proved that working people were well off – revealed that more than half the deposits were in sums greater than $300 and that the rich took advantage of tax benefits offered to depositors and obtained most of the low-interest loans. The report was accompanied by severe strictures on bankers who had refused to give information and obstructed the inquiry as much as possible. The issue became highly controversial: the bureau's bleak picture of working-class conditions was said to be exaggerated and unrepresentative; and in the prosperous year 1872, with support for labor reform withering away, the future of the bureau was in doubt. It was saved largely by the advocacy of Governor Washburn, who argued strongly for a bureau, though for one inspired by different principles.

William B. Washburn had already made known his social philosophy in an address to the legislature in 1871.

It is so natural to feel that what always has been must always be, that we are too apt to content ourselves with things as we find them. But this is the dictate neither of wisdom nor of prudence. Standing still is not the province of society; it must either advance or retrograde.

The working people, he continued, were not separate from but an integral part of society, and "the least addition to their comfort is a gain to the whole community." The Bureau of Statistics should be a principal way of discovering what was both practicable and just. In 1872, with the bureau under attack, he said that failure to fulfil the expectations of all who supported it did not justify its abolition. If poverty, bad housing, lack of education, and distress caused by sickness or old age existed, legislators should know their extent. Inquiries into private affairs were certain to cause resentment, but "if there were businesses which could not operate without keeping laborers in poverty, they should cease operation." On the other hand the bureau existed to collect facts and statistics "calculated to assist statesmen in working out the problem of industrial reform," and not "to further some pet scheme of this theorist or that mere enthusiast."

Its object should be to deal with statistics, to keep back nothing, to present no one-sided picture, but as far as possible to collect all the facts, and leave them to speak for themselves.

When the legislature agreed to continue the bureau, Washburn appointed, as Oliver's successor, a quiet but politically ambitious young man called Carroll D. Wright.[6]

Of Wright his admirer and successor, Horace G. Wadlin, would later claim that

he created the peculiar department of the public service to which his life was mainly devoted. When he entered this service bureaus of original investigation devoted to the collection and presentation of statistical information relating to sociology included under the broad term "the labor question," were practically unknown; when he left the office of [Federal] Commissioner of Labor such offices were recognized as important and necessary branches of government.[7]

At the outset he sought the advice of Francis A. Walker, who had been a member of the first Massachusetts commission and director of the 1870 census, and who was regarded as the foremost American statistician of his day. He advised Wright to cultivate scientific detachment and steer clear of political commitment:

If any mistake is more likely than others to be committed in such a critical position, it is to undertake to recognize both parties as parties, and to award so much in due turn for each. This course almost inevitably leads to jealousy and dissatisfaction. If an office is strong enough simply to consider the body of citizens, and to refuse to recognize or entertain consideration of parties, success is already, in the main, assured. Public confidence once given, the choice of agencies, the selection of inquiries to be propounded, are easy and plain.[8]

Wright reprinted this letter in the first report of the bureau for which he was responsible, and clearly intended it as a declaration of his own policy.

Many years later, as the acknowledged leader of the profession he had helped to create, Wright would see in the pursuit of statistical evidence an almost magic quality. In a society bedevilled by the consequences of political patronage, the worst of appointees would somehow yield to the imperatives of accuracy and impartiality.

[6] Quotations and abstracts from Governor Washburn's addresses are given in Charles F. Pidgin, *History of the Bureau of Statistics of Labor in Massachusetts* (Boston, Mass., 1876). This book was issued with a foreword by Carroll D. Wright and may therefore be regarded as an "official" view of the bureau's aims and methods under his direction. The later history by C. F. Gettemy (1915) is far less useful for the early years of the bureau.

[7] Quoted Gettemy, 14.

[8] Massachusetts Bur. of L. S., 5th R. (1874), vii–viii.

No matter for what reasons they were appointed, no matter how inexperienced in the work of investigation and of compilation and presentation of statistical material, no matter from what party they came and whether in sympathy with capital or labor, and even if holding fairly radical socialistic views; the men have, almost without exception, at once comprehended the sacredness of the duty assigned to them, and served the public faithfully and honestly, being content to collect and publish facts without regard to individual bias or individual political sentiments.

As soon as a man accepted responsibility for recording a fact, he became aware of an obligation which overrode partisanship and neutralized bias. Distortion would be "to commit a crime worse than ordinary lying, because it would mislead legislators . . . and fix a falsehood in the history of the State."[9]

Impartiality was not necessarily impassive. In 1904 Wright gave instances of results achieved by the presentation of statistical evidence. These were not always immediate, but the facts remained on record to provide arguments which endured. Looking back to Kemble's work in Massachusetts, he recalled the tenement house investigation which had "crystallized in a reform movement having for its purpose the improvement of tenement houses." In child labor there had been marked results; and in factories safety had been improved, the employment of women and children regulated, and an inspectorate established. A ten-hour law had been passed in Massachusetts in 1874, and when manufacturers complained that it cut production a further investigation demonstrated that more goods were produced both per man and per machine. The inequitable common law on employer liability had been modified to give labor better compensation for accidents at work. Truck payment had been reduced, and wages were paid more frequently and regularly. Convict labor had been cut and industrial training expanded. But the services of the Massachusetts bureau had not been exclusively for the benefit of labor. In 1873 there had been alarming reports of vast numbers unemployed – 200,000 or perhaps 300,000 in Massachusetts – but an investigation had shown that the peak figure was not much over 28,000. In 1890 there had been concern over the extent of indebtedness in the United States, but statistical inquiry had shown that the figures were grossly inflated.[10]

Though the Massachusetts bureau under Wright disclaimed advocacy of policy, it achieved much (as Francis A. Walker had predicted) by its choice of subjects for investigation. A list of inquiries in the Massachusetts reports

9 "The Value and Influence of Labor Statistics," *Bulletin of the Bureau of Labor*, 54 (1904), 1,087.   10 *Ibid.*, 1,090–5.

during Wright's tenure of office suggests a systematic plan, extending over years, to cover all the major topics which affected the condition of labor:

1873: wages, cost of living, savings, ownership of property, the labor movement, co-operation, housing, elementary education, and the effect of reducing the hours of labor

1874: the education and employment of young persons, sanitary conditions in places of work, a comparison between wages in Massachusetts and foreign countries, laws on the safety of machinery, the cost of living, and savings banks

1875: the education of working children, female health, factory laws, and co-operation

1876: the comparative income of wage and salary earners, and the history of labor legislation

1877: arbitration, co-operation, a census of blind, deaf, insane, and idiotic persons, pauperism and crime, and fire precautions in places of work

1878: employment and living standards in 1875 and 1877 compared, the education of working children, private and corporate businesses, conjugal conditions of the people, and literacy

1879: unemployment, the condition of labor, convict labor, wages and prices, hours of labor, drunkenness and rules for the sale of liquor

1880: strikes, convict labor, crime, and divorces

1881: arbitration and conciliation, drunkenness and liquor sales, and uniform hours of labor

1882: French Canadians in Massachusetts, labor conditions, wages, prices, and profits

1883: employers' liability for injury to work people

If the topics became fewer as the years went on, the reports did not become shorter. Indeed the question was not whether the bureau was active, but whether the sheer weight of evidence collected might not defeat the purpose of making people informed on the issues. When Wright became the first federal commissioner of labor, this tendency was intensified. Three-quarters or more of the federal reports consisted of close-packed tables, and though invaluable for historians one wonders how many contemporaries got the message they were intended to convey.

The Massachusetts bureau was the pioneer and in many respects the model, but each state bureau encountered its own problems and evolved its own methods and priorities. A frequent complaint was of insufficient authority conferred by law, or, where the terms of reference were broad, of inadequate staff and miserly appropriations. In its first report presented in 1873 the Pennsylvania bureau explained that it had been empowered to investigate the conditions of labor but had been given no authority to require information and no money to pay agents: "We had, like the

Israelites of old, to make bricks without straw . . . and, like the busy bee, we have collected from every wayside flower; from books, reports, our own observations, and voluntary contributions from others." Nor could the most diligent research overcome deficiencies in the existing records of the state. In Pennsylvania no central office received reports on revenue collection from counties, cities, wards, or townships, so that the greater part of the taxes paid by the people appeared in no official document.[11]

The majority of bureaus were set up in the wake of the depression which began in 1873, and were even more clearly established in response to agitation and alarm. In its first report in 1877 the Ohio bureau observed that "the Labor question is becoming, if it is not now, the leading question before the people . . . That they are not content at the present time, that a spirit of discontent is rife, and open revolt only prevented by the hope of speedy change, needs no elucidation." A general statistical office would not meet this need, and in its second report the Ohio board said that the plan for a *separate* Bureau of Labor Statistics was deliberately framed to foster "a thorough and continuous investigation . . . into the conditions of labor."[12] In Illinois the establishment of a bureau in 1879 was attributed directly to the election of several working men to the legislature.[13] In its report for 1890–1 the Maryland bureau, created in 1884, asserted that "It becomes the duty of the government to protect and defend labor against such encroachments as would degrade and coerce it in operation."[14]

Circumstances enabled the Illinois bureau to make an immediate impact upon policy. In response to alarm about mining accidents the state legislature had passed a safety law, which went into considerable detail in prescribing what should or should not be done. But the administration and enforcement of this highly technical law had been left to counties without additional funds or the benefit of expert advice. The bureau was therefore presented with an issue in which the intention of the sovereign people had been declared, but an appalling accident record bore witness to the frustration of their purpose.

The report for 1883 revealed that not all counties had appointed inspectors of mines, and those that had paid low salaries for part-time work without requiring inspectors to possess professional qualifications. Nor

[11] Pennsylvania Bur. of S. of L., 1st R. (1872–3), xiii.
[12] Ohio Bur. of L. S., 1st R. (1877), 10.
[13] Illinois Bur. of L. S., 2nd Bienn. R. (1883), vi.
[14] Maryland Bur. of Industrial Statistics and Information, 4th R. (1890).

were the salaries in any way uniform. La Salle county, with sixty-five mines and 3,000 miners, paid its inspector $500 a year; St Clair, with seventy-six small mines and 1,600 miners, paid $480; Macupin, with twenty-one exceptionally deep and difficult mines, settled for $180. On the other hand, some counties with few mines paid high salaries for what were probably treated as political sinecures. The bureau pointed out that an efficient inspector required many skills and should work full time. He ought to have practical experience of mining, some scientific training, enough tact to secure voluntary compliance with his recommendations, and enough knowledge of the law to prosecute recalcitrants. To clinch its argument the bureau calculated that the total cost of inefficient county inspection was greater than the hypothetical cost of a well-organized state inspectorate. Ohio had a fully qualified chief inspector with a salary of $2,000, and a significantly better safety record. In Pennsylvania four state inspectors at $2,000 a year were appointed by the governor on the recommendation of a board of examiners. The men who paid the price for incompetence were the miners themselves. There were over 20,000 of them in Illinois "peculiarly exposed to hardships and perils, and who in their daily life go hand in hand not only with poverty and hardship, but with sudden death." The major error had been to delegate to counties "the duty of the State."[15]

This vigorous report made a deep impression. A state inspectorate was established by the legislature, and in its next report the bureau reported significant results. In one district sixteen escape shafts had been ordered and constructed, and two mines had suspended operation because they were judged unsafe; in another district injunctions had been sought against four owners, and three of these had then complied with the law; in a third district, with the greatest number of deep mines, twenty escape shafts had been sunk at an estimated cost of $100,000, and legal proceedings had been instituted against others. By one means or another the owners of 147 mines had been compelled to sink escape shafts, in twenty-two more the additional shafts were under construction, and in forty-one new ventilating fans had been installed. There was already a noticeable and welcome drop in the number of fatal accidents.[16]

In the same report the Illinois bureau also presented an ambitious survey of the conditions of the industrial working class. Data had been obtained from 2,129 families, engaged in 163 occupations, and living in fifty-three

---

[15] Illinois Bur. of L. S., 2nd R. (1883), 107–10. For later mining legislation see Earl R. Beckner, *A History of Illinois Labor Legislation* (Chicago, Ill., 1929), 292–5.

[16] *Idem*, 3rd R. (1884), 421ff.

cities. The report included tables giving family financial statements, sources of income, earnings of women and children, an analysis of average expenditure, and a summary of retail prices. The result was an extra-ordinarily full survey, and a mine of information about working-class conditions of life.[17]

In Ohio the move to establish a bureau began in 1873 but did not succeed until 1877. Again the prime movers were representatives of organized unions, and the first commissioner, H. J. Walls, was highly favorable to labor. His reports supported trade unions, opposed truck payments, and condemned convict labor.[18] Advocacy may have prevented the Ohio bureau from winning the reputation for impartial accuracy so much valued by Wright, but it made for interesting reading. Faced with a legislature which was notorious for spending more time on partisan wrangling than on economic, social, or humanitarian questions, the bureau may have decided that the best plan was to enlist public sympathy and to bring pressure upon the legislature from the grass roots. If this failed, there was still a chance that labor might win a fair deal once employers and the public became aware of the issues.

Whatever the reasoning, the methods of the Ohio bureau were in sharp contrast to those of Massachusetts. Its reports contained fewer statistical tables, and more attempts to expose the inadequacy of existing institutions and ideas. Its second report exposed slum housing in Cincinnati. In 1868 1,410 tenement houses had contained six or more families and 9,894 families occupied 16,197 rooms. In 1871 306 dwelling houses had no water, 862 no yard space, 251 no privies, and 480 cellars were inhabited.

Two rooms, front or back, in the second, third, fourth, or even fifth storey of a barracks, hemmed in on all sides but one, is the average home of the working man in the Queen City of the West, and for these two rooms, he pays on average in excess of four-roomed tenements in most of the towns and smaller cities of the State.[19]

In 1873 a cholera epidemic killed 207 persons, of whom 142 were tenement dwellers; in 1874 scarlet fever carried off 687, with 486 from the tenements; in 1875 and 1876 smallpox killed 1,651, and in these two years the five most densely populated wards contained 33.9 and 41.0 per cent of all reported cases.

The most interesting work of the Ohio bureau, from the point of view of

---

[17] *Ibid.*, xxff. (with tables and analysis of replies).
[18] The members of the legislature who took the lead were M. A. Foran, president of the Coopers' International Union, and John Fehrenbatch, president of the National Association of Mechanical Engineers.
[19] Ohio Bur. of L. S., 2nd R. (1879), 287–92.

social theory, was its analysis of the causes of strikes and the way to avert them or mitigate their consequences. It strongly backed arbitration tribunals, and gave detailed accounts of some of the more successful schemes. In common with other bureaus it also investigated child labor, and the related problem of education for working children. It found many reasons why children were employed, but all were reduced to the single incentive – to increase profits – and it was not employers alone who perpetuated the evil. Where piecework was the rule, children were often hired by the workman in charge of the contract, while parents in mines often brought in their children as helpers; but the most general cause remained the desire to cut labor costs, and boys were hired wherever they could do men's work. In the furniture trade about half the labor consisted of boys from ten to fifteen. The bureau concluded that "it is reasonably certain that so long as there is an abundance of child labor offered, so long will places be invented for children in manufactories, stores etc."

There were laws requiring schooling, but no one enforced them; and those who attempted to do so found themselves frustrated at every step: "Unless the laws are made more stringent and compulsory, the evil must continue to grow." Incidentally, the bureau noted that school boards systematically, if not intentionally, excluded poor children by the simple expedient of changing about half the books required for courses every year. The booksellers gained, but poor parents might have to take their children out of school.[20]

The Ohio bureau may not have been very effective in securing direct action from the legislature, but it could not be ignored. In 1891 its spokesman at the National Conference reported that its duties had been enlarged and its appropriation increased. Moreover it had maintained the right to investigate in the name of the State, and to publicize its findings. Taken together its reports present a gallant attempt to understand the problems of industrial society.

The New York Bureau of Labor Statistics was not created until 1883, and then with inadequate powers. One of the earliest tasks of the commissioner, Charles F. Peck, was to draft a bill requiring compliance with requests for information from the bureau and imposing penalties for misrepresentation. Although he was confident of its passage during the session of 1884 the bill was not reported out of committee. It was passed in 1886, but the commissioner reported that it was still difficult to obtain

[20] *Idem*, 5th R. (1882), 327–32.

information, and, ironically enough, that the most reluctant to answer requests were trade union officials. Why they should not supply information to a bureau "created solely at the request of organized labor, and whose special interest it is supposed to protect, was puzzling."[21]

In 1884 the sole topic for investigation in New York was child labor, and the bureau had asked for a ruling from the state attorney general on whether the commissioner or his agents could enter and inspect places of work. He replied that such power was not specifically conferred by the act establishing the bureau, and though it might be implied from the instruction to report it would be unwise to assume this as the law would be strictly construed. The law, he said, gave the commissioner power to require the attendance of witnesses, but expressly declared that no witness should be compelled to answer any question regarding his private affairs; from this it might be inferred that the commissioner could not enter premises to obtain information which he could not require from a witness on oath. "This opinion," reported the bureau, "was to a certain extent fatal to the investigation." In addition appropriations were inadequate, and the bureau reported that without more money its work would be gravely hampered.

The handicaps encountered by the New York bureau were partly political. The Democrats had won control of the state under Grover Cleveland, and retained it when he moved to the White House, and, though ostensibly favorable to labor, the party was traditionally hostile to the extension of state authority. In addition all questions in New York became enmeshed in rivalry between the state and the city. These factors gave employers unusual opportunities for exerting influence, either by direct pressure on the legislature at Albany or by alliance with the Democratic party bosses of New York city. The worst days of the Erie Railroad and the Tweed Ring belonged to the past, but there were more discreet ways in which inconvenient investigations could be thwarted. This was offset, to some extent, by lack of unity among business interests. Railroads were opposed by rural business, retailers of consumer goods, and exporters; manufacturers and importers had conflicting interests; and no one welcomed open alliance with the notorious employers of sweated labour in New York city. A wide social gulf separated the massed financial power of Wall Street and the dozens of small entrepreneurs, many of them recent immigrants, who were responsible for the ready-made clothing or cigar

---

[21] New York Bur. of L. S., 2nd R. (1884), 5–6; 4th R. (1886), 10–11.

trades. There was therefore no straightforward confrontation between labor reformers and the massed battalions of capital; it was rather that in every area of investigation there was someone ready to obstruct, and that political protection was too often available for those who would neither co-operate with the bureau nor comply with the law.

In 1887, reviewing ten years of labor legislation, the New York bureau complained that the laws were numerous, but their effectiveness doubtful, because nobody was specifically charged with their enforcement, and even if the responsibility were established the appropriation was "wholly inadequate." The compulsory school law – the so-called Truant Act – was a striking example. If rigidly enforced it would have virtually ended the employment of children in factories, but there seemed to be a tacit but general understanding that it would remain a dead letter. A law required the provision of seats in shops for female employees, but these were found in few stores and an employee detected in using them was liable to instant dismissal. The board of health could require bakeries to provide proper sanitation, but no appropriation was made to enable its officers to inspect premises or prosecute offenders. The bureau itself lacked the staff and the voluntary co-operation which were necessary for compiling accounts information.[22]

Despite these difficulties the New York bureau was not inactive, but its enthusiasm was manifested in general and sometimes impressionistic reports rather than in the prosaic compilation of statistical evidence. The reports were short on figures, and tables were frequently accompanied by explanations that they were not comprehensive. On the other hand, the difficulty in performing the primary duty of a statistical bureau inevitably forced it into the field of what would now be called investigative journalism. A bureau short of statistics was forced to be sensational.[23]

The third report included the results of an inspection of working-class housing in New York city.[24] There was "a terrible packing of people, absence of actual light or ventilation, and a total disregard of sanitary contrivances." The commissioner described his own visits to a number of "these horrible rookeries." He had heard so much of the wretchedness of life in the slums that the idea had grown stale and he went "impressed with an idea that the terrible representations made in connection with the

[22] *Idem*, 5th R. (1887), 84.
[23] It had some success in reaching the public. The demand for the fourth report (dealing with apprenticeship, immigration of skilled labor, the protection of native-born labor, and technical education) was greater than the supply (5th R. (1887), 12).
[24] New York Bur. of L. S., 3rd R. (1885), 174–7.

subject were but the extravagant recitals of scientific theorists and sentimentalists." Reality proved worse than rumor. He gave a detailed description of two large tenement houses in New York City. Two five-storey buildings were separated by a courtyard ten feet wide. As one came in by the main entrance to one building, one became aware of the water closets behind a seven-foot partition and consisting of nothing more than an iron trough running below a row of seats; in addition to excreta, all kinds of other refuse were thrown into the trough, in which there was no running water though it was flushed down once a day. As one mounted the staircase the smell rose from below. Other apartments used vaults at the rear of the courtyard, and the foundation walls of the building formed the sides of a sewer. Some gratings over the sewer allowed surface drainage to enter and gas to escape, and in them accumulated filth which was never carried away· by running water.

It would seem as if a spirit of common humanity would prompt the owner of such property to prevent a continuation of these awful health-destroying and disease-infecting cesspools that are to be found in and around their tenements. Humanity, however, has little or nothing to do with the case. The main and all-important question with these people seems to be to get the largest possible revenues from their wretched rookeries with the least possible outlay.

There was one puzzle. The city of New York had a board of health, and the city government had power to act on its recommendations. "What should be said to the board of health of a great city that tolerates such a state of affairs?" Illustrations accompanied the report, but did less than justice to the revelations of the text.

Despite the difficulties in getting laws passed or enforced, the bureau made some impact on the statute book. Manufacturing in state prisons by convicts was restricted, and it became illegal to contract for the employ- ment of children in reformatories; the making of cigars in tenements was forbidden; the wages of employees were made exempt from attachments for debt, and homes were exempted from seizure; and an eight-hour day for state laborers and mechanics became law, though overtime was allowed.

While strongly supporting the principle of labor organization, the bureau frequently criticized irresponsible action, particularly by leaders of new unions anxious to show results. While power was in the grasp of working men, if properly led, all might be jeopardized by misuse of influence. Working men were too apt to quarrel among themselves, and leaders were divided over trivialities and petty jealousies. Weakness and false arguments gave victory to their opponents. Matters might improve if political economy were taught in the public schools, for surely it was possible "to present, in a condensed form, the infallible scientific truths which govern the social and business world."

Viewing its own contributions in 1885 the New York bureau took a philosophical view. The "social question" was one of the great problems of the age, but must go through various stages before a solution could be found.

The labor question, like the slave question, must pass through its periods of agitation, discussion and action. If the period of discussion has only been reached at the present time, then it is the fault of the agitators themselves, because they did not begin the agitation at an earlier day and press it.

In New York the bureau had been late on the scene – fourteen years after the Massachusetts bureau and five or six after those of Illinois, Pennsylvania, and Ohio – which indicated lack of skill on the part of labor organizers and ignorance of the issues on the part of the public. But things were on the move, even though the stage of decisive action had yet to be reached. "There is . . . no reason to fear that it will not resemble the slave question in its solution."[25]

Maryland set up a small and understaffed Bureau of Industrial Statistics and Information in 1884, and its first report expressed the hope that it would soon be allowed to move beyond the experimental stage and assume wider powers. Maryland suffered more than most from the sluggish apparatus of state government. The legislature met every other year in the small, pleasantly antiquated city of Annapolis and was dominated by representatives of rural areas, of whom many came from the exceedingly conservative eastern shore. Though Baltimore shared with other great cities the problems of overcrowding, immigration, and conflict between capital and labor, a third of the labor force was black, and many of the white working men and women had come recently from backwood areas of the south. There were, however, factors which saved Maryland from stagnation. Baltimore was prosperous, less affected than other great cities by depression, and as a great port it had a cosmopolitan outlook without being overwhelmed by immigration. The state had what contemporary reformers regarded as one of the best prison systems in the country, and (as already shown) an active board of public health. Finally, though the state was firmly under Democratic control, the party's ascendancy had been achieved with less bitterness than in former Confederate states and business

25 *Ibid.*, 615, 618–19.

leaders were "bourbons" neither in their attitude to social change nor in their relations with labor.

In 1884 Governor Robert M. McLane devoted most of his biennial message to labor questions. He recommended legalization of trade unions, an eight-hour day for state employees, no employment of children under ten, and an eight-hour law for women and children under sixteen.[26] The Bureau of Industrial Statistics was one outcome of this initiative, and the first commissioner, Thomas C. Weeks, was an active friend of organized labor. From the beginning Weeks saw it as his duty to present positive recommendations to the legislature. Even if he had wished to, he had not the resources to collect statistics which would speak for themselves. Moreover, looking at the experience in other states, he might well have felt that the time had come for action in Maryland; and the politics of the state being what they were, no action was likely to occur until someone took the initiative. He recommended greater powers for the bureau to examine witnesses on oath and require answers to requests for information, and could cite the existing powers of other bureaus in justification. He recommended state arbitration courts, and was able to refer to precedents in New Jersey, Massachusetts, New York, and Ohio.[27] Stringent laws for fire escapes in factories were required, as shown by experience in Illinois and Ohio. In 1891 Weeks recommended a factory inspectorate on the New York model, "with power to enter the private and secret places at present absolutely closed to the public view, where young girls and women are employed, laboriously working for scant wages, under the 'contract system' in the clothing trade."[28]

Inevitably his recommendations led to accusations that his reports were one-sided, and Weeks saw fit to reply in 1891: "I have endeavored to serve no faction or party, to hold myself free from labor unions on the one hand, and associations of capital on the other, and I have used my best effort to present only the actual facts and figures I could obtain and to present them uncolored by my own individuality." The disclaimer was no doubt sincere, and he did supply the legislature with a great deal of information about economic life in the state; but his major recommendations were certainly "colored by his own individuality." The "actual facts and figures" might speak for themselves, but his interpretation was unquestioned: the state of Maryland must act with a sense of urgency to get abreast of changes taking

[26] State of Maryland, *Senate and House Documents, 1884,* "Message of the Governor."
[27] Maryland Bur. of Industrial Statistics and Information, 2nd R. (1886), 83.
[28] *Idem,* 4th R. (1890–1), 7.

place elsewhere, and only a sympathetic view of the needs of labor could save the state from distressing and debilitating industrial conflict.[29]

Of the former Confederate states only North Carolina had set up a Bureau of Labor Statistics by the end of the nineteenth century. Created in 1887, the bureau was to "collect information upon the subject of labor, its relation to capital, the hours of labor, the earnings of laboring men and women, their educational, moral, and financial condition, and the best means of promoting their mental, material, social, and moral prosperity." To accomplish these wide-ranging tasks the commissioner was paid a salary of $1,500, and could appoint a chief clerk at $900 and other assistants, provided that the total cost, in addition to his own salary, did not exceed $5,000 for the first two years and $2,000 a year thereafter. The bureau was required to present an annual report in pamphlet form and to send copies to every member of the Assembly, every newspaper published in the state, county officers, and any other person who might request it. In addition one copy went to each other state, and 100 to labor organizations in the state. $3,000 was appropriated for publication and distribution in the first year, and then $2,000 annually, appropriated from the proceeds of a tax on fertilizers.[30] These elaborate requirements for publicity are interesting. Clearly the legislature expected the findings of the bureau to work upon opinion rather than lead directly to legislative action.

One salient fact revealed by the investigation was widespread illiteracy and very low attainment amongst those who knew enough to put a few words on paper. From the returns it also appeared that a high proportion of working men's children were not attending school, even if they lived in towns where the educational facilities were good. In rural districts non-attendance was very high.

Progress must, to a large extent, remain fettered among working people, till the school teacher dispels some of the darkness which now pervades this state.[31]

In the past it had been possible for a man to be successful in life who could not write his name, but in the future this would change. "The ignorant will be the hewers of wood and drawers of water, whoever they may be, with hardly a possibility of bettering their condition." However there was a different emphasis from what might have been expected in a northern state; though there was a vague reference to the importance of furnishing "the necessary school advantages," the main admonition was addressed to working men to become aware of "the benefits to be derived from public

[29] *Ibid.*, 5.   [30] North Carolina Bur. of L. S., 1st R. (1887), iii–iv.   [31] *Ibid.*, 4–5.

education." North Carolina was still a long way from discussing compulsion, truancy laws, or minimum periods of education for children in employment.

The most common complaint from working men was of excessive hours – twelve to fourteen a day – and the bureau strongly endorsed the proposal for a ten-hour day. Another common complaint was "truck" payment. Working people were paid in part in vouchers redeemable only at the company store, or there was a tacit understanding that a man who did not buy at the store would lose his job. The bureau condemned the practice but made no specific recommendation for a law to end it.

It is unnecessary to pursue further the history of the North Carolina bureau, but it illustrates very clearly the limitations which nineteenth-century inquiries encountered. In collecting its statistics the bureau was, in fact, taking a sample without any clear idea of how it should be weighted. Replies from employers were skewed towards those who had a sense of public responsibility and adequate records. Replies from working men were skewed towards those who were literate and intelligent. The report does not say whether the inquiries went to blacks as well as to whites, but one suspects that few of the former answered. The figures given for average wages show some quite surprising variations from county to county, and as most of the anomalies show figures well above the average, suspicions are aroused. Did the replies come from a small number of skilled men who were able to earn high wages, or from employers anxious to demonstrate their generosity? Despite these defects, the North Carolina bureau continued its work. If the legislature was difficult to move, the bureau spread information about real conditions in a backward state and prepared the way for the new era which lay ahead.

As a compiler of statistics the North Carolina bureau had far to go, but this is not to minimize its importance. Despite the niggardly appropriation, the legislature had set up a body with specific duties assigned to it. It was to inquire, report, and make public its findings. On questions affecting labor it was required to become informed, and to use its information to influence public policy. The legislature and the bureau thought of that influence being exerted primarily upon employers and working people and only indirectly upon law-making; yet this did not alter the fact that a bureau of the state was now charged with investigating a vital aspect of social life. At every session of the legislature there would be a report to consider; and on many occasions the report would suggest action by the State. Public responsibility had been enlarged, even if the first steps were halting.

In the industrially more advanced states an element of self-congratulation crept into many reports in later years. If less was heard of the role of the bureaus in response to pressure from organized labor, there was a good deal more emphasis upon their contribution to general welfare, their acceptance by employers, and their recognition by the people at large. In its early days the Pennsylvania bureau encountered a good deal of hostility, and mere inquiry was attacked as an "inquisitorial and unwarrantable interference with the private affairs of business men." So long as the bureau had no power to demand information, employers solved their own problems by ignoring its requests, but in 1874 the legislature conferred the necessary power upon the bureau and this led to a concerted effort to repeal the act and "practically abandon the work that those who asked for its establishment believed should be done."[32] The Philadelphia Board of Trade denounced the bureau as "communistic." However, it survived these attacks, and was soon accepted as a permanent and useful agency of state administration. The Wisconsin bureau, which had complained bitterly of inadequate staff and funding when first established, claimed that by 1889 its scope of work and duties was "constantly broadening and increasing." In that year new laws had raised the age at which children could be employed in factories from twelve to thirteen and extended the prohibition to commercial establishments.[33] Another law recognized statistical information supplied by the bureau as an essential part of government. A comparison between the sparse information provided in departmental reports before 1850 and the massive output of 1900, is a true measure of a fundamental change in ideas of government.

Indeed the thirst for information was in danger of exhausting those who had to supply it. In 1891 Wright suggested that the time had come to effect greater centralization in statistical work: "With various bureaus and departments calling for the particular information which each specifically wants, manufacturers sometimes get weary of well-doing and seriously object to furnishing information. Some plan for harmonious cooperation, to avoid duplication of effort, seems to be necessary."[34] One result was to expand the range of the federal census; another was to require the Federal Department of Labor to undertake inquiries which lay outside its original terms of reference. Whatever the means, the end was clear; the acquisition of precise information on every aspect of working life had been accepted as

[32] Pennsylvania Bur. of S. of L., 2nd R. (1873–4), 421.
[33] Wisconsin Bur. of L. S., 4th R. (1888–9), v–vi.
[34] Commissioner of Labor, 7th Ann. R. (1891), 5.

a responsibility of government. For good or ill twentieth-century governments would have at their disposal an accumulation of knowledge beyond the imagination of any previous age, and its volume would continually increase.

For the time being, however, the responsibility for most social and economic regulation lay with the states. It had always been hoped that information would not be sterile, but would breed action. What had been done? In 1895 Wright, attempting an answer, gave twenty examples of labor legislation, adding that though not all were to be found in every state, they were "so general as to entitle them to be considered in the body of labor legislation." This somewhat clumsy phrase meant that one could see a moving frontier in labor law with many states going through a similar evolutionary process, some later than others, but all working to change the pattern of laboring life.

Prominent among the laws enacted were fixed hours for women and children, safety and fire regulations, the inspection of factories, new health and sanitation standards in places of work, modifications in the law of employers' liability, and encouragement of education in industrial and evening schools. Each apparently straightforward heading meant complex statutes and codes in the states where they were enacted. National conferences of the officers of bureaus, the influence of the Federal Department of Labor, and, after 1895, frequent issues of the *Bulletin of the Department of Labor*, all helped to produce some degree of uniformity in practice and interpretation, even where state laws were somewhat idiosyncratic.

Enough has been said in the preceding pages to drive home the point that enactment of a law did not mean its enforcement; but over the years legislatures had slowly come to make larger appropriations, appoint more officers, and define precisely the responsibility for executing the laws and prosecuting offenders. The frequent complaints incorporated in reports of state bureaus also indicate changing expectations of what government should do. The generation which spanned the years between 1865 and 1900 had to learn wholly new lessons in public responsibility, and inevitably there were mistakes, omissions, and resistance to change. An experienced bureau head, looking back to the early days, said that "every legislative body found it necessary to consider a mass of proposed legislation directly affecting the right of free contract as it was then held, nearly all of which carried the police power far beyond its existing bounds."[35] The steady

[35] C. F. Gettemy, *History of the Massachusetts Bureau of Statistics,* 8, quoting Horace Wadlin, Carroll D. Wright's successor as head of the bureau.

enlargement of responsibility for the protection of labor could not take place without some second thoughts and attempts to delay action or nullify laws; but in time public responsibility was accepted for a wide range of issues affecting the conditions of labor. Taking a long view this was of far greater significance than the questions of currency and tariff which generated such passionate concern amongst politicians and theoreticians.

There was a broad division between bureaus that confined themselves wherever possible to investigation, compilation, and advice, and those that eagerly sought executive power to enforce the law. In practice the distinction might become blurred as external pressure forced executive functions on some unwilling bureaus, while others had grasped the right to inspect and enforce but used more sparingly their right to prosecute. A bureau which followed at first the course marked out by Wright was that of Connecticut. The first commissioner, Arthur T. Hadley was not a union man but an academic economist, and in his report for 1885 he discussed the functions of a bureau mainly in negative terms. It should not make the investigation of complaints and redress of grievances its primary task, but should act as an aid to legislation by "showing where the present system, as *a system*, works injustice." This might mean the statistical study of problems that had only a remote connection with labor conditions. It should not undertake a roving commission to expose existing practice, for "the surest way to influence public opinion was to concentrate attention upon a few well-chosen subjects." It should not espouse or even examine ambitious plans for the reform of society. It should not accept responsibility for the inspection of factories.[36]

In his second report Hadley amplified his somewhat veiled promise to study the system as a system. There were certain symptoms which, when found in combination, meant that society was on "a low industrial level." Among these symptoms were child labor, long hours, and irregular or infrequent payment of wages. Child labor meant that parents could not afford to keep them at home or put them in school; long hours meant reduced efficiency; monthly wages meant store credits and accumulating debts. Until child labor had been dealt with there was no point in going further, but in Hadley's analysis parents and local authorities carried most of the blame, while employers could not be expected to obey the law unless first assured that all would do so. It is no surprise that Hadley's successor, Samuel M. Hotchkiss, reported that he had traveled around the state, conferred with all classes and found among laboring people "a general feeling of distrust of the Bureau," and a belief "that it was organized in the

[36] Connecticut Bur. of L. S., 1st R. (1885), 105–13.

interests of capitalists and employers, and that their interests would be practically ignored."

Hotchkiss argued against the idea that there could be free contract when working men were allowed little freedom of choice. An employer might be humane, generous, and well-intentioned, "but circumstances have given him power to dictate terms to his workmen." An immediate consequence of this new approach was a Factory Act which established an inspectorate as an independent agency reporting to the governor. The bureau also departed from Hadley's precept of tackling one thing at a time, and embarked upon a three-year study of capital, profits, and wages. The resulting report came to the rescue of employers by claiming that middlemen had reaped the benefit derived from lowered costs of production, and that the hostility of low-paid workers was therefore directed against the wrong people; but it went on to attack employers for not complying with the ten-hour law for women and children and pointed out that there was no way in which the law would enforce itself. If no state agency took the initiative, the individual's only remedy was to levy complaints and offer testimony, which few were able to do. A law required the weekly payment of wages and employers claimed they were ready to obey it if requested to do so; "but employees do not dare to enforce this right." The factory inspectors should be empowered to enforce the law, for no one else could do so.

The Connecticut bureau now sought publicity, which was a deliberate departure from its earlier role as a largely invisible agency advising the legislature on economic affairs. It saw itself standing between capital and labor, advocating justice to both but impressed by the validity of labor's grievances, and passing on both facts and judgments to the public. This was not a subversive role, but conservative in the truest sense: "The stability of society is based largely upon publicity, and properly regulated bureaus of statistics furnish an authentic public representation of facts, gathered from careful investigation, that even a myriad-minded newspaper cannot secure." Its usefulness was demonstrated by public demand, as 5,000 copies of the report for 1888 were quickly exhausted and 10,000 more had to be printed.[37]

The Wisconsin bureau presents an example of advocacy and enforcement. From its inception it had executive authority, and despite an inauspicious start was soon acting as a Department of Labor rather than as a Bureau of Statistics. Launched in 1883 it had a mandate to investigate "all

[37] *Idem*, 2nd R. (1886), xvi; 3rd R. (1887), 10; 4th R. (1888).

matters relating to the commercial, industrial, social, educational and sanitary condition of the laboring classes." It was specifically given authority to enter factories, examine safety devices, supervise laws for the employment of children, minors and women, and prosecute offenders. There was one flaw in this grant of power: the whole task was to be performed on an appropriation of $2,000, which included $1,500 for the commissioner, $500 for expenses, and nothing for inspectors, clerks, or printing. It was housed in two small rooms in the Capitol. "No other state," complained the commissioner, "requires so much for so little or furnishes such inadequate facilities for performing public business."[38]

Fortunately for the future of the bureau the commissioner, Frank A. Flower, was a man of imagination and energy, and in good standing with the Republican party. Denied the money for systematic investigation, he made his reports impressionistic but effective accounts of labor conditions. Forced to go short on figures he made a virtue of the omission. He believed that his second report would interest the people of Wisconsin as much as it would disappoint "Eastern metaphysicians."

They have expressed a desire to have the various states compile phalanges of abstract figures, because by running through their metaphysical alembics they can, like the alchymists they are, produce results which, though of no practical value, are nevertheless very mystifying to the groundlings and very serviceable in advertising the conjurors.[39]

Confronted with the perfunctory way in which businessmen furnished information, he counterattacked by accusing them of inefficiency. There was an "utter lack of intelligent systematic method . . . no reliable system of keeping accounts . . . and, ignorant of their own business, they guessed at this and that with ridiculous results."[40]

Flower won his first victory with the addition of a deputy commissioner, a factory inspector, and a clerk to his staff, and with a more realistic appropriation. Undeterred by possible objections to the polemical character of his reports, he declared that the real purpose of the bureau was not the compilation of tables but "the enforcement of labor laws, annihilation of child labor, securing new legislation, and general activity on behalf of wage-earners." Though in name a statistical bureau it was in practice "the most far-reaching and comprehensive piece of machinery in the state for the enforcement of law." A second inspector was added in 1887, and a new labor code – including the prohibition of factory labor for children under

[38] Wisconsin Bur. of L. S., 1st R. (1883–4), 7–10.
[39] *Idem*, 2nd R. (1885–6), v.   [40] *Idem*, 1st R. (1883–4), 105.

twelve – was enacted. In 1889 the age was raised to thirteen, and the prohibition extended to all places of employment. At the same time the inspectors' sphere was enlarged to include tenements, offices, hotels, theatres, and public halls.

Flower's expansionist policy was continued by his successor, H. M. Stark, who was able to report that employers were complying with requests for information and acting without protest upon suggestions made by the inspectors. There was even a request from some manufacturers for the appointment of an additional inspector with responsibility for the safety of steam boilers. There is perhaps a hint of accommodation. If employers no longer regarded the bureau as their natural enemy, the bureau was no longer arguing the case exclusively from the point of view of wage earners. Manufacturers were coming to realize that, though regular inspection might sometimes be embarrassing, it also protected them against less scrupulous competitors.[41]

The changing mood on both sides did not diminish the work of the Wisconsin bureau. In 1885, its first year, it had issued 138 orders for the improvement of safety and sanitation; they increased each year, and the report for 1897–8 recorded 1,217 written orders and many verbal orders issued and acted upon. Nor was the bureau complacent about conditions. In 1887 the bureau's report claimed that its officers could "never cease their goings and comings, never lift their eyes from the field of inspection." Wide knowledge was required, and much experience:

We must understand how to deal pleasantly and successfully with the multitudinous characters that make up our population. Meet their subterfuges, expose their tricks, and watch the shrewdness of those who propose to evade or disobey the laws; and do it, too, without betraying our knowledge of their motives and purposes.

Ten years later the bureau undertook a physical examination of some 5,600 children and revealed a dismal story of weakness, injury, disability and chronic ill-health brought about by premature and illegal employment. This led to the passage of tougher laws that marked "a turning point in factory legislation."[42]

Whether bureaus were responsible for enforcing the law or merely recommended that this should be done, they were setting up new criteria by which not only employers but also government itself should be judged. The

41 *Idem*, 4th R. (1888–9), v–vi.
42 *Idem*, 9th R. (Synopsis of the Reports of the Bureau of Labor of Wisconsin) (1900), *passim*; 3rd R. (1886–7); 9th R. (1899–1900).

significance of this may easily be overlooked. Here was an agency of the State showing up the inadequacy of state law. Judges had traditionally protected subjects against the unlawful exercise of power; now another body, relying upon its understanding of social science, declared what laws or what lack of law created injustice. To perform this task effectively the bureaus had to master the modern technique of gathering information and new methods of law enforcement.

Official requests for detailed and precise information have become so much a part of modern life that we are liable to forget their novelty. In the past it was the duty of office holders to satisfy official curiosity, but accuracy was hardly expected, and if it had been the means to achieve it seldom existed. The ordinary citizen became familiar with the censuses taken from 1790 onwards, but was normally required to give no more than name, sex, marital condition, occupation, and race. Though the range of questions grew with each census these were directed to educated employers and dealt with matters that could be readily ascertained: number employed, real property owned, type and volume of products, and so on. Moreover the answer required was that which was true at a particular moment in time, and required no historical retrospect. The bureaus of labor statistics often wanted answers to more difficult questions – the number of days' employment in a year, the average wage, expenditure, and costs – which often required recapitulation over a long period. They might also ask for statements which involved judgment as well as a knowledge of fact. In oral hearings they might be required to give opinions as well as provide facts.

All bureaus began by sending out question sheets (or "blanks" as they were called). The preparation of these sheets was no simple matter, and the evaluation of the information collected required experience and intelligence. Though bureaus continued to use blanks sent by mail, they preferred to collect or at least to verify information by making personal visits. Most of them persuaded the legislature to appropriate money for the employment of agents to conduct these visits, but in 1904 the California bureau was still complaining that it was a waste of time to collect statistics by mail, and pleading (unsuccessfully) for more agents so that it could do the job efficiently.[43]

When a bureau had enough men to collect information it still encountered much resistance. Indeed the unfamiliar spectacle of a man with some official designation, armed with a notebook and pencil, raised

[43] California Bur. of L. S., 11th R. (1904), 5.

suspicion. The Pennsylvania bureau encountered "a jealous dread of unwarrantable interference," and in 1874, when it obtained an act making it unlawful to withhold information, there was a storm of protest, including the denunciation by the Philadelphia Board of Trade of the man who had sponsored the law as a "mischievous busybody" and "communist."[44] There was nothing more resented by the average American, said the New York bureau, than "inquisitorial visits," and neither employers nor workmen were easily convinced that the bureau was not "prying into business affairs for underhand purposes or for personal or political uses."[45] The bureau had been told by the State Attorney General that "the right of a citizen to be secure in his property against unnecessary searches and inquisitorial examinations is sacredly regarded" and warned that the courts would not sanction inspection unless explicitly authorized by statute.[46] Yet "inquisition" was necessary, and it had to be persistent, comprehensive, and time-consuming for interrogator and respondent. The New York bureau pointed out that the details of even one manufacturing business could not be obtained "by perfunctory inspection," and that its task was to understand the whole factory system.[47]

Sometimes it was simply incomprehension that made accuracy impossible. Aware that many returns were incomplete or unintelligible, the North Carolina bureau explained that "the working men of North Carolina have not been in the habit of keeping an account of their receipts and expenditure, loss of time, accumulations, etc. and were therefore unable to answer some of the important questions asked."[48] In 1892 it was said that the people of California had not "been educated up to the point of giving information for statistical purposes." Though the questions had been simplified and agents worked enthusiastically "no account of energy would get results."[49] In 1884 the New York bureau failed to get replies from many manufacturers about convict labor, but charitably attributed this to the fact that many who received the paper thought that it was advertising matter and destroyed it on receipt.[50]

Sooner or later these inhibitions and obstacles had to be overcome if a modern administrative system was to evolve and make hopeless the cause of individual objectors; but much effort and the reversal of deeply rooted

[44] Pennsylvania Bur. of L. S., 2nd R. (1873–4), 421.
[45] New York Bur. of L. S., 5th R. (1887), 40–1.   [46] *Idem*, 2nd R. (1885), 19.
[47] *Ibid.*, 10.   [48] North Carolina Bur. of L. S.
[49] Speech by Commissioner Watts of California at National Conference of Officials of Bureaus of Labor Statistics, 1892.
[50] New York Bur. of L. S., 1st R. (1884), 36.

opinions were required before the change could come about. Nevertheless the New York bureau was on the side of history when it proclaimed that

This information, collected and classified, would be a sound basis on which the legislator and the philanthropist could take action; without it we work in uncertainty, tentatively; efforts at legislation are piecemeal and inharmonious, always experimental, sometimes contradictory. We have reached a point in our development of governmental conscience, that *laissez faire* policy, on the basis of every man for himself, is no longer possible.[51]

If there was resistance to investigation it may be imagined that enforcement would be a stupendous task; indeed in Massachusetts and several other states the bureaus steadily refused to accept the responsibility and left to others the duty of making orders and instituting prosecutions. Ohio had two reasonably efficient inspectorates of mines and factories, which functioned separately from the bureau, and the same was true of Illinois. Connecticut had no system of factory inspection until 1887, and then the chief inspector reported directly to the governor. On the other hand, as already noted, the Wisconsin bureau had, from the start, responsibility for enforcing labor laws. In Minnesota the bureau inspected and reported deficiencies, but not until 1893 was it given the duty of enforcing factory and railroad laws.

Inspectors were in the front line; they entered factories, went down mines, heard complaints, encountered racalcitrant employers face to face, issued orders for improvement, and, if necessary, instituted prosecutions. In Wisconsin, Frank Flower had occasion to reprimand his inspector of factories at Milwaukee, and his letter gives an insight into what was expected:

The inspector is the stinger of the hornet, the snapper of the whip. . . You say pretty bluntly that you will not offend anybody. You will have to enforce the laws or make room for someone who will.[52]

Shortly after this he decided to dismiss this inspector and replace him by a man who would enforce the law "with vigor, industry and impartiality for the benefit of wage earners." In Minnesota at the end of the century the Inspector of Factories had authority to order immediate compliance with the law, and to lay down how this should be done. In one year he issued 195 orders on safety, 220 on child labor, 78 on sanitary improvements, 36

[51] *Idem*, 5th R. (1887), 34.
[52] Flower to Henry Sieber, May 28, July 23, 1887, Frank Flower Papers, Wisconsin Historical Society, Madison.

requiring external fire escapes, and 25 concerning stairways, ladders and passages. In addition he dealt with a number of minor matters relating to safety and comfort of employees, to make a grand total of 570 orders or almost two for every working day.[53]

The history of mines inspection in Ohio illustrates the obstacles to be overcome and the successful evolution of a powerful state agency.[54] The inspectorate was set up in 1874 as a result of a movement led by three immigrant Scottish miners – William Thomson, John Pollock, and Andrew Roy – who had had experience of the British mining law. A bill was drafted in 1871 and Roy lobbied for it; what he got was a commission of inquiry with himself as one of three members. His two colleagues wrote a temporizing report, and he himself produced a well-informed minority report in which he accused the other two of ignorance and of failure to remedy it by visiting mines. In response the legislature passed a mining law, but without an inspectorate. Lobbying at a constitutional convention in 1873 obtained a clause requiring the legislature to provide for mining safety and inspection, but the constitution was rejected by the voters on other grounds. In 1874, thanks to the personal support of Governor William Allen, an inspection law was passed by a large majority, and Roy was appointed. He failed to get a second inspector; no qualifications for inspectors were prescribed; and a proposal that mine managers must produce certificates of competence was lost. In the event, as so often happened in the development of social policy, success depended upon what one man, short-handed, could accomplish and what influence he could bring to bear upon the legislature in future sessions.

By this time Roy knew more than most men about the techniques and law of mining, and this made him a formidable critic of the mine operators. Despite intense efforts to undermine his position he was reappointed in 1876, but in 1878 he was dismissed by the Democratic governor, Richard M. Bishop. His successor, James D. Poston, inspected no mines and wrote no report. In 1880 Governor Charles Foster reappointed Roy for a four-year term, giving him a commanding position from which he could overreach any mine owner in expertise, access to the press, and influence with the legislature. He also built up a national reputation as an expert on the regulation of mining, and Ohio earned an enviable record for mine safety.

[53] Minnesota Bur. of L. S., 7th R. (1899–1900), 155.
[54] K. Austin Kerr, "The Movement for Coal Mine Safety in Nineteenth Century Ohio," *Ohio History*, 86 (1977), 3–18.

Illinois had an inspector of mines in 1884, as a result of the first major investigation undertaken by the Bureau of Labor Statistics, but no inspector of factories until 1894 when an independent commission of inquiry revealed shocking conditions in Chicago workshops. Governor Altgeld appointed Florence Kelley as chief inspector, and for three hectic years she battled against employers who infringed the law and especially against the Illinois Glass Company, the state's largest employer of child labor.[55] She also lobbied vigorously for a law restricting the hours of women working in textile factories to eight, but the law was declared unconstitutional by the Illinois Supreme Court in the notorious case of *Ritchie* v. *the People*. Her father had had a good deal to do with the passage of the fourteenth amendment and it was therefore with personal knowledge that she could observe: "It remained for the Supreme Court of Illinois to discover that the amendment to the Constitution, passed to guarantee the negro against oppression has become an insuperable obstacle to the protection of women and children."[56] The most enduring part of Florence Kelley's work was the creation of a strong organization. She insisted upon trained subordinates, regular reports to her office, and immediate action against offending employers. She left a staff of twelve inspectors, a large volume of statistics, and a reputation for effective lobbying.

Almost unnoticed a new profession had come into being. In 1886 factory inspectors held their first annual convention at Washington, attended by representatives from five states, and membership grew each year.[57] There was also a growing literature in which the reports of inspectors played a considerable part. The foundations of efficient and systematic inspection had been laid, but the edifice was far from complete. Chief inspectors invariably complained that their staffs were too small. The commissioner of mines in Colorado told the Federal Industrial Commission of 1901 that he had two assistant inspectors but required four more. He himself had never visited a mine outside the Cripple Creek district, and systematic inspection was impossible because the whole time was taken up in hearing complaints. A Colorado miner told the same commission that in ten years he had seen only one deputy inspector, who had spent twenty minutes at a mine employing 200 men.

[55] Sandra D. Harma, "Florence Kelley in Illinois," *Journal of the Illinois State Historical Society*, 74 (1981), 162–78; Dorothy Rose Blumberg, *Florence Kelley: the Making of a Social Pioneer* (New York, 1966), *passim; Industrial Commission*, VII, 244, 225: evidence of Florence Kelley. [56] Blumberg, *op. cit.*, 133.
[57] *Industrial Commission*, VII, 75; evidence of Rufus R. Warde, president of the first convention.

By contrast New York seemed advanced. The Chief Inspector of Factories had thirty-six inspectors, of whom nine were women; but even this was inadequate in a large state, with many manufacturing centers, and a large concentration of very poor people, almost all recent immigrants, in the workshops and sweatshops of New York City. The task was formidable and the rewards meager.

We can force them to clean their toilets, use disinfectant, and apply all sanitary suggestions that we think necessary to make more wholesome the surroundings in which they work. We have gone back . . . perhaps a week later or sooner, and found the conditions worse than they were in the first instance.

This was the view of the Chief Inspector, and Clare de Graffenried of the Federal Department of Labor, who had first-hand experience of New York, agreed that the number of inspectors should be doubled or trebled. What was needed was not "infrequent inspection from overworked officials," but frequent and regular visits with immediate prosecution of offenders.[58]

These depressing facts should be seen in context. If there was still much to be done it was now possible to see what *ought* to be done. Thirty years earlier it would have been wholly unrealistic to suggest frequent and regular inspection by government officials as a remedy for social ills. If thirty-six inspectors were not enough for a large state, not long since there had been none. The principle had been established and accepted. It remained to persuade reluctant legislators and suspicious taxpayers to spend enough money to do the job properly.

Despite the change in thirty years the achievements often appeared painstaking and prosaic when set beside the early hopes. Representatives of organized labor, who did so much to promote the establishment of Bureaus of Labor Statistics, had hoped for the discovery of some rule by which the demands of wage earners could be met without conflict. A scientific investigation of the causes of disturbance was expected to show that grievances ought to be remedied, that conciliation was the true interest of employers, and that changed attitudes would, in large measure, dispense with the need for enforcement. Law must set the outer limits rather than prescribe the detail of agreements between capital and labor, and given their growing strength, union leaders were reasonably confident that they

[58] *Ibid.*, 26ff.: evidence of David O'Leary; 237–8: evidence of Claire de Graffenried. In 1904 the California Commissioner of Labor said that cuts in his appropriation made it impossible to inspect throughout the state (California Bur. of L. S., 11th R.).

could get a fair deal within such a framework. They did not expect the regulation of wages, but hoped that certain things would be withdrawn from the bargaining process by law. Prominent among these expectations were the prohibition of child labor, maximum hours of employment for women and minors, definition of the working day (that is, the point at which overtime pay would normally begin), weekly payment of wages in money (thus outlawing payment by credit on company stores), and fixed standards for safety, sanitation, and ventilation. On arbitration labor leaders were inconsistent, but broadly speaking they wanted compulsory arbitration when employers were obdurate, but voluntary arbitration as a part of the bargaining process when there was a chance of gaining their points. The bureaus were expected to provide the arguments to carry these points.

Against this many middle-class Americans, who were not committed to the employers, nevertheless believed that better information should convince labor that political economy condemned strikes, disruption, and intervention by law. A typical point of view was expressed in 1871 by Lyman Atwater, editor of the influential *Princeton Review*.[59] He began by admitting that it was impossible to close one's eyes to the reality of conflict, yet since the interests of all were ultimately the same all interruptions of the process of production damaged both capital and labor, "just as manacles impair the working power of the human body." Law might protect the young and encourage the introduction of new branches of industry, but "the conditions of labor could not be improved by any eight or nine hour laws or by any mere legislation whatever." Combinations against employers were condemned by reason, and those who conspired to deprive men of their God-given right to work "should find the whole power of the state put forth to thwart them as enemies of the human race." The advice to employers was to spread Christianity among the laboring masses, and promote education to teach "the laws of nature, of men, and of political economics."

These arguments reflected the view of a great majority of Americans in the business, professional, and property-owning classes, and it was the historic role of the Bureaus of Labor Statistics to confute them. In contrast to an imaginary condition governed by "the laws of nature" the findings of the bureaus exposed a real world in which no such laws applied. In contrast to the harmony of interests they presented the actual record of conflict, and

[59] "The Labor Question in its Economic and Christian Aspects," *Princeton Review*, 1: 3 (1872), 48.

threw doubt upon laws of political economy which accepted degradation as the price of progress. In contrast to enlightened self-interest which was supposed to mitigate the harshness of the system, they presented an appalling picture of the world that self-interest made. They drew conclusions which ran counter to the "laws" of political economy, and sometimes departed from statistical purism to point where the evidence led.

Was legislation in the interests of labor futile? It was true, said the Pennsylvania board in its first report in 1873, that the best legislation was the least; "Yet it is none the less true that the rights and interests of all the people in the general prosperity and progress may not be justly left at the mercy of the ignorant, or vicious, or reckless, or grasping contentions of a portion."[60] When the disturbing element threatened great industries and whole communities, it was the right and duty of the legislature to interfere. With more experience behind it the Massachusetts bureau asked in 1875 what the wage system should and did achieve. The majority of working men could not maintain themselves without the earnings of wives and children, nor provide for education, sickness, or old age. The system "used men and women when they were strong, and left them to shift for themselves when they were sick, infirm or without employment," put children in factories when they should be in school, and paid ten per cent of employed men such low wages that they sank into debt and poverty without hope of improvement.[61]

The New York bureau presented a rigorous essay on social theory in its report for 1885. There could, it asserted, be no doubt that working men were made to work excessive hours for low wages, and that women were "subjected to more frequent and greater abuses." When wages were fixed by the employer alone there was no limit to what he could force desperate men to accept, and the situation was made worse by the presence of so many immigrants who would work for wages on which a native American could starve.

In so far as this makes tramps and paupers, it is the duty of the State to place some restrictions upon it, for preventative legislation will be found to be better than correction.[62]

In 1890 the same bureau was dogmatic in asserting the right of the State to intervene and the wisdom of its doing so: "The constitutional right of

---

[60] Pennsylvania Bur. of L. S., 1st R. (1872–3), 316.
[61] Pidgin, 87–8; from Massachusetts Bur. of L. S., 7th R. (1875).
[62] New York Bur. of L. S., 3rd R. (1885), 609–11.

legislative bodies to interpose between employers and employed will scarcely be disputed in the question of hours any more than in health or morals." The State had all the power needed to protect "the rights of wage earners in the matter of hours of labor." The report concluded that all labor laws hinged upon the need to protect the poor against "the inhumanity or ignorance of their employers."[63]

It was totally irrelevant to argue as though strikes were due to transient causes, malevolent agitators, or failure to understand economic theory. The Ohio bureau spent much time in investigating actual strikes that had occurred and none in protesting that they were contrary to nature:

Reason, denunciation, and at times the whole power of the law have been brought to bear to prove the folly of, or to prevent strikes; yet . . . the best that has been accomplished by all the efforts put forth to prevent strikes, is to render them less destructive to both parties, as well as less injurious to the general public.[64]

No amount of argument had prevented a strike when grievances were so acute that men saw no alternative; nor had strikes been stopped in their course so long as hope of victory remained. "Strikes seem to be an absolute part and parcel of our industrial system, and may be truthfully attributed to the desire of men to improve their condition, a desire that will not be stayed." The New York bureau pointed out that it was no longer any use to preach to working men that hard work would better their prospects: they knew, and everyone knew, that the greater part of the laboring force, however virtuous and industrious, would remain in its present status. A few might climb from the unskilled mass to the skilled minority, but this could bring no comfort, for skilled men were notoriously more prone to strike.[65] Practice of the virtues preached by moralists and political economists led either to frustration or to discontent; looking at recent history, working men knew that every advantage won had been fought for and saw no reason to suppose that things would change in the future. When men were liable to lay-offs without notice, it was of little moment to point out that they lost wages by striking; common sense suggested that time lost would be made up for later.[66]

In seeing strikes as a natural phenomenon the bureaus received some unexpected support from William Graham Sumner, disciple of Herbert Spencer and arch-exponent of laissez faire. In an article in *Forum*, with the provocative title "Do We Want Industrial Peace?", Sumner argued that

[63] *Idem*, 8th R. (1890), 13–14.
[64] Ohio Bur. of L. S.
[65] New York Bur. of L. S., 3rd R. (1885), 612.
[66] *Ibid.*, 618.

industrial warfare was "an incident of liberty"; it was an inconvenience but not an evil: "Industrial war is an attendant upon liberty. It has come just because industry has been unfettered and has been allowed to shape itself freely. How can it shape itself freely unless it works out the full effect of all the forces that are in it?" Industrial war was the inevitable means by which the redistribution of capital and labor was brought about. Interference which sought to stop war meant that one party or the other would be able to escape, for the time being, the consequence of changes forced upon it by economic conditions, and would thus produce much chaos and misery at a later date.

That is the dilemma which repeats itself over and over again in the social development of our time, and brings up one after another these "great social questions."[67]

While accepting Sumner's argument that industrial conflict was inevitable, the bureaus did not share his view that nothing could or should be done about it. His view might be a long one, but their concern was with the conditions revealed by the statistics they compiled. Human decision as well as impersonal forces explained the data on wages, prices, regularity of employment, child labor, housing, and labor organization. The problem was to accept the necessity of conflict but to institutionalize it in such a way that violence was avoided and reasonable hopes for improvement were satisfied.

The New York bureau noticed that recently formed labor organizations resorted to strikes far more readily than the long-established ones. Young unions wanted to demonstrate their strength; old unions knew that a reminder of strength might be sufficient to gain their objectives. When one of the older unions struck, the cause of the breakdown could usually be traced to exceptional obstinacy on the part of an employer. It followed that treatment of industrial conflict should aim to make new unions behave like those with experience, and intransigent employers behave as though they were reasonable.[68]

The Ohio board described in great detail a voluntary system of arbitration set up by shoe manufacturers and employees in Cincinnati.[69] All other bureaus endorsed arbitration in principle, and in so doing they implicitly subscribed to the idea that in all disputes there was room for concession on both sides. They drew back from the idea of compulsory

[67] *Forum*, 8 (1889), 406–16.   [68] New York Bur. of L. S., 3rd R. (1885), 610.
[69] Ohio Bur. of L. S., 6th R. (1882), 255ff.

arbitration, but recognized that arbitration was not likely to be resorted to if the machinery had to be set up for each dispute. The solution was for the states to set up arbitration courts which would always be ready to accept cases; and the number of strikes revealed by investigation suggested that these courts would seldom be idle once people acquired the habit of using them.

Arbitration was not a new idea, but an arbitration system administered by the State was. The idea tied in with other work of the bureaus, because arbitrators would be able to draw upon a wealth of information about wage rates, real wages, cost of living, hours of work, and productivity. The bureaus knew that the majority of strikes were small local affairs, often precipitated by ignorance of conditions elsewhere, while large strikes were often triggered by minor incidents. A well-informed arbitration court would be able to put both in their proper perspective.

Arbitration may seem a tame remedy, and a mockery in a period which saw violence at its height in the Homestead strike, and the most dramatic repercussions of local misunderstandings in the Pullman strike. More violence would follow in other strikes and in later years, but the United States did not experience another year such as 1877, in which class warfare threatened to become general. The bureaus, both by publicity and by influence on legislatures, did something toward establishing a rule of reason in industrial disputes.

It would be idle to suggest that the Bureaus of Labor Statistics offered any formula to end industrial conflict. They stood at the beginning of a chapter which is not yet closed. In 1896 Wright wrote: "The time is rapidly coming when the Community will assert its rights to perpetual peace, and so bring to bear on all parties engaged in industry a great moral influence which will secure all the benefits of voluntary arbitration and render the resort to any compulsory measures unnecessary."[70] The dream remains a dream; but this is no reason to denigrate the hopes inspired by the bureaus. They advanced the thesis that the empirical study of conditions of industrial work would lead to an era in which there could be broad agreement between capital and labor on what served both. They entered an effective protest against the belief that labor could be subjected to the discipline of abstract propositions, which always seemed to serve the interests of employers. They helped to produce a situation in which it was no longer the workers but the employers who seemed to act irrationally.

[70] *Industrial Evolution of the United States*, 29.

Some working parents might wish to send their children to earn money in factories, but organized labor was uniformly opposed to child labor. Some working men might be improvident, but it was the companies who insisted upon the "right" to refuse regular payment in legal currency. It was not the employers but the labor leaders who could appeal to the vast mass of information accumulated by the bureaus to support their case.

The accumulation of statistics, the quest for policy guided by scientific method, the regulation of social life by law, and inspection to ensure that the laws are understood and obeyed, are hallmarks of the twentieth-century state. The evolution of agencies to carry out these purposes has been a major theme of history in the century which began about 1870. If the bureaus of labor statistics had stood alone, it might have been possible to write them off as interesting experiments which succeeded in producing a great volume of reasonably accurate statistical data, but had little direct influence on public policy. However, they take their place with other new agencies charged with investigating prisons, poor law institutions, public health, railroads, and other social problems – and among them the emergence of an official body charged with responsibility for the scientific investigation of social data was a major contribution to the formation of modern American society.[71]

[71] The number of bureaus in existence at the close of the century is not certain. In 1895 Wright said that there were thirty-one (*Industrial Evolution of the United States*, 275); the *Index of all Reports issued by Bureaus of Labor Statistics*, prepared under the direction of Wright in 1902, listed twenty-nine, to which might be added the Kentucky Bureau of Agriculture, Horticulture, and Statistics. In 1904 G. W. W. Hangar claimed twenty-seven ("Bureaus of Labor in the United States," *Bulletin of the Bureau of Labor*, No. 54, 991 ff.). Hangar included the Kentucky bureau, and also Idaho and South Dakota, not in the 1902 list. The 1902 list included New Hampshire, Virginia, West Virginia, Washington, and Montana, which are not noted by Hangar. The addition of three to the 1902 list and of six to Hangar's list gives thirty-two in both instances. In 1895 Wright could not have included Virginia (which did not report until 1898) but he may have known that the Washington bureau (first biennial report 1897–8) had been authorized; this would reconcile his total of thirty-one with the later figures. There were no bureaus in South Carolina, Georgia, Alabama, Mississippi, Louisiana, Texas, Arkansas, or Florida, nor in Oregon, Idaho, Wyoming, or Oklahoma; in the east and mid-west only Delaware was without a bureau.

7

THE RAILROAD COMMISSIONS

Railroads presented the most formidable problem for society. Never before had private decisions entailed so many public consequences; never had public responsibility been called upon the shoulder such extensive powers of regulation. They presented in addition a question of such complexity that it has been as much misunderstood by later writers as it was by contemporaries.

Indeed there was not one railroad problem but several. At one stage railroads were desperately needed; counties, cities and towns spared no effort to persuade the companies to divert main lines or build branches; money for railroad bonds was raised locally and handed over with few conditions attached; rights of way were generously conceded; legislatures granted charters which gave corporations the widest possible latitude, often including the power to fix rates without public supervision. Parts of many western states remained in this condition until late in the century and produced a curious alliance against regulation between giant corporations and representatives from the poorest districts. Men who desperately hoped for railroads to be built readily succumbed to the argument that hostile legislation would put an end to construction, while charters which lightly conceded exclusive rights remained to plague future discussion of the railroad problem.[1]

Once constructed a railroad might have a monopoly of communication between a district and its markets, and at this stage pressure of a quite different kind was generated. Railroads were accused of raising rates to an extortionate level, of charging far more where there was no competition than elsewhere, and of allowing services and facilities to deteriorate. The rhetoric of anti-monopoly was at hand to express opposition to the corporations and their managers. Yet in practice this kind of anti-railroad

---

[1] The generalizations in this and the following paragraphs owe much to George H. Miller, *Railroads and the Granger Laws* (Madison, Wis., 1971).

185

movement seldom produced much legislation of consequence, save in rare instances when the aggrieved district was large, politically important, and able to find allies among the major economic interests in a state. The rise and temporary success of the Grangers were the product of such a situation, but more often representatives from farming counties were likely to be divided between those who wanted new railroads and those who wished to regulate those that already existed.

A far more fruitful source of support for the principle of regulation sprang from discrimination between towns, districts, and commercial centers. The railroad case was usually straightforward. The most profitable business was to carry freight for long distances from major terminal to major terminal; the least profitable was to carry freight for short distances between intermediate points. Between these two extremes there was room for much variation, but there was always a good prima-facie case for charging higher rates per mile for short than for long hauls. In many instances the total rate for a long distance might be less than for a short one, and this was likely when there was competition for traffic between the distant terminals. These reasons, which seemed so clear to railroad managers, were not going to appeal to shippers who found themselves at a disadvantage, when competing with rivals from other parts of the state, in gaining access to major marketing centers; nor did discrimination end at state boundaries, as there were many reasons why railroads might find it advantageous to encourage through traffic to very distant points rather than serve a regional market. Milwaukee found itself by-passed when rates to Chicago were cut, but Chicago itself was in danger of losing trade when the railroads offered attractive terms to shippers who would consign directly to New York. New York might find itself at a disadvantage in competition with Boston. The Baltimore and Ohio was desperately anxious to preserve the competitiveness of Baltimore as an outlet for mid-western produce and to undercut rates to other Atlantic ports.

Railroad managers were often called upon to make nice calculations. Very adverse rates might discourage traffic over certain sections so severely that they became unprofitable, and this might be the moment to reduce short-haul rates. In the area of the Great Lakes managers had to watch the rates charged for water-borne traffic to ensure that too much freight was not being sent by the longer but cheaper method. Indeed they often argued that competition would automatically correct rates which were truly extortionate. At the same time the larger companies might try to limit wasteful competition by forming pools, associations, or informal agreements. Whether the corporations were exploiting monopoly or curbing competition they seemed (at least to those who depended upon them) to be stupidly indifferent to future development. In 1891 San Francisco merchants, organized in a Traffic Association, argued that steamship service should be launched with the express purpose of carrying freight more cheaply to the east and even to the Mississippi valley than by the Central or Southern Pacific railroads.[2]

Excessive rates and discrimination between shipping points were mainly western and south-western problems, as highly capitalized and expensively operated railroads there served thinly populated regions. In the east, where the networks were fully developed, competition intense, and water navigation often a viable alternative, the most frequent complaints were likely to be of rebates or discounts to large shippers and agreements between railroads to cut competition. Everywhere there were also complaints of a different order about poor services on less profitable lines, inadequate passenger and inconvenient terminal facilities. Excessive charges by express companies were another source of complaint. Nor could all railroads run profitably, and their situation was worsened by the enormous amount of construction undertaken between 1866 and 1873. By the 1880s half the railroads in the country were in the hands of receivers, and many stockholders could hardly recall the time when they had received a dividend.[3]

The weightiest demands for railroad regulation came from influential groups of merchants in commercial cities. In his important study of railroads and the Granger Laws George H. Miller observed that the law that was subsequently tested in *Munn* v. *Illinois* was passed in 1871 by a legislature with a solid Republican majority and a heavy preponderance of representatives connected with business and the professions. There was a Legislative Farmers' Club but it was divided on the question of railroad regulation, and the major split on the issue was between representatives from districts where railroads were strong and those where local interests wanted to encourage new construction or support weak railroads. The former wanted a uniform rate law, an end of long- and short-haul discrimination, and a supervisory commission; the latter opposed a general

---

[2] Stuart Daggett, *Chapters on the History of the Southern Pacific* (New York, 1922), 297.
[3] In a memorandum on government ownership of railroads dated April 20, 1886, Thomas M. Cooley wrote that the majority of corporations paid no dividends and were unlikely to do so – either on actual cost or on the market value of shares: "Numbers of them are steadily sinking into bankruptcy," and not one in twenty could pay a dividend of 8% (Cooley Papers, Bentley Library, University of Michigan).

rate law but were prepared to accept a commission. A revised act of 1873 was a compromise providing for flexibility on rates but for a strong commission with power to prosecute for infractions of the state law. In New York the whole movement for regulation was initiated by the Chamber of Commerce of New York City. The chairman of the Ohio Railroad Commission took a dim view of this movement, describing it as "a League in New York who are covertly trying to hedge the commerce of the West so that it must go through the port of New York." In California dissatisfaction with a somewhat inert commission led to the formation of a Traffic Association by San Francisco merchants. In Texas the first move toward the establishment of a commission came from a Freight Convention in Dallas attended by representatives of farmers, merchants, and businessmen, where it was asserted that "the great masses of the farmers and dealers in heavy merchandise were much dissatisfied with the railroad rates."[4]

It is necessary to make these points to dispose of the once prevalent notion that the movement for railroad regulation was an offshoot of "agrarian radicalism." It is true that the cost of carrying agricultural produce was often at the heart of the local controversy, but the men prepared to press for legislation were normally the merchants who handled the produce, feared that high rates placed them at a competitive disadvantage, and suspected that rivals elsewhere were being given unfair discounts or rebates. In this controversy it was natural to use the rhetoric of anti-monopoly, and to invoke the cause of oppressed farmers, or, more generally, to claim to represent the interests of "the people" against the corporation. This need not suggest that the grievances were unreal or that the behavior of the railroads did not deserve censure, but does indicate that the whole movement for railroad regulation was a response to the needs of an expanding society; not a radical critique of free enterprise, but the reaction of business to threatened profits and high-handed attempts to direct the patterns of trade. It was this character that earned the new commissions acceptance and a reasonable degree of success.

There were other good reasons why government should take an interest in railroads. In 1865 Sir Morton Peto, reporting on American railroads for

---

[4] George H. Miller, 182ff.; Lee Benson, *Merchants, Farmers, and Railroads: Railroad Regulation and New York Politics 1850–1887* (Cambridge, Mass., 1955), 39–43, 55–79, and *passim*; Gerald D. Nash, *State Government and Economic Development: Administrative Policies in California, 1849–1933* (Berkeley, Calif., 1964), 159–60.

the benefit of British investors, found much to criticize.[5] The operating costs averaged more than twice the cost per mile in England; too great a proportion of the earnings went on maintenance and repair (the price of shoddy or incompetent construction); and investors were not getting a fair share of the profits, which were used instead for new capital projects. The Express Company system was open to abuse, especially when the Express directors were also officers of the railroads and sure to see that profits which ought to be earned by the railroad came their way. The large number of lines led to lack of co-operation, cost-cutting economies, neglect of safety, and poor service. These shortcomings anticipated the construction boom that would make matters worse. High speeds were uncommon because the tracks were poor, most railroads were single-track, causing delay in populous regions, and management was inefficient. Few Americans could make comparisons with foreign countries, but there was a general feeling that the companies were not doing enough – either for their stockholders or for users – to justify the privileges conferred upon them by charter.

One obvious cause of complaint was the bad safety record. Accidents were frequent, but even more shocking was the toll of death and injury inflicted by railroads on their own employees. Brakemen who had to run from car to car were the most vulnerable, but switchmen were too often pinned between cars that they were attempting to couple or uncouple. In 1886 the chairman of the Massachusetts Railroad Commission estimated that over 1,000 were injured and over 200 killed every year when coupling or uncoupling cars. This was probably an underestimate, for in 1888 the Federal Commissioner of Labor gave the official figures for the year ending 30 June: 315 passengers had been killed and 2,138 injured; 2,070 employees had been killed and 20,148 injured; while 2,897 others had been killed and 3,602 injured, mainly when crossing tracks or when trains ran off the rails. In Texas alone in the year ending June 30, 1891, eighty-three employees were killed, together with three passengers and one hundred and eight others.[6] Three years later the figures were even worse. These appalling figures date from late in the century and may be interpreted either as a failure of the great number of safety laws passed by the states or as an indication that things could have been much worse without efforts to impose caution by law; but however interpreted they show that the

[5] Sir Morton Peto, *The Resources and Prospects of America* (London, 1865), 280–90.
[6] Senate Documents, 49th Congress, 1st session (1886), *Report No. 46* (Cullom Report), 235: evidence of Thomas Russell; Texas R.R. Comm., 1st R. (1892). (There had been some improvement in 1891–2, for which the commission claimed credit.)

railroads had a case to answer at the bar of opinion. Though the number of passengers killed or injured was much lower than that of employees, passengers usually suffered in accidents that attracted maximum publicity, so that the hazards of rail travel were widely known. Nor could regular travelers be unaware of the inconvenience and delays caused by damaged track, unsafe bridges, and defects in the locomotives. The corporations might have friends, but few could deny that in this field the law should be tough, explicit, and strictly enforced.

Despite these defects railroad corporations made the most of their power in the decade after the Civil War. Charles Francis Adams Jr, who had unrivaled opportunities for observing railroad practices, wrote that by 1870 "the railroad corporations were . . . rapidly assuming a position which could not be tolerated. Corporations, owning and operating the highways of commerce, claimed for themselves a species of immunity from the control of the law-making power." They received regulatory laws in a manner that was "at once arrogant and singularly injudicious." In law they sheltered behind the Dartmouth College decision, and acted as though a corporation once chartered was immune from legislative regulation.[7] In March 1873 *The Atlantic Monthly* published an article entitled "Railway Despotism," which claimed that "as to the evils of the present condition of things, there is remarkable unanimity of opinion. . . . The railroads are gigantic monopolies over which the principle of competition has no control . . . A railroad today means, to the great number of people who project and create it, simply a fraudulent device for extorting a quantity of money from the public under the guise of a public service." In the face of this threat the writer could, however, suggest no easy remedy. Incorporation implied the right to regulate but "instead of the State's supervising the railroads, the railroads supervise the State."[8]

Yet nothing seemed to abate the truculence of the companies. When western states first passed regulatory laws the typical railroad action was to behave as though nothing had happened. The telling phrases of Adams can be quoted once more: "If a railroad official was asked what course the companies proposed to pursue in regard to the new legislation, the usual answer was that they did not propose to pay any attention to it . . . Naturally this impolitic course not only incensed the commissioners, but, what was of far more consequence, it strengthened their hands."[9]

---

[7] Charles Francis Adams Jr, *Railroads: their Origins and Problems* (Boston, Mass., 1878; repr. New York: J. & J. Harper, 1969), 127.
[8] *The Atlantic Monthly*, Mar. 1873, 381–3.   [9] Adams, *Railroads*, 127.

The surprising thing was that despite the Dartmouth decision the legal position of the railroads was weak. The police power of the states had still to be fully tested in the courts, but it was certainly known to exist. As common carriers the railroads had obligations which were deeply implanted in Anglo-American law, and which were also affected by the more purely American development of "eminent domain," under which the states could appropriate private property when required for public use provided that fair compensation were given. To this power the railroads owed the land on which tracks were laid, depots built, and their rights of way legalized; they could also anticipate many future occasions on which there would be need to ask the legislature for further use of eminent domain.

In the event the doctrine of the Dartmouth College case crumbled with few authoritative voices raised in its defense. The argument was put by two obscure delegates to the Illinois Constitutional Convention of 1869–70, Reuben M. Benjamin and Jesse Hildrup. Benjamin argued that privileges granted to corporations were vested rights that could not be impaired, but that there were sovereign rights that no legislature could give way beyond hope of recovery. The people were the source of authority and they alone could relieve a legislature of its right to exercise constitutional powers. The right to fix rates came into this category, for it derived directly from the police power to regulate common carriers; if a legislature could deny to its successors the exercise of this right it had, in effect, altered the constitution. The charter could not therefore have intended to yield to railroads the *exclusive* right to fix rates, or, if it had so intended, was itself unconstitutional. To this Hildrup added an argument based on eminent domain. If the police power was not sufficient, none could deny the right to take all or part of a corporate franchise for public use. As this power had existed before the railroads, all charters must be construed as granted without impairment to eminent domain. George H. Miller has observed that "no part of their argument has since been refuted by the United States Supreme Court." The great authority on constitutional law gave his general approval when Thomas M. Cooley remarked, in *Constitutional Limitations*, that if a legislature had the power to bargain away its powers under the guise of incorporation it was certainly "a very dangerous power, exceedingly liable to abuse."[10]

If the legal protection claimed by the railroads proved to be fragile, there were serious and practical obstacles to effective regulation. No one in

[10] Quoted Miller, *Railroads and Granger Laws*, from *Constitutional Limitations*, 1st ed. (1868), 280.

America had experience of problems on this scale, and knowledge of British and European practice was superficial. Was regulation to take the form of statute enforced by the law officers? States did try to fix maximum rates by law, prohibit discrimination, and require annual reports, but soon found themselves immersed in a sea of technical reasons why the laws could not or ought not to be enforced. *Munn* v. *Illinois* vindicated the right, but by the time it was decided Illinois had already moved on to experiment with a regulatory commission. Maximum rates fixed by law could be inflexible and might well be above some rates already charged.

A favored alternative was to create a railroad commission, but there were considerable variations as to form and power. A commission might consist of three or more members, or there might be a single commissioner with a staff of subordinates. The commission might be appointed or elected. It might do no more than investigate, give publicity to its findings, and make recommendations for legislative action. It might itself institute proceedings or rely for enforcement upon the state law officers. It might be required to execute a rate-fixing law, with discretion to vary the rates when necessary, or it might itself have power to publish the schedule of rates, and where it did so its findings were normally to be accepted as prima-facie evidence that the rates fixed were reasonable.

Whatever the form of the commission it faced a task that was far more difficult than appeared on the surface. It was apparent that large railroads were powerful, but they also had the enormous advantage of continuity and fixity of purpose. The political authority, wrote C. F. Adams Jr, was "continually trembling for its retention of temporary power," but the railroad officials served a corporation which did not change. It was not only that continuity strengthened political influence, but that their case always rested upon detailed knowledge of particular circumstances. It might be assumed that a commission had only to reach a decision on the fair rate per mile and then apply it, but on investigation it might be found that a fair rate for one line was grossly unjust for another. When J. H. Osborn became Wisconsin's first Railroad Commissioner in 1877 he sought advice in various quarters and received a long reply from A. H. Ferguson, secretary of the American Cheap Transportation Association, on how to fix a rate. The basic considerations were the real cost of a railroad and its equipment, a reasonable return for the investor, and the interests of users. If there had been fraud and over-capitalization who should pay the price? Operating costs were affected by grades, curves, and frequency of service, the condition of equipment, maintenance, and depreciation. Close investigation with professional advice was required to obtain the answer, and premature action would "do more to hurt the cause of the people than anything you might leave undone." If commissioners mastered the technical side of their job, they had still to tread warily, for highly paid lawyers were employed to detect and exploit any error.[11]

Charles Francis Adams Jr would later claim to have invented regulation by commission, but the idea was in the air before he persuaded the Massachusetts legislature to act upon his proposal. As early as 1866 Warner Bateman, chairman of the railroad committee of the Ohio Senate, suggested a four-man commission to examine the physical condition of railroads, require defects to be remedied, and prosecute for non-compliance with its orders. New railroads would require approval of their plans by the commission, and a safety code was to be enforced. He did not mention the regulation of rates, but this was not an issue in Ohio at that time. Bateman also relied upon a ruling by the Ohio Supreme Court that no judicial proceedings were necessary to subject private property to public use. Like the power to tax, the right of eminent domain belonged exclusively to the legislature, and might be exercised directly or indirectly by that body. Other cases supported his contention that the right to value railroad property might be delegated to a commission, but no action was taken on a bill that his committee reported and Ohio had to wait for its Railroad Commission.[12]

If Charles Francis Adams Jr does not deserve exclusive credit for the commission idea he was certainly its foremost advocate and as a Massachusetts commissioner set the pattern for others. Adams was unlike other members of his distinguished family in that he sought a career in public administration and subsequently in business rather than in high politics, but he inherited other distinctive characteristics from his father and grandfather. These included clarity of mind, impatience with those who thought less clearly than himself, and a strong sense of duty. He was also ambitious, somewhat self-righteous, and occasionally introspective. Like other members of his family he kept a diary and confided to it both doubts of his own achievement and sharp criticisms of others. He was, in many ways, unlike his brother Henry, but he shared with him an ambition to be both an actor in the public play and a critic of it. Emerging from the war with a colonelcy but no clear idea about his career, he resolved to make the study of railroads his special claim to recognition and reward.

Apart from his disclosure of scandals in the Erie management, the first

[11] R. H. Ferguson to Osborn, May 22, 1877, J. H. Osborn Papers, Wisconsin Historical Society, Madison.
[12] Warner Bateman Papers, Western Reserve Historical Society, Cleveland.

notable contribution by Adams to railroad literature was *Railroad Legislation* published in 1868.[13] He assumed that eminent domain was both universal in its application and inalienable. A state could not give to any person the right to use another's land in perpetuity, and a grant to a railroad must have always contained the implied condition that ownership might be recovered and transportation operated as a public service. The situation was, he argued, precisely analogous to that of turnpike roads which had once been operated by private companies but had since been restored to public ownership and control. If the exigencies of the present time made such a proposal premature for the railroads, the fact that they were left "in private hands as a source of profit was, at best, a necessary evil." One obvious difficulty was that state governments were clearly unable to take over the whole complex business of managing railroads and probably lacked the knowledge or competence to supervise their operation in private hands. It followed that the best solution would be the establishment of a state agency armed with power to investigate, take evidence on oath, compel the attendance of witnesses, and require the production of accounts. Apart from rules that were purely procedural Adams did not believe that this agency should make and enforce regulations or fix rates. It would be a quasi-judicial body; but law was the province of the legislature, enforcement that of the executive. The formal duty of this agency or commission would be to advise the legislature; its informal but more important function would be to make public all aspects of the railroad question.

These views were elaborated and given wide publicity in *Railroad Problems*, published in 1869 in the *North American Review*, but by this time Adams knew that the legislature had acted upon his suggestion and that he was to be one member of the three-man commission. The powers granted were even weaker than he had advocated, but in retrospect he came to approve what had been done:

Undesignedly the Massachusetts legislators had rested their law on the one great social feature which distinguished modern civilization from any other of which we have record – the eventual supremacy of enlightened public opinion.[14]

On all questions affecting the relationship of the railroads with society there would, in future, be "a body of experts . . . clothed with full inquisitorial

---

[13] First published in the *American Law Review*, then as a separate pamphlet (Boston, Mass., 1868), from which the citations which follow are taken (11–19).
[14] Wright, *Railroads: their Origins and Problems*, 13.

powers." As the commissioners were appointed for three-year terms some degree of continuity and accumulated experience was assured, and Adams was to serve for nine years as a commissioner. He was always the most active member and from 1872 the chairman. Knowledge, thoroughness, and a reputation for fairness won for the Massachusetts commission a position of unrivaled authority, respected by the public, attended to by the legislature, and ultimately winning the confidence and co-operation of the companies. The Adams legacy was still living in 1893 when the commission recorded that "The legislature has . . . placed in the hands of the Board a more persuasive and effective appliance for the regulation of rates than legal compulsion – that of investigation, criticism, and publicity."[15]

Adams conceded that in some other states – and by implication those with less active, informed, or wise makers of opinion – stronger coercive power might be necessary, but he believed that all states should evolve toward advisory commissions. He was most critical of those that tried to fix rates by law, or gave to their commissions judicial, legislative, and executive power. Once the Massachusetts railroads had learned to co-operate with the commission he grew increasingly tolerant of their actions, believing that the existence of the commission, acting as a permanent arbitration tribunal, had brought together railroads and public in a harmony which had been disrupted by early misunderstanding. He did not expect a quick resolution of all difficulties, but believed that when such resolution was achieved it would be found that the government and the railroad companies had been advancing on convergent paths. This attitude made him tolerant of combination among the railroad companies, and he claimed that all engaged upon the difficult task of adjusting the interests of railroads and the public had found a few large companies easier to deal with than many small ones. The ideal would be a tribunal, charged with protecting the interests of the public, which found no work to do. These conclusions made it easy for Adams to make the transition from chairman of the Massachusetts Commission to president of the Union Pacific. In his own mind he had not changed sides but demonstrated that in an enlightened society the so-called law of competition must observe certain limits. Neither public nor profits would be served if free competition was invoked to justify either folly or injustice.

An austere, fair-minded, and professional tribunal had virtues which spoke for themselves, but it should not be forgotten that it owed its existence to the sovereign State. Somewhere behind the process of

[15] Massachusetts R.R. Comm., Report for 1893, 14.

investigation and judicious decision lay the sovereign's right to decide, regulate, and enforce. The advisory commission owed its existence to an awakened sense of public responsibility, and the difference between it and the regulatory commissions might be more apparent than real.

Massachusetts set one pattern; by common repute Illinois set another. The Constitutional Convention of 1869 paid considerable attention to the railroad problem, and the arguments used to strip from the corporations the protection of the Dartmouth case have already been noticed. Charges imposed by owners of grain warehouses and elevators were also an issue. The new constitution declared that railroads were public highways and subject to such regulation as might be prescribed by law, and applied the same principle to warehouses. The legislature was empowered to correct abuses and prevent extortion and discrimination, and in 1871, acting upon these principles, laws were passed to regulate railroads and warehouses and a commission was set up to enforce them.[16]

These laws were ultimately to be upheld by the United States Supreme Court in the justly celebrated case of *Munn* v. *Illinois*, but the early days of the commission were unhappy. The railroads claimed that apart from a few police regulations their charters protected them from all legislative interference. They relied, said the commission, on the constitutional protection provided for "eleemosynary corporations, such as country colleges or small charitable institutions." They refused to accept the argument derived from eminent domain, and did not acknowledge "that such powers as were granted to them must always be understood to have been granted with the reservation that they should be exercised for the public good."[17]

The Illinois commission encountered other difficulties. The laws affecting railroads were many, confused, and inconsistent, but an attempt to have them codified failed in 1872. Massed resistance from the railroad lobby enlisted representatives from the less developed counties in the army of the commission's enemies. The law was amended in 1873, and after a severe contest the commission emerged as a strong but more flexible body; it had the power to determine rates and its findings, if arrived at after proper investigation, were to be accepted as reasonable and complied with; but the right of appeal by the corporations to the courts was expressly

---

[16] For the legal arguments see pp. 61ff above. The laws are described by Philip D. Swenson as "the boldest assertions in Illinois history of the state's police power to enforce principles of justice" ("Illinois" in James C. Mohr (ed.), *Radical Republicans in the North* (Baltimore, Md, 1975), 109).

[17] Illinois R.R. & Warehouse Comm., 1st R. (1871), 26.

safeguarded. The railroads might have preferred no regulation, but denied this option they much preferred to have the decision rest in the hands of a commission, before which it would be possible to marshal evidence, while leaving open recourse to the courts.

The Illinois commission soon realized that long tenure would allow the accumulation of experience necessary to win respect for its decisions, and would have preferred to become an advisory body on the Massachusetts model; it was not allowed to divest itself of power but became an appointed body, though for two years only. There was, however, implicit recognition of the fact that the law of 1873 had altered its function. It was no longer a policeman enforcing the law but a tribunal charged with the duty of deciding what would be fair to both parties. This meant a vast amount of work in investigating, recording information, and hearing complaints. The commission also assumed responsibility for supervising the physical condition of railroads and giving publicity to their accounts.

The twenty-third report of the Illinois commission listed 294 laws which it was required to observe or enforce, and in 1889 it summed up the changed relations with the railroad companies:

The cessation of the open struggle so keenly waged by railway managers early in the history of railway legislation . . . has been succeeded by a need of much watchfulness over the matter of practical details of operation. The general spirit of managers is that of acquiescence in such reasonable regulations as we have from time to time adopted.[18]

Railroad men would not have been human if they had not fought against fresh regulations, claimed the benefit of every doubt, and sought to gain any advantage that could be won without open resistance; but the commission was now accepted as a permanent agency with ultimate power to enforce its regulations. Appeal to the courts remained open to the corporations (or, indeed, to users who failed to obtain satisfaction), but this was recognized as the last, not the first, resort.

The Illinois commission inspected the physical conditions of railroads and the facilities offered to shippers and passengers, and investigated all accidents; its reports often read like those of a schoolmaster rebuking recalcitrant pupils but distributing due praise and encouragement. In 1886 it said the railroads were, with few exceptions, equal to any in the Union, and in 1890 claimed "without boasting" that the better class of railroads in the state did not "suffer by comparison with the very best in the United

[18] *Idem*, 23rd R. (1893), 281ff; 19th R. (1889), 11.

States." But there were reservations. The record of the Wabash was poor, and two lines under its control were deplorable: one – the Cairo, Vincennes, and Chicago – had been allowed to deteriorate until its condition was very bad, while sections of the St Louis, Alton and Springfield had been closed to avoid a heavy repair bill and many of its 109 bridges were in poor condition. On the Peoria and Pekin a bridge had collapsed because the metal used in construction was of poor quality, while the track of the Indiana and Illinois Southern was in bad shape. On the other hand the Santa Fé got a good report, the Vandalia line was "in every way first class," and it was particularly reassuring to know that the Illinois Central – the pride of the state – was in very good condition.[19] Less attention was paid to accounts, for one interesting feature is that, while the Massachusetts commission regarded its right to demand them as the key to its success, the Illinois commission treated this largely as a formality: it was more interested in regular reports on operation, construction, alterations in service, repairs, and accidents. All this imposed a great deal of work upon the managers and it is not surprising that the commission sometimes complained of delays. In 1893 it instituted legal proceedings against two small companies but "with the larger companies, upon which devolved the greater labor in making their reports, there was no trouble whatever." The picture of the commission imposing good business practice on the corporations is interesting and intriguing.[20]

The Illinois commission was inconvenienced by the Wabash decision of 1886, which meant that it could not regulate freight loaded in Illinois but destined for other states, and that companies could cut out Chicago by offering low through-rates to the Atlantic ports. It was a question of acute concern to the merchants in the large commercial centers of the state, but of little interest to individual consigners of agricultural produce to the east or to Europe. The commission could refer to low interstate rates when hearing complaints of excessive rates in Illinois, insist that within the states all rates should be made public, or permit reductions on competitive rates to Illinois cities. The Wabash decision therefore limited influence upon the rates charged for long-distance freight, but it did not diminish the commission's work, which continued to grow with each year of operation.

---

[19] *Idem* (1890), 4–15.
[20] *Idem* (1891), 3. The increasingly close co-operation between the commission and the companies inevitably led to accusations of subservience and corporation control. This was implied by so well-informed a man as Henry Carter Adams, then statistician to the I.C.C., in 1897 (H. C. Adams Papers, May 11, 1897, Bentley Library, University of Michigan, Ann Arbor). See pp. 215–17 below.

Another state in which regulation has been associated with the Grangers was Wisconsin, but a major factor here was the ambition of Milwaukee to retain the trade of the interior and defeat attempts to attract trade into long-distance traffic. Here too were many counties without railroads, or with small, weak lines, which opposed any measure that might frighten investors or delay construction. The first regulatory law – known as the "Potter Law" – has often been cited as typical of Granger legislation, but it is found only in Wisconsin and even there was short-lived. This law of 1874 divided the railroads into four classes, fixed a maximum rate per mile for each, and set up a commission which might lower but could not raise rates. This was a clumsy measure, extremely difficult to enforce, and in many instances obviously unjust.[21] J. H. Osborn, the first commission chairman, quickly realized that inflexible maximum rates would do more harm than good; the strong railroads would survive but might retaliate by cutting services, the weak with proportionately high operating costs might go to the wall. In 1876 the law was amended, the three-man elected commission was replaced by a single appointed commissioner, and while there was a general prohibition of unreasonable and discriminatory charges there was no attempt to fetter the commissioner's discretion in deciding which charges were fair.[22]

Under this new dispensation the Wisconsin commission quickly came to adopt a position similar to that of Illinois. It heard complaints, aimed to conciliate rather than recriminate, and adopted the philosophical attitude that "time alone will furnish correction of the evils of the railway system as they have existed."[23]

Ten years later the commissioner explained that he would not "in the least abate the vigor of control," because capital uncontrolled "becomes fired with greed and unjust exaction," but would temper that control with "justice of even and unerring poise."

It is coming to be understood, in any matters of difference between parties and railroad companies, that the easier, better, and cheaper way to settle them is to present them to the Railroad Commissioner, and have him present them to the companies, than it is to rush into the courts under the advice of feud breeders and shyster lawyers.[24]

---

[21] For the Potter Law see George H. Miller, *Railroads and Granger Laws*, 81ff.; also Wisconsin R.R. Comm., 4th R. (1877), *passim*.

[22] Wisconsin R.R. Comm., 1st R. (1875), 91–7, 137–8.

[23] *Idem*, 6th R. (1879), xliii.

[24] Wisconsin R.R. Comm., 4th Bienn. R. (1889–90), 18.

Thus in Wisconsin, as in Illinois, one sees the transformation of an agency created to impose the will of the majority upon the corporations into a quasi-judicial tribunal in which both parties could expect a fair hearing. In other words these regulatory commissions ended by performing a function not unlike the advisory commission of Massachusetts, although the hand of the police power was more visible. One result of the change was the enormous amount of work required from an expert commission, and Wisconsin was fortunate in that, while commissioners came and went, its first assistant commissioner and secretary held office for sixteen years and ended by knowing more about railroads than any other man in the states.

Commissions did not all fit into this pattern of development. That of California contained all the apparent elements of strength and yet became a byword for ineptitude. Though it enjoyed the unusual distinction of being embodied in the state constitution it failed to satisfy the wishes of those who had been its advocates. In 1895 a serious critic wrote: "We have a body, created sixteen years ago for one definite purpose, and frequently renewed, with its mandate unchanged. It is impossible to imagine a better test of the question, whether, with our political machinery, the people really govern."[25] Two of the three first commissioners endorsed existing rates, apologized for them, and demonstrated that the great Central Pacific was treating Californians as well as could be expected. During the long period of Republican domination little control was exerted over the railroads, and majority reports continued to be "briefs in defence of the railroad and in denunciation of its opponents,"[26] but little improvement was recorded when the Democrats gained power in 1894.

The California commission was also strongly criticized by Stuart Daggett, twentieth-century historian of the Southern Pacific, who wrote that commissioners spent little time in their offices, were irregular in attendance even at formal meetings, and "failed to make effective the most primary requirements of the law." Of the first commission the chairman was John S. Cone, a wealthy landowner with no administrative experience, but a close friend of Stanford and other railroad men. C. J. Beerstecher, elected as representative of the Workingmen's Party, was a San Francisco lawyer with a small practice; he entered upon his office a poor man and left it richer by at least $12,000. As he invariably sided with Cone in sustaining existing rates the implications were obvious.[27]

[25] Samuel Moffett, "The Railroad Commission of California. A Study in Irresponsible Government," *Annals of the American Academy of Political and Social Science*, 6 (1895), 469–77.

[26] *Ibid.*, 475.

[27] Daggett, *Southern Pacific*, 191. A committee of the legislature reported that "Com-

In 1895 the commission contained two members elected on a pledge to reduce rates by twenty-five per cent, and proceeded, as a first step, to order a reduction of eight per cent on grain schedules. This was challenged in the courts, and the Federal District Court found against the commission on the ground that the provision in the state constitution making its findings "conclusively just and reasonable" was in conflict with the fourteenth amendment.[28] Thus, when the opposition of railroads was overcome, the weight of the judiciary was brought into play. In progressive eyes the most damning comment came in the evidence of J. C. Stubbs, a vice-president of the Southern Pacific Company, before the Industrial Commission in 1899:

I think it has been a useful commission. It has not been anarchistic or confiscatory in its actions, and for that reason some of the people condemn it, but on the whole I think its course is satisfactory.[29]

The popular ground for condemning the commission was its alleged subjection to railroad power, and the combined strength of the Southern and Central Pacific Railroads could be overwhelming when fully exerted. Even so one must marvel at railroad success when confronted with a commission possessing almost arbitrary power, with anti-railroad planks incorporated in most party platforms of the late nineteenth century, and with sustained opposition from San Francisco merchants. It may be necessary to look a little further to discover whether the commission suffered from structural weaknesses. The Constitution of 1879 declared that all railroads were common carriers and subject to legislative control. There was to be no pooling and no discrimination. An elected commission of three had power to establish rates, to examine the books and accounts of all railroads, issue subpoenas, take evidence on oath, punish for contempt, and "enforce their decisions and correct abuses through the medium of the courts." The rates fixed by the commission were to be accepted as reasonable in all civil and criminal cases. Neither the constitution nor subsequent legislation empowered the commission to investigate remedies for anything other than rates, so that a whole range of issues relating to safety, operation, and facilities – which occupied so much of the time of other commissions – was excluded from its jurisdiction. This had a somewhat debilitating effect. Rate fixing was difficult and prolonged, while the other duties were comparatively straightforward, showed immediate

missioners Cone and Beerstecher acted in the interests of the railroad corporations rather than of the public" (*ibid.*, 198).
[28] U.S. Circuit Court, Northern District of California, *Southern Pacific R.R. Co.* v. *Railroad Commissioners*, Nov. 30, 1896. Opinion of Judge McKenna (also reprinted in California R.R. Comm. Report for 1895–6).
[29] *Industrial Commission*, IX, 767.

results, and provided an incentive for the commissioners or their agents to become familiar with the detailed operations of the railroads. Lack of this experience always placed them at a disadvantage when arguing over rates.

In 1883 two of the commissioners took the view that all complaints should be subjected to the same rules of evidence as in a court of law, that the railroads should not be deemed extortionate or discriminatory until the case had been proven, and that all circumstances must be fully investigated before it was decided what was unreasonable. They quoted approvingly the statement of a railroad manager that it was necessary to reckon with fifty-eight items, all differing materially on each railroad or branch and appearing in different combinations, before fixing a rate. On lines to the east through high mountain country costs were affected seriously by climate, while all were affected by the cost of fuel, labor, and "other things too numerous to mention." The third commissioner would have none of this and advocated a uniform maximum of 3 cents per mile. Undoubtedly the majority was well-advised, but most Californians could not see why the simple and drastic action was avoided.[30] In 1892 the commissioners were at odds with the Traffic Association, organized by San Francisco merchants to press for lower rates to the east. In response to criticism for not using their statutory powers, the commissioner said:

We are of the opinion that the Traffic Association . . . is in error in demanding that this Commission shall arbitrarily fix the rates of freights and fares; that the Board shall occupy the position of prosecutors, sit in judgment, and practically render a decision in the case before the defendant has had the opportunity to be heard.[31]

The Traffic Association and the railroads were adversaries, and the commission intended to arbitrate, not to act exclusively on behalf of one party.

Though railroad power was a real danger in California, the methods adopted to curb it were well calculated to increase tension rather than to discover appropriate remedies. The commission itself was poorly constituted to deal with difficult issues. Three men, elected from different districts, without previous acquaintance or common policy, were expected to carry out mandates which even the briefest experience in the job proved to be impracticable. And having failed to cut the rates as expected, they had no other way of proving their usefulness.

Despite these limitations, it would be wrong to dismiss the California

---

[30] California R.R. Comm., 4th R. (1883), *passim*. This was despite the fact that all three Commissioners had been elected as Democrats pledged to reduce rates (Moffett, 471).
[31] *Idem*, 13th R. (1892), 8.

commission as entirely useless. It stood for the principle of public regulation and it was in the interest of the railroad corporations to give it enough respect to avoid more hostile legislation. The commission was, for instance, able to insist upon regular reports, and in 1900 these documents filled over 300 pages in its annual report. In the same year the commissioners pointed the way to real improvement if anyone was prepared to listen:

It is the duty of the Commission to secure . . . reductions in rates of transportation, and it is evident that no such result can be accomplished by any general horizontal reduction of the rates maintained by the Company; on the contrary, the only practical method of securing any reduction is to investigate each class of rates and to remove such discrimination as may be found, and to reduce any particular rates or classes of rates which may be found exorbitant, to the basis of a reasonable and fair rate.

In other words, anti-railroad rhetoric and demands for reductions across the board were no substitute for hard work, patient investigation, and exact knowledge. Most commissioners, lacking the staff, money, and encouragement to do the job properly, lapsed into inaction; yet there are grounds for accepting the conclusion of a historian of Californian administration during these years that "without the experience gained through the years of trial and error the development of more adequate administrative means to implement state policy would have been impossible." One can only add that in California the process of trial and error far outlasted the period of adjustment in other states.[32]

There are revealing contrasts between the California commission and that of Georgia, which won a reputation as one of the strongest in the country. From its establishment in 1879 it had power to make rates and prevent discrimination, and by a significant clause in the statute, its rulings were to be accepted in all disputes as, prima facie, just and reasonable. If the companies complained, it was for them to prove that a rate was unreasonable, and in the meantime that rate remained in force.[33] In 1881 the law was tested in *Tilley* v. *the Savannah, Florida and Western Railroad*, and upheld in the Federal Circuit Court, where Mr Justice Woods refused an injunction to suspend a rate fixed by the commission, on the ground that "the question whether the rates prescribed by the legislature, either directly

---

[32] *Idem*, R. for 1900, 24; Nash, *State Government and Economic Development*, 164.
[33] The 2nd R. (1880) includes a review of the history and powers of the commission. See also the U.S. Senate Committee on Labor and Capital, *Report and Hearings*, Vol v (1883), 543: evidence of James M. Smith (Chairman of Georgia Commission).

or indirectly, are just and reasonable, is a question which the legislature may determine for itself."[34] The principle was then fought out in the legislature, where a proposed amendment would have left the companies free to fix their own rates and the commission would have investigated only when complaints were received; the rulings by the commission would also have lost their "just and reasonable" status and would be liable to suspension by injunction.

It was argued that Georgia should follow the Massachusetts pattern, with its main function the investigation of complaints and recommendation to the legislature. The commission itself prepared a brief vigorously contesting the validity of this comparison. In New England there were "balanced corporate interests, alike powerful in means and organization," and the public was therefore represented directly through the legislature and indirectly through organized opinion ready to bring pressure to bear if rates were unreasonable and discrimination practiced. In Georgia there was no such balance of economic power, and regulation without the power to enforce would be in name not substance. Despite the opposition of some influential men in the state – including former governor Joseph E. Brown, who was deeply involved in railroad politics – the commission survived with its powers intact.[35]

Having failed in the courts and the legislature, the railroad companies decided to co-operate. In 1888 the commission received numerous complaints, and most were remedied without difficulty "as we have generally found the railroad companies swift to correct the error when brought to their notice." General prosperity helped the cause of the commission as predictions that regulation would cause a withdrawal of services and investment were falsified. In the nine years since the commission had been launched the value of railroad property had increased from under ten million dollars to over twenty-nine million dollars, while the value of all property in the state had appreciated by sixty-nine per cent.[36] In 1889 the commission was given additional duties to inspect and regulate station accommodation, and in 1891 to supervise

[34] 5 Fed. 641. The judgment is printed in Georgia R.R. Comm., 3rd R. (1881), 81–91.

[35] Printed argument by the Railroad Commission against proposed changes in the law (Georgia State Archives, Atlanta). They would end "all that is distinctive in the Georgia system." There was sufficient public interest to warrant the publication, as a separate pamphlet, of *Debates in the Senate of Georgia . . . to Amend the Railroad Commission.* An appendix to these debates reports an interview with ex-Governor Joseph E. Brown in which he condemned rate making and said "I suppose that no one will question the fact that the Railroad Commission of Georgia possesses extraordinary powers."

[36] Georgia R.R. Comm., 16th R. (1886), 8.

safety. First inspection of the Georgia Central revealed facts which could hardly have been welcome to the managers: while the track bed was sound the rails were poor, worn, and sometimes dangerous; maintenance and replacement had not kept pace with increased demand; and travel had been reduced to depressingly slow speeds. The commission was also given the duty of regulating express and telegraph companies.[37]

Though the work undertaken by the Georgia commission was onerous, its annual reports were often cursory and uninformative. There was little attempt to enlighten the public about the intricacies of the railroad problem. The commission was an agency of government, not a forum for debate, but this remoteness may help to explain its success. There was a long tradition of public promotion and operation in Georgia, so state involvement was no novelty. Indeed the Western and Atlantic Railroad was still state-owned, though leased to private operators.[38] It was therefore comparatively easy to make the transition from ownership to regulation and to hand over responsibility to a commission that would be shielded from immediate popular pressure. Members were appointed by the governor, with the consent of the Senate, for six-year terms. The first chairman was James M. Smith, a former governor and man of considerable influence, and on his retirement in 1886 he was succeeded by Campbell Wallace, who had been one of the first commissioners. Wallace was succeeded by L. N. Trammel, and at the turn of the century the chairman was T. C. Crenshaw; both men had previously served as commissioners for some years. The high standing and experience of the Georgia commission were recognized in 1895 when one of its members, Allen Foot, presided at the first national convention of railroad commissioners. The California commissioners were elected for three-year terms; from 1880 to 1898 there were five chairmen, none of whom had had previous experience on the commission; and only one commissioner served for more than one term.

In 1898 the Georgia commission departed from the normal brevity of its reports to express some confidence in its work. Its regulations had been observed and put into operation promptly: "Gradually a better feeling between the roads and their patrons is becoming manifest." The commis-

---

[37] *Idem*, 18th R. (1890), *passim*; 20th R. (1892), 9.
[38] The State leased the railroad to Joseph E. Brown and his associates in December 1870 for twenty years. When the lease was due to expire there were lengthy and involved arguments about the terms. The lessees wanted to be compensated for improvements; the State admitted that it had been handed over in very poor condition but argued that this had been recognized in fixing a low rental and that a condition had been its restoration in good working order.

sion attributed this improvement to the enforcement of reasonable rates and uniform rules throughout the state. As a consequence "arbitrary acts and unjust discriminations, and consequent strife and discord" had been prevented.[39]

The history of the Iowa and Texas commissions shows how state power increased in the later years of the century. The Iowa commission was remodeled in 1888, that of Texas was established in 1892, and both had powers as extensive as any in the nation. Iowa had a Granger law in 1874, fixing rates by law but with no commission to enforce them.[40] After *Munn* v. *Illinois* had put the power to regulate beyond the reach of litigation, railroads tried to discredit the law by charging maximum rates even when the commercial rate might have been lower. There were other reasons why the law was impracticable, and in 1878 a commission was created to exercise general supervision, with power to modify unreasonable rates but not to take the initiative by declaring what a reasonable schedule should be. This attempt to follow the example of Massachusetts was a dismal failure, with excessive rates and discrimination continuing unabated. Rates on the long haul from points west to Chicago were keenly competitive, and the railroads sought to recover losses by raising charges on non-competitive short hauls within the state. The railroads regarded their freedom to make rates in Iowa as crucial to their western strategy, and were prepared to use every effort to avoid regulation. In the state elections of 1887 the railroad question was a major issue, and the new legislature prepared to make changes; as one advocate of regulation wrote, "never before had so formidable a railroad lobby assembled at the state capitol. The dogs of war were let loose from all quarters."[41]

Articles were planted in the *New York Times, Tribune* and *World*, in the Albany *Argus*, and the Boston *Advertiser*, to demonstrate that eastern opinion regarded the Iowa proposals as socialistic, wild, confiscatory, and disastrous for the railroads; "especially did they bewail the losses that would fall upon the widows and orphans who had confidingly invested all their hard earnings in this property."[42] These articles were copied in the Iowa press, but to no avail; a new law was passed in both houses without a

[39] Georgia R.R. Comm., 26th R. (1898), 18.
[40] William Larrabee, *The Railroad Question* (1893; 3rd ed. repr. New York, 1971), Chapter 11, *passim*. He was governor of Iowa when the law of 1888 was passed and supported it vigorously.
[41] Larrabee, *The Railroad Question*, 339.   [42] *Ibid.*, 341–5.

single adverse vote. It took over much from the existing law, but the new commission had power to make and revise maximum rates which were to be accepted in all suits if arrived at after proper investigation. There were also provisions for enforcement. Below the legal maxima the railroads retained the right to make their own rates, and could bring suit in the courts to demonstrate that the commission rates were unreasonable, though none did so. The railroads were able to delay implementation of the law by injunction, but when the commission had made minor changes a second injunction was refused. They then tried to discredit the law by withdrawing services on the ground that the legal rates made them uneconomic; but this backfired as demand at the lower rates was so great that the companies soon faced an embarrassing flow of earnings. Indeed their prosperity was greater than it had been in the once happy days of freedom.

The move to regulate began in Texas in the late 1880s, but it was not until 1891 that serious proposals for a commission were discussed. A. W. Terrell, the leading advocate of regulation, realized the crucial importance of getting an agreed rate into operation without encountering legal delays. He wrote that while the *Chicago, Minneapolis, and St Paul* decision meant that the railroads must have the benefit of due process they should have it "as against a rate once fixed, only by direct action against the Commission, and let the rates fixed be enforced until a final judicial decision."[43] As finally enacted the commission had unqualified power to make, publish, and enforce schedules of rates which would go into operation immediately, while the burden of proof that rates were unreasonable would lie with the complainants.

One curious feature of the Texas debates was the degree of ignorance shown by delegates and lawyers hostile to regulation. As one observer noted, "Many of the critics posed as learned lawyers, and yet they were not aware of the fact that the Supreme Court of the United States had many times held that a law such as we had enacted was not only within the power of the Legislature but was one that it became its duty to enact for the protection of the masses."[44] The advocates of regulation were fortunate in being able to avoid the pitfalls of ignorance because they had the advice of Senator J. H. Reagan, who had taken a leading part in Congress in all the moves that led to the establishment of the Federal Interstate Commerce

[43] Terrell & Reagan, J. H. Reagan Papers, Texas State Archives, Austin.
[44] M. M. Crane Papers, Materials for an Autobiography, II, 21, Texas Historical Society, Austin. There is also much material on the Railroad Commission in the J. S. Hogg Papers.

Commission in 1887. After the Texas commission was established Reagan was persuaded to become its chairman, thus bringing to the post unusual prestige and experience.

The power of the Texas commission was brought to the test in the case of *Reagan* v. *the Farmer's Loan and Mercantile Trust*. The trust was the principal stockholder in a railroad that had not paid a dividend for several years, and challenged both the constitutionality of the commission law and its right to set a "reasonable" rate that would postpone still further any prospect of making a profit. On the first count the Supreme Court had no difficulty in deciding that the case was ruled by *Munn* v. *Illinois* and that the Texas law was constitutional. In order to get this point settled quickly, the commission withdrew the rate in question without offering any evidence to support it. Nevertheless, Mr Justice Brewer decided to discuss the issue raised, and decided that such a rate would be found "unreasonable" by the courts.[45] This settled no point of law, but could be taken as a strong directive to the courts to interpose if the earnings of a railroad were jeopardized by a commission ruling. In practice the case had little effect. Brewer had argued exclusively from evidence supplied by the railroad, and if the issue was raised again it would be open to the State to introduce evidence of mismanagement, over-capitalization, and poor service. It was doubtful whether a railroad itself would wish to raise these embarrassing questions, while stockholders might be deterred by the knowledge that regulations had often ended by increasing profits. In 1899 Reagan told the Industrial Commission that in Texas "we make the rates, regulate them, and have absolute control."[46]

The work of the Texas commission developed one interesting aspect of policy. Reagan was quite clear that the power to determine rates should be used to favor the interests of Texas. Producers in the western parts of the state might be tempted by low interstate rates to ship directly to New Orleans or Mobile, and to prevent this very low rates were fixed on cotton and other products consigned to Texas ports from points in the state more than 200 miles away. He wrote that this would help "to make our own seaports the principal markets for our own products and draw to them as far as practicable the merchandise of other states and territories." This action also involved the tacit co-operation of other states and territories in sanctioning similar low rates to their own borders on lines connecting with the Texas network. Other states had no doubt resorted to similar tactics, but only Texas avowed so openly the intention of using low long-haul rates

[45] 154 U.S. 362.   [46] *Industrial Commission*, IV, 345.

to promote its own interests. In its fourth report in 1895 the commission claimed that its policy had been "to encourage the interests of Texas merchants and manufacturers, and to do this by reductions in rates have frequently been necessary." The railroads serving Texas found that two could play the long-haul/short-haul game; the principle of regulation won powerful friends among Texan businessmen; and the port of Galveston owed much of its twentieth-century prosperity to rate-fixing by the commission.[47]

What, then, was the work of the State Railroad Commissions in the later years of the nineteenth century? An authoritative statement was given by Balthasar Henry Meyer in a report to the United States Industrial Commission and published separately in a slightly enlarged form.[48] Meyer was a lawyer who had specialized in railroad law, and had a wide knowledge of the character and work of the commission. He devoted little attention to rate-fixing and a great deal to safety, which had been, he said, one of the most prolific sources of legislation. There existed, he wrote, "few topics about which so many different laws have been passed, and perhaps none in regard to which more separate acts have been approved by the various legislatures."[49] A majority of these laws related to the standards of equipment and the physical condition of the tracks. Many others sought to improve cars and stations, in so far as the comfort, health, and safety of passengers were concerned. A very common law required that fresh water and necessary conveniences should be supplied on trains and in stations. The general laws of nearly all states provided that trains should run at regular times, that bulletin boards should announce times of departure, and that notification should be given when trains departed from schedule. This emphasis upon the practical details of operation can be found in many commission reports.

The lengthy Illinois report for 1890 pointed out that even weak lines served a function, and that however small their operations, some people depended on them. It was therefore an important function of the commission to ensure that these lesser railroads were well maintained and provided good service. This was one of the tasks that made "a judicious

---

[47] Texas R.R. Comm., 4th R. (1895), 15; Reagan to W. A. Shaw (Dallas Aug. 20, 1895) said that in making freight rates the commission "is cooperating with the States and Territories north and west in the effort to build up commercial cities on our coast" (Reagan Papers, Texas State Archives, Austin).

[48] "Railway Regulation under Foreign and Domestic Law," *Industrial Commission*, IX, 897–1004; Balthasar H. Meyer, *Railway Legislation in the United States* (New York, 1903).

[49] *Ibid.*, 126.

regulation of railways by law so necessary to the public welfare." The commission also took the lead in pressing that continuous brakes and automatic couplers should be made compulsory. During the preceding year 7,057 persons in the United States had been killed or injured when coupling or uncoupling, and 2,011 by falling from trains (most of them when setting brakes). It all meant that the Illinois commission had plenty to do, and its success depended upon continuous activity, investigation, advice, and, if necessary, enforcement.[50]

The Massachusetts commission had no power to fix rates, though the right of the legislature to do this was "beyond question." The commission had, however, "a more persuasive and effective appliance for the regulation of rates than legal compulsion – that of investigation, criticism, and publicity."[51] The western commissions, ostensibly with stronger legal powers, relied mainly upon the same strategy to achieve results. In 1891 the Minnesota commission observed that a large amount of its business never reached the stage of formal complaint lodged against the railroad: "The commission has found itself able to arrange a large number of misunderstandings . . . satisfactorily to both sides, by personal conference with the parties interested."[52] It pointed out that the commission could issue two kinds of order: the first affected repairs, safety, operating standards, and so on; the second determined rates. It noted that following the Supreme Court decision there must be a formal hearing, with due notice given, before a rate was fixed, and there was a right of appeal to courts. As to the other types of order the commission claimed that its decision on matters of fact ought to be final.

The very wide range of duties that a railroad commissioner might perform is illustrated by the Michigan report for 1887.[53] His duties had originally been defined in an act of 1873, and additions were made in subsequent years. He could take statements on oath, and conduct additional interrogatories on management and the state of equipment. He could inspect, require repairs to be carried out, restrict the speed of trains, and even suspend operations until repairs were carried out satisfactorily. In case of disputes between railroads he could arbitrate and his decision would be final. When there were two terminals in the same city, he must ensure adequate arrangements for the transfer of passengers and freight, and

---

[50] Illinois R.R. Comm., 30th R. (1900), *passim*.
[51] Mass. R.R. Comm., R. for 1893, 14.
[52] Minn. R.R. Comm., R. for 1891, 18.
[53] Mich. R.R. Comm., R. for 1887, Appendix.

again his decision on disputed points would be binding. He could order flagmen to be placed at any gate, crossing, or bridge, and was required to inspect stations. He was also required to investigate the application of any village for railroad facilities, and could order such sidings and other track as he might "deem for the public interest, and to be just and reasonable." Fences came naturally under his jurisdiction, as did rules for providing signals, the investigation of accidents, and many safety requirements. As to the financial affairs of the railroads, the commissioner prescribed a uniform system of accounts, required a monthly statement of earnings, estimated the tax due from a railroad, filed this information with the Auditor General, and did the same for express, station, and depot companies. In 1883 this was made a general power to compute the tax due from each "person, association, co-partnership, or corporation" connected with railroad operation. The commissioner was to appear on behalf of the State when any proposal was made to abandon track or stations constructed wholly or in part with state aid. Last, but far from least, he had to make an annual report to the legislature.

In 1889 the Michigan report noted that railroads complied with state and national laws against rate discrimination but were challenging them in the courts. The state laws fixing rates were not being complied with in all cases, but apart from this difficulty there were few complaints and the railroads were in excellent physical condition. In Michigan, as in other states, it was noted that the relationship between the railroads and the state authorities had greatly improved:

The present condition of the railroads in the State is better than ever before. The service continues to improve; laws are more closely observed than heretofore; and, as a whole, the relations of the railroads and the people are in a very satisfactory condition.[54]

A similar note was struck by the Missouri commission when its report for 1891 noted "a very general disposition on the part of railroad companies to render prompt compliance with the laws regulating them," and a willingness to comply promptly with orders and recommendations. Formal complaints, followed by mandatory hearings, were becoming less frequent, and adjustments were normally secured by personal visits and correspondence.[55]

James F. Jackson, one of the Massachusetts commissioners, stated in 1899 that numerous recommendations on rates, the condition of stations,

[54] *Idem*, R. for 1889.   [55] Missouri R.R. & Warehouse Comm., 17th R. (1891), 14.

new services, changes in schedules, and other operating details were made by the commission. In many cases these required changes in existing practice, but the companies usually complied. There were a few examples of recommendations ignored, but the commission itself made a distinction between recommendations which expected compliance and those which were tentative and suggestive. Commissioner Jackson agreed that the companies usually complied because the recommendations were "sustained by the public sentiment of Massachusetts." Though styled "advisory," the commission's decisions on a large number of issues affecting convenience and safety were final and enforceable at law. Business was voluminous; in 1900 three hundred questions were considered and hearings were held almost every day.[56]

The path of good administration did not always run smooth, but there was often more difficulty with small than with large companies. An Illinois statute of 1871 required every railroad company to file its report with the commission by 1 September. Twenty years later the commission reported that few had filed by 1 September, many not until November, and that a few delayed even longer. The report commented that "the delinquency of a few companies . . . has grown to be a positive abuse, which it will be necessary for the Commission to resort to harsh measures to correct, if the practice continues." In these cases it was often difficult to decide whether the fault lay in deliberate defiance of authority or in sheer incompetence, but perhaps the inefficient were more likely to shelter behind an alleged objection to regulation. A marked improvement followed this complaint.[57]

A. K. Teisberg, secretary of the Minnesota commission, said in 1899:

As far as State legislation is concerned, I think we are pretty well fixed in our State. I think we have good laws covering every conceivable point, and we have now obtained the decision in the highest courts on several points sustaining us. We know where we are at.[58]

As for the *Chicago, Minneapolis, and St Paul* case, he said, the decision had been salutary rather than destructive. The legislation had been amended. The commission was required to give notice of an investigation and to take evidence as in a court before deciding. Appeal to the courts against a decision was allowed in conformity with the Supreme Court judgment, but the state Supreme Court had taken a narrow view of its right to review evidence. In 1894 the commission had ordered a reduction of about twelve

---

[56] *Industrial Commission*, ix, 841–8: evidence of J. F. Jackson, 842.
[57] Illinois R.R. Comm., 21st R. (1891).   [58] *Industrial Commission*, IX, 372.

and a half per cent in grain rates, and the railroad had appealed. The company won in the District Court, but the decision was reversed in the state Supreme Court and remitted for retrial. The case was then dropped, because the railroad lowered its rates. In the course of its judgment the Minnesota Supreme Court had said:

The fixing of rates is a legislative or administrative act, not a judicial one. Under the constitution a court cannot place itself in the shoes of the commission and try *de novo* the question of what are reasonable rates . . . The court can review the acts of the commission only so far as to determine whether the rates fixed by it are unreasonable and confiscatory, and to what extent, in much the same manner as an appellate court determines whether or not the verdict of a jury [awarding damages] is excessive and to what extent.[59]

In other words the court did not claim the right to review the evidence heard by the commission, and would reverse a decision only if the company could prove that the rate fixed was unreasonable or would mean that they were operating at a loss. The court accepted the finding of the commission on matters of fact, and would intervene only if the rate ordered was unreasonable in the light of this evidence.

In matters affecting details of operation and safety the Minnesota commission established important points. In *Jacobson* v. *the Wisconsin, Minnesota and Pacific* the United States Supreme Court upheld an order of the commission to instal a connection between the tracks of two companies to facilitate the transfer of traffic. The other issues did not reach the courts. A state law required trains to come to a full stop where two railroads crossed, unless interlocking signals approved by the commission were installed; as a consequence approved signals at crossings were "getting to be very numerous." There were many examples of reduced rates in the state. Greater efficiency was the major cause; but "the rulings of the commission and the moral effect of these rulings have had a good deal to do with it." Or, to put it another way, the presence of the commission guaranteed that lower costs would be passed on to the public in the form of lower rates.[60]

There was one interesting difference between the regulatory commission of Minnesota and the advisory commission of Massachusetts. In both states the railroad companies had to obtain the consent of the commissions for all issues of new stock or bonds (or additions to old issues). In Minnesota this was thought to be of little practical significance, but in

[59] *Rippe* v. *Becker et al.*, 57 NW 331, decided Jan. 1894.
[60] 179 U.S. 287, decided 1900. *Industrial Commission*, ix, clxxii.

Massachusetts it was regarded as the keystone of public responsibility. In one state the most prized right was the regulation of rates, in the other control over capitalization. In Massachusetts the scrutiny of accounts was no formality. Company books were regularly submitted and inspected, so any proposal to raise new capital could be seen in context. The commissioners knew precisely the value of assets, earnings and profits, and the likely use for new capital. Indeed they might well know more about financial prospects than the railroad managers; and as their consent was necessary they could impose prior conditions for new issues of stock. This power, exercised behind closed doors by men who had the benefit of inside knowledge, was the real sanction behind other recommendations which had no force in law.

Not all commissions were as efficient as those of Massachusetts, Illinois, Michigan, and Minnesota, and some were reputed to have developed too close a relationship (to put it mildly) with the corporations that they were supposed to regulate. In Ohio the major issue had never been high rates, as the state benefited from intense competition between the railroads as this kept charges low. The Railroad Commissioner sometimes found it necessary to defend the railroads against attack. In 1886, anticipating by twelve years the doctrine of *Smyth* v. *Ames*, he wrote that though they must accept regulation and limitation upon their charges, "Property rights are not of the public. While the use is public, the property is not the public's."[61] He believed that his task was to keep a close eye on railroad finance and physical condition, rather than to press continuously for lower rates. While Massachusetts had gone furthest in subjecting railroad accounts to scrutiny, "the state of Ohio is far ahead in critical examination of structures." Particular attention had been paid to bridges, and useful works on railroad engineering had been published under the auspices of the commission.[62]

There was some dissatisfaction with the Ohio commissioner, and in 1886 he was ordered to investigate all complaints, and report his findings and action to the legislature if in session or to the governor. The commissioner reported in the following year that few complaints had been received, and retaliated by claiming that too little money was appropriated for him to carry out his major task of inspection. Following these disputes the commissioner was dismissed from office. His successor found that the

---

[61] Ohio Commissioner of Railroads, 20th R. (1886), 12.
[62] *Idem*, 19th R. (1885), 193.

appropriation was already overspent, and that there was therefore even less to carry out the inspection required by law.[63]

This episode in Ohio history illustrates a familiar tension. Was the primary function of a commission to deal with complaints – most of which would relate to high or unfair charges – or to keep a watchful and informed eye upon safety, services, and technical efficiency? In the former capacity a commissioner must necessarily adopt the role of prosecutor and adversary in facing the railroads; but as a technical expert he might well be regarded – at least by the efficient railroads – as a friendly critic whose advice would improve their service, their record for safety, and even their profits.

In 1894 the powers of the Ohio Railroad Commissioner were increased to give him "the power of police supervision in relation to safety and protection of persons and property." He reported that the companies had complied with all orders relating to public safety and had, in many cases, voluntarily anticipated formal requests. The inspectors had found the Baltimore and Ohio in good condition, while the Erie, which had had a poor reputation for so long, had made great improvements. The commissioners were appointed for only two years – and while the reports of some were massive volumes others were content with thin recitals of unexciting fact – but the inspectors and their assistants provided continuity and professional knowledge.[64]

Wisconsin had begun with the "Potter's Law," and thus earned a reputation for unwise display of legislative strength, but in 1876 this policy was reversed. The maximum rate law was repealed. An act created the office of railroad commissioner, who could investigate rates but not fix or enforce them. He was to hear complaints, and report on them to the Attorney General. It has been generally assumed that under this law the railroads had their own way in Wisconsin until a new reform movement in 1905. This belief is reinforced by the adoption of the rates charged by the Chicago, Milwaukee and St Paul in 1872 as the standard for all first class railroads. In 1881 the commissioner also claimed credit for dispelling the idea that the railroads were making enormous profits from the people of Wisconsin. Under the policy adopted in 1876 construction had gone vigorously ahead and "timid capitalists" had been convinced that they would suffer no

[63] *Idem*, 21st R. (1887); *Annual Message of Governor James E. Campbell for 1891*, 10. In his report for 1886 Commissioner Henry Apthorp had vigorously attacked rate regulation that would deprive the railroads of all profit. This did not win him friends or popularity.
[64] Ohio Commissioner of Railroads, 28th R. (1894), xvii–xviii.

injustice.[65] Few complaints were received, and the inspection of railroad track and equipment went forward vigorously. In 1890 the commissioner could recall no case in which his decision or recommendation had been rejected by the railroads; the cases had been "amicably settled" without involving the Attorney General.[66]

In matters of safety the state commissions felt able to express guarded satisfaction at the close of the century. The number of casualties and accidents seemed to have levelled out, especially after the commissions' requests, repeated over many years, led to the passage of a federal Safety Appliances Act in 1893. By 1900 sixty-eight per cent of all rolling stock had continuous brakes, while nearly all had semi-automatic couplers. The reduction in accidents to switchmen fell from 11,700 in 1893 to 2,265 in 1903. Unfortunately the improvement was deceptive; an almost imperceptible rise in casualties in the last two years of the century proved to be the beginning of a sharp upward trend which reached an all-time peak in 1913.[67] Track improvement and maintenance had not kept pace with the increasing weight and speed of trains, especially with companies more keen to spend money on acquiring control of other lines. While the national total of accidents mounted, the incidents were widely scattered, and many lines escaped for several successive years. Consequently hard-headed managers might calculate that it was cheaper to clean up after an occasional accident than to pay for expensive improvements. So far as employees were concerned many companies set up mutual aid funds, ostensibly to compensate for injuries but in fact to shift the cost to employee contributions. Some companies were honorable exceptions, but it was a melancholy fact that, though they were approaching their zenith in power, speed, and durability, with the techniques of safety better understood than ever before, more lives were lost each year. A further battle for safety had to be fought and won, but it lies outside the chronological limits of this study. Meanwhile the setback should not obliterate the many successes of earlier years in making railroads accountable to the public and in setting and raising operational standards.

In 1896 the Wisconsin commissioner contrasted the current situation with that prevailing thirty years before. Then the service was poor, there were no through rates, transfers from railroad to railroad were difficult and

---

[65] Charles Fairman, "So-called Granger Cases," *Stanford Law Review*, 5 (1953), 610.
[66] Wisconsin R.R. Comm., 5th Ann. R. (1881), lii; 4th Bienn. R. (1889–90), 18.
[67] Christopher Clark, "The Railroad Safety Problem in the United States 1900–1930," *Transport History*, 7:3 (1977), 54–74.

expensive, and the trains ran slowly over poorly laid rails of inferior quality. All this was changed. The cars were "models of comfort and convenience," transfers were easily made, and fast, heavy trains ran on good rails laid on solid and well-drained beds. Freight rates had fallen to little more than half their former level, the effect of new construction had been to bring producers "a thousand miles nearer the markets," and thousands of acres had been brought into cultivation.[68] In 1900 the Wisconsin commissioner of the day observed that "the trend of public thought for a generation has been toward statutory regulation of railroads and supervision of them by commissioners, acting under authority of law."[69] The underlying principle had been that charges should be reasonable and just for the services performed, but this opened "a vast field of inquiry." There is an implied defense against the alleged inactivity of the commissioner. The more he became immersed in the technical aspects of the job, and the more he sought to persuade rather than confront the corporations, the less conspicuous he became. There was, of course, a paradox in that the more official pressure increased the efficiency of railroads the more powerful these were likely to become in state politics. Once they adopted the strategy of winning friends rather than ignoring enemies, their prestige and support were bound to grow. For those who believe that the proper relationship between business and the public is antagonistic, this outcome must be unwelcome; for others it may give food for thought.

State railroad regulation had come to stay, but the relationship between the commissions and the companies had greatly changed. In 1899 Edward P. Wilson, representing the National Association of Manufacturers, the Cincinnati Board of Trade, and the Ohio Valley Improvement Association, described this relationship to the Industrial Commission in the following words:

A sort of everyday neighborly relation obtains. The managers of the railroads are very well acquainted with all the commissioners along the lines of the roads in the various States. Their work in the States comes very near to corresponding with the wishes of those commissioners. It allays dissatisfaction, although they have had some pretty fierce discussion.[70]

A cynic might say that the commissions, having found that they could not beat the railroads, had decided to join them. The evidence surveyed in this

---

[68] Wisconsin R.R. Comm., 7th Bienn. R. (1895–6), 147.
[69] *Idem*, 9th Bienn. R. (1899–1900), 21.
[70] *Industrial Commission*, ix, 591.

chapter suggests that the roles should be reversed: the States had established their authority, the railroads had decided to acquiesce. If this conclusion is accepted, it means that many generalizations about government and business in the late nineteenth century must be revised.

8

TOWARD THE FUTURE

The activities of the states described in this book take their place in the great change of modern times from acquiescence to intervention. Faced with deprivation, disease, and untrammeled economic power the former counsel had been submission to the will of God; when it appeared that God had placed remedies in the hands of men, laws of nature had been discovered to curb action; when it appeared that economic ruin did not follow in the steps of government action it was revealed that "paternalism" undermined character. Self-regulation was claimed as the only remedy for the failures of an unregulated society, and this principle was applied to the complex working of a modern economy, to biological survival, and to individual moral character. In retrospect these themes can be seen as temporary defenses against the advance of the great rationalist principle that man was master of his world and could make of it what he wished, and the great principle of popular government that, in the long run, ends and means must be settled by representative government; but at the close of the nineteenth century they had been questioned rather than discredited. The walls had been breached but had not yet crumbled. Yet the current was surely set toward an era in which public responsibility for care of the unfortunate, for regulation of economic activity, and for control of the environment would be accepted as a matter of course. The agencies of the states take a place in these great changes, but their significance cannot be gauged without considering their relationship to federal regulation and their contribution to the changing climate of opinion.

The following inquiry falls naturally into two parts. The first will consider the direct and indirect influence of experience in the state upon the development of federal authority, and the second will consider its more far-reaching but less easily identified contribution to the broad stream of opinion favoring the enlargement of public responsibility.

The Anti-Trust Act of 1890 set up one model for federal regulation, the agencies of the states another. Under the first offenses, procedures and penalties were laid down by statute; prosecution was the responsibility of law officers, interpretation and punishment the duty of the courts. Codes of practice would evolve from administrative and judicial precedent. The alternative model consisted of an autonomous commission with members enjoying fixed tenure, deriving authority from the law, and empowered to carry out its own investigations, make rulings, issue directives, and prosecute offenders. Once a commission had been established it would build up its own body of precedents, accumulate information, recruit and train an expert staff. While members would retire at the end of their legal terms and vacancies be filled by the incumbent executive, the commission would not be responsible to him or to any departmental head. Its reports and recommendations were submitted directly to the legislature.

There were thus two distinct ways of exercising federal responsibility, but it was not always certain which would prevail. While the Interstate Commerce Commission retained its separate character, the federal Bureau of Labor Statistics, which might have become an autonomous agency for investigating labor conditions, became instead a part of the Department of Labor and subject to normal political control. The Federal Board of Health, which had had an unfortunate and abortive career, also came under departmental control when re-established in the twentieth century. On the other hand the powerful Federal Communications Commission was to enjoy the same autonomy as the Interstate Commerce Commission.

The legal foundation of federal intervention differed from that of the states. The federal government relied mainly upon the power latent in the right to regulate interstate commerce, reinforced by the common law doctrine that contracts to restrain trade were void and by the political anti-monopoly tradition. The men of the late nineteenth century could hardly anticipate the enormous and ever-growing weight that would later rest upon the commerce clause and were therefore acutely aware of the constitutional restraints upon federal action. Earlier attempts to read more authority into the general welfare clause had been treated unsympathetically by the courts. The power in Congress to protect citizens against injustice committed by the states had little relevance when positive intervention in social or economic life was desired. By contrast, action by the states had developed from the police power and the willingness of the courts to bring more and more state activities into its orbit.

Another obstacle to be overcome when intervention moved from state to federal levels was simply that of scale. The state agencies worked in close proximity to the activities that they were deputed to investigate, supervise, or regulate. The legislators whom they had to convince lived equally close to the problems and could be sensitive to the complaints of the voters. Most important was the geographical concentration of the leadership in influential groups, which made it comparatively easy to inform and enlist "public opinion." Massachusetts was particularly fortunate in that the cultural and commercial center was also the state capital; Boston thus provided a stage on which it was easier than anywhere else to rally interests and opinion once a reasoned case had been presented. This explains why all the Massachusetts agencies made a virtue of reliance on public opinion and lack of coercive power. For a federal agency the problem would be very different: Washington was neither a cultural nor a commercial capital, there was limited interest in local issues, and so many diverse pressures operated on Congress that it was difficult to mass support in favor of any particular measure. If a federal agency was purely advisory it was difficult if not impossible to know who would listen to the advice.

In some fields the existing state agencies were foremost in pressing for federal authority to supplement their own; yet they seldom spoke with one voice, while rare unanimity on aims might conceal disagreement on methods. It might, for instance, be thought that the case for uniform federal law on quarantine, pure food, and child labor was so strong, and supported by so many state agencies, that federal authority would be exerted at an early stage; yet federal action in each of these fields was long delayed. Moreover successful state agencies built up vested interests opposed to encroachment upon their own authority, and a federal agency might encounter new versions of state rights. This was most apparent in the history of the first and short-lived Federal Board of Health, and in the later efforts to obtain a national food and drug law. The early failure of Congress to pass any law to control the adulteration of food, prevent the sale of harmful drugs, or require accurate labeling of products led several states to develop elaborate laws of their own. Variations in the law from state to state, laxity in some, severity in others, and different standards caused confusion to producers, distributors, and vendors; but efficient state administrations were reluctant to alter their own procedures or weaken the authority of their own scientific services in the interests of national uniformity.

The erection of an upper tier of federal agencies and the application of state experience to central government therefore presented problems that were not easily solved, and methods evolved in the close-knit state societies might be misleading when accepted as guidelines for national action. The problem was complicated by the division of state agencies into those which were purely advisory and those which insisted that they must have the power to regulate and enforce.

Yet one can also ask whether the federal government would have shifted from non-interference to intervention without the experience of the states to build upon. In one fundamental aspect of modern administration the states had marked out a path of great significance. This was the creation of agencies which acted upon the authority of the State while maintaining and indeed strengthening their autonomy as experts in the field. While reserving ultimate political control, many of the states had been content to leave the investigation and supervision of important aspects of social and economic life to bodies which outlasted executive and legislative authority, acquired knowledge of a subject which went far beyond that which any legislative committee could hope to match, evolved codes of practice which put flesh on the original statutory bones, developed professional services, and added a new and most significant institutional element to society. In the twentieth century the federal government would move far and fast along the same lines, but the extent to which its innovations depended upon earlier innovations in the states should not be ignored. This is the vantage point from which should be viewed the first approaches to federal regulation examined in the following pages.

The first attempt to set up a federal regulatory agency was initiated at state level, took little account of state views or experience, and soon ended in unrelieved failure. The yellow fever epidemic of 1878 caused President Hayes to set up a three-man commission to investigate and report. It recommended complete quarantine, rigorous enforcement by federal authorities, and a National Board of Health. The consequent bill was passed by Congress with unusual alacrity and became law on March 3, 1879. Four years later Congress failed to renew the board's appropriation and it therefore ceased to exist. A writer in the *Journal of Social Science* commented acidly upon the willingness of Congress to vote money for a naval hospital benefiting a small minority while giving nothing for a board which acted "for the good of every citizen of the country, and even of humanity throughout the world."[1]

---

[1] Dr Henry E. Baker, in a communication to *Journal of Social Science*, 16 (1883), 26; cf. William G. Carleton, "Government and Health before the New Deal," *Current History*, 45 (1963), 71–6.

The one state board with extensive experience of the fight against yellow fever was that of Louisiana, but its stormy and controversial career, resisting attacks upon its authority from inside the state and from other states, has already been recorded.[2] After a short period of co-operation between federal and state boards bitter rivalry developed. In 1881 Dr Stanford Chaillé, a member of the National Board and formerly of the Louisiana Board but personally hostile to its then head, Dr Joseph Jones, summed up the issues in dispute.[3] Should suspected cases of yellow fever be reported to other states by the National Board, or await action by the State Board? Should other states keep observers in New Orleans and at the quarantine stations? Should Louisiana allow ships to proceed to its own quarantine station before they had been inspected at Ship Island, the federal station? The State Board raised the rallying cry of state rights and federal interference, and unfortunately it was not an abstract constitutional argument but a very concrete dispute over what action federal officials should take on the spot, how far they could be instructed from Washington, and what happened when an order from the National Board, which had no coercive power, was over-ruled by the State Board. Lobbying in Washington by Louisiana against the National Board, and lack of effective support from other states, led to its demise in 1883.

In 1887 the Ohio Board of Public Health made a strong plea for the restoration of national responsibility, and asked all medical men and sanitarians to bring pressure upon Congress: "Our representatives in that body should be cognizant of the fact that the grave responsibility is resting upon them of protecting our nation against the invasion of an epidemic which may devastate a great portion of our country, and ruin its prosperity for years to come."[4] Nothing came of this initiative, and despite recurrent complaints from other state boards nothing was done to co-ordinate quarantine measures except through an administratively weak sanitary council of the Mississippi valley. In 1893 the federal government did obtain some control over quarantine by extending the responsibilities of the Marine Hospital Service; but the whole question remained to be plagued by interstate rivalries, by the refusal of the state boards to trust each other when great commercial interests might be affected by quarantine or even by reports of cases, and by extra-legal action to impose what was called "shotgun quarantine" against infected localities.

---

2   See pp. 139–42 above.
3   *National Board of Health Bulletin* (1881), Supplementary Report by Dr Chaillé.
4   Illinois St. B. of H., 2nd R. (1887), 29; Ohio B. of P. H., 2nd R. (1887) 29; Carleton, "Government and Health."

It was ironic that when pressure for complete national responsibility was revived twenty-three years after the end of the National Board it was New Orleans that gave it most determined support and other states that showed hesitation. In the intervening years most state boards had become effective agencies employing large medical and scientific staffs and extremely suspicious of a quest for uniformity which might well force them to relax their own standards. On March 3, 1906 the Mayor of New Orleans introduced fifteen business and professional men from the city to the House Committee on Interstate Commerce to give evidence in favor of a bill to extend the powers of the Marine Hospital Service.[5] The difficulties of co-operation between states were explained. In the preceding November there had been a convention of southern states at Chatanooga to agree upon action in the event of an outbreak of yellow fever, but the principal spokesman from New Orleans asserted: "That agreement worked very well until the first case of yellow fever came. Upon the outbreak of the very first case that agreement went to pieces . . . It appears that there is absolutely no authority in this country that can give us any assistance except the Federal government." He confessed that this was not a pleasant fact for a southerner to face, "but the moment that the Federal authorities took hold" during an outbreak in 1905 "the confidence of our people began to be restored."

Other witnesses from New Orleans gave similar evidence, yet there remained intractable difficulties. If inspection were carried out by the Marine Hospital Service, would state boards of health accept their findings or insist upon doing the job over again, perhaps with different methods and working upon different theories? The committee chairman, William P. Hepburn, said:

Is not this the trouble – is it not the boards of health of the different states that have thrown impediments in the way of legislation of this kind? I do not hesitate to say that if there was not a board of health in the United States there would be no difficulty at all in getting a proper quarantine system.[6]

This was ungracious and overlooked the enormous amount of work done by the states to improve health when no one else had been willing or able to act; yet it underlined an important point. If the advance of state and federal responsibility had got badly out of step, uniform, efficient, and national regulation became increasingly difficult to achieve.

[5] House Committee on Interstate Commerce, *Hearing on a bill to further enlarge the powers and authority of the Public Health and Marine Hospital Service* (H.R. 14,316) (3 Mar. 1906).   [6] *Ibid.*, 7.

A somewhat similar situation developed in the regulation of food, drink, and drugs. By the early years of the twentieth century every state had a pure food law and had taken steps to prevent the sale of harmful drugs; most of them had laws about the labeling of products; many had set up advanced scientific services. Different requirements and varying standards made for confusion, but some of the states which had traveled furthest were most opposed to any attempt by the federal government to legislate for uniformity. Former Senator William E. Mason of Illinois told a House committee that he was opposed to federal standards with the power to decide what they should be vested in the Department of Agriculture. "I think you ought to leave every State to adopt its own laws and to attend to its own business."[7] F. H. J. Knocke, Commissioner of Agriculture of New York, said:

What can be done with a national pure food law without machinery to enforce it, as compared to an able and forceful combination of the dairy and food commissioners of the various States working together with a singleness of purpose, not with envy to beat one or the other to get some temporary advantage, but to help this one and that one . . . A Federal law, if there be a Federal food law, is good as far as it will help the work of the various dairy and food commissioners . . . but it should be only as a convenience, and not to supersede the States and be the great "It."[8]

Indeed in 1905 the National Association of State Dairy and Food Departments resolved without dissent that standards should be set by them acting in concert and not by the Department of Agriculture. The one obstacle to effective control by the states was the Supreme Court decision in the original package case, according to which state jurisdiction over imported foodstuffs could not begin until the package had been broken and its contents introduced into the commerce of the state. The State Food and Dairy Commissioners argued that the proper course was to pass a law correcting that decision, and not to use it as an excuse for undermining by federal action all the good that had been done – and more that could be done – by co-operation between the states. This was reinforced by the argument that in a country with such wide climatic divisions laws appropriate in one state might be harmful or absurd in another.

There is a tendency to assume that those who pressed for federal responsibility always had the best of the argument, yet the case for building

---

[7] House Committee on Interstate Commerce, *Hearings on the Pure Food Bill* (H.R. 4,527) (1905), 44.
[8] *Ibid.*, 50. Knocke was not a witness but his speech was inserted in the record by W. E. Mason as a part of his evidence.

upon state agencies and utilizing existing services was often cogent and worthy of consideration. It is true that it was always possible to cite examples of laxity and to question the ability of the states to discipline such powerful interests as the meat packers; yet in retrospect it can be asked whether a requirement to co-operate might not have been as effective as a federal agency with all its top-heavy structure and inevitable delays. One difficulty in pursuing this path was clearly constitutional. To build an edifice, brick by brick, upon the commerce clause might be easier than to discover a constitutional doctrine by which states could be required to use their police powers collectively; but the elastic constitutionalism of the twentieth century has done stranger things. Leaving aside these specu-lations, it is enough to emphasize a paradox of the progressive period: advances in the states made it more difficult to enlarge federal respons-ibility, yet without these advances where could the experience which made central regulation possible have been found? When a National Health Service was finally established in 1912 it had at its disposal a vast range of information and expertise accumulated by the state boards.

The next federal agency to be established was from the first closely linked with state experience, and made it a rule to supplement and co-ordinate state activities rather than to regulate from the center. In 1883 the Senate set up a committee on the relations between labor and capital.[9] This was the first major investigation by Congress of a social issue, and its hearings were lengthy, revealing, and balanced. Many witnesses, and especially those representing organized labor, advocated the establishment of a Federal Bureau of Labor Statistics. This suggestion was taken up; the first Bureau of Labor was set up in 1885, and in 1888 it became a separate department though its head was not given cabinet status. The first head was Carroll D. Wright (with twenty years of experience in Massachusetts behind him), who would remain in office under six presidents.

What most witnesses before the 1883 committee wanted was a voice for labor in the national government; what they got was a bureau which took up the Massachusetts principles of objectivity, impartiality, and faith in the healing power of statistical fact. Personally Wright was strongly committed to fair conditions of work, the abolition of child labor, arbitration in industrial disputes, and a wage system which would allow honest men to better their own condition and plan for the future of their children; but he believed that these objectives could be obtained only by the patient and

---

[9] Senate Committee in Education and Labor, *Relations between Labor and Capital*, 47th Congress, 1st session; 48th Congress, 1st session.

undramatic investigation of the facts. In Massachusetts the facts had spoken loudly enough to persuade the legislature to enact the most advanced factory law in the country, but was this relevant when planning the strategy for a federal agency? Congress could not pass a factory law, abolish child labor, enforce health and sanitary laws, or provide for safety. Its responsibility in strikes was limited to some control over presidential use of the military or perhaps to altering the law under which federal courts issued injunctions.

As a statistical bureau the new agency entered an already crowded field. The Treasury, the Departments of Commerce and Agriculture, and the Bureau of the Census were already busy. They would shortly be joined by the Interstate Commerce Commission, which set up its own statistical service. Was there a special field of *labor* statistics to be marked out and won? The question was not answered by the vague phrases in the act establishing the bureau, and Wright decided to concentrate at first on problems which lay within the orbit of national financial and fiscal policy. His first major investigation was into the causes of depression. It was an ambitious task for a new agency, with an inexperienced staff, to step in where generations of economists had failed, and in this case the facts told no coherent story. An investigation of marriage and divorce was then commissioned by the Senate Judiciary Committee and produced valuable results, but not of the kind expected by the original advocates of a labor bureau. Even more remote from their thinking was a mammoth investigation designed to provide a scientific basis for the perennial tariff debate; it was published in 1890 and 1891, demonstrated no clear-cut or scientific answer to the problem, and was used only to furnish both high- and low-tariff men with occasional scraps of information to support their cases. More significant were a number of less intensive studies of subjects nearer labor's heart – women and children in industry, employer liability, industrial education, railroad labor, and urban housing – but the results were normally presented in column after column and page after page of figures which only a statistician could interpret. They remain a voluminous source for economic historians but had little contemporary impact.[10]

An important part of the bureau of labor's work lay in drawing together the state bureaus and disseminating information. The first National Convention of Labor Commissioners met at Boston in 1885, agreed to work for a uniform system of gathering statistics, and drafted a

[10] For information in this and the following paragraphs see James Leiby, *Carroll Wright and Labor Reform*, Chapters 5, 6, and 7, *passim*.

bill for presentation to the legislature of the fourteen states represented. This bill subsequently passed in some states but not all; the proposed authorization for more investigatory visits, additional staff, and larger appropriations encountered resistance, though in practice most state bureaus were able to approach national uniformity by internal administrative change. The conventions continued to meet every year, and there were sometimes sharp exchanges between impartial statisticians and labor activists over the proper function of bureaus. The *Bulletin of the Department of Labor* began publication in 1895, and continued with many supplementary issues and special reports. These functions were in line with Wright's original plan for federal action. In evidence before the 1883 Senate Committee he had suggested power to establish bureaus in states where they did not exist, and annual reports and other reports and bulletins as the need arose. With energy, professional skill, and adequate staff it would become "one of the strongest auxiliaries to the educational forces of the nation."[11]

The most common hope was that the new bureau would find answers to distressing industrial conflicts. In his first report as Federal Commissioner Wright tried to allay fears about the progress of labor organization. Writing at a time when the Knights of Labor were at their peak, he saw hope in complete organization on both sides: "Each force must treat with the other through intelligent representatives, and such treatment would result in doing away with passion, with excitement, and with all that comes of the endeavor of a great body of men to treat with employers."[12] When organized force met organized force in this way disputes over the hours of labor would be settled more satisfactorily than by legislation. Wright regarded freedom of contract as illusory; not so much because labor was weak but because an employer could always withhold his products from the market without risking disaster, while laborers could pay their bills only by selling their labor. One party could afford to wait; the other could not. He was a strong believer in arbitration and hoped that the time would come when it would be made compulsory. At the instigation of President Cleveland, Congress passed a law in 1888 to make arbitration available in all disputes affecting interstate commerce, provided that one party requested it; failing this the president might appoint a special commission to investigate and recommend.

The commission procedure was used in 1894 to investigate the great

---

[11] Senate Committee, *Relations between Labor and Capital* (1883): evidence of C. D. Wright, 571.   [12] Commissioner of Labor, 1st Ann. R. (1886), 287.

Chicago strike originating with the dispute at Pullman. Wright was chairman and wrote a report which rebuked violence but rejected most of the employers' arguments and recommended compulsory arbitration in future strikes. The important issue raised was whether the government should accept a commitment to intervene in strikes affecting interstate commerce, and, if it did so, who should see that findings or recommendations were accepted. A weak act of 1898 avoided compulsion, failed to set up a permanent arbitration tribunal, and said nothing about the responsibility for carrying out the recommendations of special commissions. Neither employers nor labor welcomed the act – the former because they were confident of winning most of the time and rejected government intervention in principle, and the latter because no government was trusted.

Suspicion of government mediation on the part of the unions partly reflected disappointment that the Department of Labor had not won them influence at Washington. Whatever had appeared in reports or recommendations the unhappy fact was that interventions by federal government, though infrequent, had invariably been against the strikers, under the pretext of protecting property, preventing violence, or moving the mails. In this delicate area the hope that scientific investigation and impartial findings would satisfy all parties was vain.

From other points of view the first Department of Labor was of outstanding importance in the evolution of modern government. It won national endorsement for the idea that the lives of working people were of concern to all, that investigation of wages, earnings, and social conditions should be carried out by government, and that intervention might be justified when the facts demonstrated its necessity. It was a momentous step to establish a federal agency with exclusive responsibility for finding out how people lived and worked, what trends could be discerned, and how truth could be separated from prejudice. Suspicion of "agitators" might be hard to dispel from the middle-class American mind, but at least an administrative instrument had been forged to demonstrate that industrial disputes could be rationally analyzed and might be remedied by intelligent action. The department was also evolving the statistical apparatus without which no modern government can function. Between 1888 and 1890 the department broke new ground by analyzing the earnings and expenditure of 8,544 families, selected as a cross section of the population. In an article published in 1892 Wright stressed the importance of these studies for the future management of labor. Working in collaboration with Professor Roland P. Falkner of the University of Pennsylvania, the department supplied the statistics for a study commissioned by a Senate committee; from this came the first use of index figures to measure general trends and fluctuations in prices and wages. This required not sporadic investigations of selected occupations but continuous collection of data. In 1900 Wright made "the regular annual collection and presentation of data concerning wages and prices" the major function of his department. Wright was also the influential advocate of changes in the census, though he failed to merge it with the department to form a general statistical agency for the United States. Hitherto the census had been a decennial enumeration which had been required, on each occasion, to answer more and more questions. The assessment of the information spilled over into the following years, but with reduced staff and without any opportunity for gathering supplementary information. After a trial run in the census of 1900, a new system was established with the Bureau of the Census as a permanent body.[13]

In 1903 both the department and the census bureau were assigned to a new Department of Commerce and Labor. This was not entirely happy; too many things had been drawn together which might have been better left separated, while the enlarged department became subject to too many political pressures; but once again the long-term consequences outweighed immediate fumbling. The federal government had taken a decisive step toward the assumption of modern responsibilities, and this had come about as a direct consequence of experience in the separate states. The Massachusetts Bureau of Labor Statistics can claim to be the progenitor of modern labor administration and of the statistical apparatus to sustain it. Other state bureaus had also played their part in pressing for solutions, molding opinion, and creating professional support for the new developments.

The first attempt to regulate interstate commerce by commission owed something to pressure from the states but little to the experience of state commissions. A bill to regulate commerce passed the House on March 26, 1874 by the narrow majority of 121 against 116.[14] It proposed to treat all but purely local lines as interstate commerce, to prohibit unfair rates, and to set up a commission with power to take evidence on oath, fix maximum rates, and revise tariff schedules. If it borrowed the idea of a commission

---

[13] For Wright's own history of the census and analysis of its problems see Carroll D. Wright, *History and Growth of the United States Census* (Washington D.C., 1900).

[14] This bill seems to have escaped the notice of historians. For passage of the bill see *Congressional Record*, 43rd Congress, 1st session (1874), 2,493.

from Massachusetts, the sweeping powers owed more to legislation in the
western states and the idea probably originated in that part of the Union.
The Senate committee on commerce had received a resolution from the
legislature of Kansas asking for a law fixing maximum rates and forbidding
discrimination, while Wisconsin had urgently requested "such national
legislation and action as will best secure to western produce an un-
obstructed channel of transportation to eastern and foreign markets at
reasonable rates." Iowa also asked for regulation of freight rates and fares
where they could not be controlled by state legislation. A body styling itself
the National Agricultural Congress asked for the improvement of competing water routes under government direction, and joint action by the states
to control through-railroad rates. Another proposal was the construction
of a government-owned freight line from the Mississippi to the Atlantic.[15]
Despite this evidence of interest and concern, the House Interstate
Commerce Bill was not reported out by the Senate committee.

A bill of 1876, which proposed regulation by the courts rather than by
commission, died, as did a similar bill sponsored by J. H. Reagan, chairman
of the House committee on interstate commerce, in 1878. These proposals
were favored by New York merchants but not by the National Board of
Trade, which preferred a commission. By this time some railroad leaders
were becoming concerned about the effects of unregulated competition and
rate wars, and in 1882 a bill which had been drafted by Charles Francis
Adams Jr proposed both legalized pooling and a three-man federal
commission to collect information and hear complaints. This was the first
overt attempt to graft the Massachusetts principle onto the national stock.
In Congress a contest was developing between a group led in the House by
Reagan, who wanted a tough law against unreasonable rates, discrimination, and prohibition of pooling, with enforcement by the courts, and
others, who wanted a committee to examine the case for a commission,
which would, they believed, look sympathetically upon pooling or traffic
associations while being capable of preventing discrimination. A committee
set up by the Senate under Shelby M. Cullom contained a majority of
commission men, and the list of questions distributed to witnesses was
designed to make the point.[16]

One interesting thing about the Cullom committee was that it made, for
the first time, an effort to draw upon the experience of the states, though its
report confessed difficulty in doing so. The history of the state commissions

---

[15] Senate Committee on Transportation Papers (1874), National Archives, Washington
D.C.   [16] *Senate Report No. 46*, 49th Congress, 1st session (1886), *passim.*

had not been written, and little was known of them as an institution. Nevertheless the Cullom committee discovered enough to report confidently that the commissions were a success, proved the possibility of regulation, but also demonstrated the need "to supplement, give direction to, and render effective State supervision."[17]

The committee heard witnesses from eight state commissions. The two commissioners from Wisconsin were so new to the job that they did not feel qualified to give general advice; the same was true of one from Iowa, but a more experienced colleague was on hand. Of the remaining states two were unequivocally in favor of a federal commission on the Massachusetts model: that is, with power to investigate, to make public its findings, and to recommend legislative action. The Massachusetts commissioner himself naturally preferred such a commission but had reservations about the need for a national body. Minnesota favored an advisory commission, and Nebraska leaned in that direction but was somewhat undecided. New York wanted a commission to fix reasonable rates, and the more experienced Iowa commissioner thought that the commission should have this as a reserve power after a complaint had not been remedied. Illinois was divided, with one commissioner supporting regulation and the other advice.[18]

Thomas F. Russell, chairman of the Massachusetts commission, said that opinion in Boston was opposed to fixing rates at the level charged by the Grand Trunk of Canada in an attempt to capture western trade. He also expressed some doubts about the way in which a federal commission would work in practice. In Massachusetts, he said, the commissioners knew "every railroad president and every railroad superintendent and freight manager"; they could bring personal influence to bear, and this was the crucial factor in the generally acknowledged success of his commission.[19] This was a warning that might have been given more weight.

The most experienced of all the state commissioners, Campbell Wallace of Georgia, was flatly opposed to a federal commission. He confessed that he had once favored the idea but had come to reject it: "The regulation of interstate transportation and of local transportation is so entirely different that you cannot take the workings of one and adapt it to the other."[20] He wanted a federal law against unreasonable and discriminatory rates and a special judge in each federal circuit to hear complaints, make decisions, and

---

[7] *Ibid.*, 63, 64, 179.
[8] Data extracted from Senate Committee on Interstate Commerce Hearings, 49th Congress, 1st session (May–Nov. 1885).   [19] *Ibid.*, 308.   [20] *Ibid.*, 1422, 1428.

issue orders. There might be appeals to higher federal courts, but on questions of fact the determination by the special court would be final. The reasons why Wallace, who ran a very strong state commission, rejected the idea of a federal commission were interesting. The primary duty of the state commission was, he said, to ensure that shippers within the state, the majority of whom were farmers or small merchants in rural areas, got a fair deal. As they were unlikely to have the knowledge or resources to tackle a large company, it was the business of the state commission to act on their behalf; but complaints involving interstate commerce were almost always lodged by merchants in large commercial centers who were either organized in associations or easily able to combine. They were quite capable of protecting themselves provided that the law was on their side.

The suggestion that there should be federal railroad courts in each circuit was interesting. They would become expert tribunals, but avoid the blend of investigatory and judicial functions which subsequently made life difficult for the Interstate Commerce Commission. As there was an essential difference between the state and federal problems there was a good case for treating them in different ways. This argument by Wallace may have led to the inclusion, in the Interstate Commerce Act, of proceedings in federal district courts as an alternative to lodging complaints with the commission, but the main thrust of Campbell Wallace's advice was ignored. The committee had its mind set on a federal commission, and accepted the view of the majority of railroad commissioners in preferring an advisory commission on the Massachusetts model. Most railroad men who gave evidence were also opposed to a commission with power to fix rates. With this weight of opinion in favor of an advisory commission, the committee would have had to argue explicitly for rate fixing if this was what they had intended.

After more than a year with Congress the Interstate Commerce Act incorporating these recommendations was passed. The first part declared that all rates must be reasonable and just; prohibited special rates, rebates or drawbacks, and all other discrimination between individuals, companies, or localities; and forbade higher charges per mile for shorter than for longer distances "under substantially similar circumstances and conditions." It forbade pools or any other agreement between competing railroads to divide freights or revenue. This anti-pooling clause was inserted at the insistence of Reagan, who insisted that he would block the bill in the House unless it were added. The second part of the bill set up a five-man commission to be appointed by the president with the consent of the

Senate and retire in rotation. In the future the full tenure would be six years. The commission was given power "to inquire into the management of the business of all common carriers," compel the attendance of witnesses, and require information. Complaints could be made to the commission, which might also initiate inquiries on its own. Whenever a company refused or neglected to obey "any lawful order or requirement" the commission would apply to a circuit court sitting in equity, which should have power to hear and determine the matter. The findings of the commission on questions of fact were to be accepted as true prima facie. This procedure was much quicker than a normal suit under common law.

It was clear that the commission could find that a rate was unreasonable, issue an order to lower it, and if resisted apply to the courts. There was no explicit statement that the commission could declare what rate was reasonable and require a railroad to charge no more. It might be inferred that the commission could not decide what was unreasonable unless it also decided what would be reasonable; nor was there anything to prevent a commission from communicating this information to the company. The crucial issue was whether the commission could order the reasonable rate to be charged and prosecute if no action were taken. Was this a "lawful order or requirement"?

The weight of opinion in evidence before the Senate committee had been heavily in favor of an advisory commission without the power to fix maximum rates. A year of debate on the issue had not added a clause explicitly giving the power. Yet there was a widespread belief that maximum rates could be fixed. It was four years before the power was challenged and nine before the Supreme Court decided that it did not exist.[21]

A characteristic of the Massachusetts commission was reliance upon publicity to prevent a company from acting unreasonably. In a compact society, in which historical accident had concentrated political, commercial, and literary influence in one city, "public opinion" was a real force. The railroad owner who was known to charge unreasonably would quickly lose the good will of his commercial clients, was certain to suffer attacks in the press, and might expect to find himself facing hostile action when the legislature next met. A federal commission had to act in a very different environment. The commission was central, the complaints were local.

[21] 162 U.S. 184, decided Mar. 30, 1896.

Dissatisfaction might reach Congress through pressure from constituents, but in the large national assembly even the largest state made a minor impact. When the complaint came from a western state it was also likely that control over the railroad in question was exercised from a distant city, and there was no way in which the owner met his critics face to face in the course of daily business. The commission certainly had the good will of a large majority in Congress, and there would be strong resistance to any concerted move to abolish or emasculate it; but general support was quite different from backing the commission in a dispute over what was reasonable in a distant part of the Union. Expectations, based on the Massachusetts example, about the effect of publicity failed to reckon with these very real differences between state and nation.

These difficulties need not be exaggerated. A law was a law, and the threat of prosecution was real. In the fight against discrimination almost everyone was on the same side except the individuals, corporations, and cities which had succeeded in playing off railroad against railroad. Sensible railroad men knew that stability was worth a price, and the more far-sighted knew that they might gain in the long run if users came to believe that existing rates had the sanction of the federal commission. These things combined to give the commission a good start, and for five or six years it was regarded as an outstanding success. Business was voluminous, and its scope is indicated in a letter of February 1891 from the secretary to the chairman:

My own work is constantly growing. There is much more activity than ever before in the effort to bring the violators of the law to justice, and I am in constant communication with the various United States District Attorneys who are receiving information of violations, and who are constantly asking for suggestions, making inquiries, etc.[22]

The secretary believed that the indictments already laid had had the effect of "entirely changing the condition of affairs," and that "the law was observed far better than when it first went into effect." The greatest success was in wiping out discriminatory rates. Special arrangements with individuals remained difficult to detect, but across the country there was no shortage of commercial associations keeping a close watch on the large corporations and on advantages given to competing cities, and their complaints crowded in upon the I.C.C. The temporary advantage gained

[22] E. A. Moseley to T. M. Cooley, Feb. 21, 1891, Cooley Papers, Bentley Library, University of Michigan, Ann Arbor. Hereafter cited as Cooley Papers.

by securing business through offering a special rate became hardly
worthwhile, and many railroad presidents welcomed a law which allowed
them to discipline over-enthusiastic freight managers.

Success in the honeymoon period of the commission owed much to the
first chairman, Thomas M. Cooley. There could hardly have been a better
choice. His *Constitutional Limitations* had been widely recognized as an
authoritative commentary and was much quoted in the courts; he had been
a state judge, and was receiver of the Wabash railroad. Cooley was
respected by railroad men, but his appointment was also welcome to those
who hoped to see the rule of law imposed upon railroad operations. In 1893
William Larrabee – former governor of Iowa, an authority on railroad
legislation, and no friend to the companies – wrote that Cooley had been
"particularly well-qualified for the office of chairman," that under his
leadership the commission had become "more than a purely executive
board," and that its decisions were "in many cases the equivalent of judicial
rulings."[23]

In 1886, when rejecting the idea of government ownership, Cooley added
that nothing could be more unnecessary, "for a government railroad
Commission under popular laws may accomplish all the good that can be
accomplished by government purchase."[24] In his first commission report
he surveyed the results of the first nine months, and wrote of the moral
issues involved; the evils of railroad practice had not only worked injustice
upon individuals but "blunted the sense of right and wrong," while class
feeling had been built up between those who "for every reason ought to be
in harmony." Examples of railroad tyranny had become all too frequent,
and "It was high time that adequate power should be put forth to bring
them to an end. Railroads [were] a public agency."[25] Underlying his
approach there was a conviction that railroads must learn both to obey the
law and to respect it. The rule of law meant its voluntary acceptance as the
principle of rational conduct, and men who might lose business or income
must be given a fair hearing; if possible, they must be brought to the point

---

[23] It will be observed that my judgment of Cooley differs sharply from that of Gabriel Kolko,
Railroads and Regulations, 1877–1916 (Princeton, N.J., 1965), 47–8. Kolko says that
Cooley's position "was best represented in the Supreme Court by Justice Stephen J.
Field"; he was "completely identified with the railroads' interests from at least 1882 on";
"For several years he aligned himself with the most conservative railroad opponents of
federal regulation." He was opposed to granting judicial powers to commissions. By 1887
he was "advocating the legalization of pooling with public sanction and control." The first
statement misunderstands both Cooley's views on constitutional limitation and Field's
views on legislative powers.

[24] Draft dated Apr. 30, 1886, Cooley Papers.

[25] *1st Report of the Interstate Commerce Commissioner, December 1887*, 9.

of compliance with informal recommendations rather than carry defiance into courts.

One danger was that the companies would try to make the law ridiculous by irrational compliance. When Bishop Knickerbocker of Indianapolis complained that following the passage of the law the local railroads had withdrawn the passes that they had customarily given to clergymen traveling on duty, Cooley replied that no one would penalize men for exercising sensible discretion: "Penalties are for willful violations of law; not for errors of judgment."[26] Another danger was an expectation that the commission was out to harass the railroads. In May 1887 Cooley deplored the prevalence "of a vague notion that power has been conferred upon the Commission to interfere anywhere and for any reason satisfactory to itself in order to prevent what it may think likely to be harmful . . . The Commission must find its authority in the law, and not in its own ideas of right or policy."[27] Commissioner W. L. Bragg was following Cooley's guidelines when he wrote, in an official communication: ". . . The Railroads fix their own rates, but any person may have them arraigned for being in violation of the statute."[28] This of course meant that when a railroad fixed a rate it must always bear in mind the possibility of complaint, formal proceedings, and an adverse decision. The law would be most effective when railroad managers asked themselves at the outset whether a rate proposed would pass the test of reasonableness.

This was not to imply that the commission should be an inert body, taking no action until a complaint came before it. It was not going to scrutinize every tariff schedule for irregularities as soon as it was received – even if desirable this would be impossible, with some 180,000 tariffs filed in the year ending December 1, 1889 and covering thousands of stations in all parts of the country; but at the same time the tariffs were filed for a purpose and a large portion of the commission's administrative staff was employed in analyzing them. The commission was not merely passive.

The statute contemplates that complaints shall be made against rates as one of the means of enforcing the law, and it also contemplates that the Commission shall exercise a general supervision over the methods of railroads as far as this can be done.[29]

[26] I.C.C. Commissioner's Letterbook, Apr. 18, 1887, National Archives, Washington D.C.
[27] Cooley to J. A. Handley, traffic manager of the Minnesota and North Western, May 18, 1887, *ibid.*
[28] Bragg to F. B. Rice, president of the Board of Trade of Waterbury, Connecticut, Feb. 26, 1890, *ibid.*
[29] Bragg to Hon. B. W. Arnold, Richmond, Virginia, Jan. 17, 1890, *ibid.*

It would be the duty of the commission to draw the attention of the companies to any irregularities that might appear in the tariffs or accounts and expect them then to be rectified; only in the last resort would prosecution be undertaken, but the threat of proceedings would ensure voluntary compliance.

To facilitate the commission's function as a watchdog it was necessary to insist, wherever possible, upon uniformity in the publication of schedules and presentation of accounts. This meant that an expert staff must be gathered at Washington. Cooley brought young Henry Carter Adams from the University of Michigan as chief statistician, despite some qualms about "his peculiar notions which seem to verge on socialism." Adams was to continue to combine this post with his academic duties for several years and built up his own staff of assistant statisticians.[30] There was also an Auditor of Rates and Transportation, with a large clerical staff to work on the tariffs. There was to be much work behind the scenes but little in the limelight.

A great deal of correspondence was generated by Section 4 of the Interstate Commerce Act, which forbade long- and short-haul discrimination but allowed the commission to suspend this clause after considering a plea from a company. An early rush of applications was referred to the various state railroad commissions in April 1887, and the further the commission went into this question the more difficult it became to lay down clear principles of action. Was a shipper to be deprived of the advantages of cheap rates over long distances? If competition brought down the rates at one center, should the railroad be forced to concede the same advantage to shippers at intermediate points? Must a company be forced to lose business by holding its rates for competing points at a level which was recognized as reasonable at other points? This question required careful investigation in every instance and a careful balance between all the interests affected. The commission had also to take into account any rulings by state commissions and the reasons for them, so that no disparity developed between state and interstate practice.[31]

The commission was far less active in trying to curb pooling. As a railroad receiver Cooley knew all too well the effects of ruinous com-

---

[30] In March 1886 Cooley had been consulted privately by James B. Angell, president of the University of Michigan, about "the fear that he [Adams] might do and say foolish things." Cooley expressed regret at his indiscretion but thought that he intended well, and was "undoubtedly conscientious in his views and in their expression." "Personal Memoranda," Mar. 30, 1886, Cooley Papers.
[31] I.C.C. General Letters, Apr. 1887, National Archives, Washington D.C.

petition, and was prepared to sanction agreements between companies provided that the resulting charges were monitored by the commission and did not impose upon shippers and consumers too high a price for stability. In common with other well-informed commentators, he regarded the anti-pooling section of the Act as a late and unnecessary addition. The general requirement that rates should be reasonable was sufficient safeguard, because any pooling arrangement was subject to it. Reagan, the principal author of the anti-pooling section, came to recognize the wisdom of this argument, but it proved difficult to repeal the section once it was incorporated in the Act.

All experienced men knew that selfishness was not concentrated exclusively in the railroad companies, and that local commercial associations might be as predatory in their small way as the big railroad corporations were in theirs. In March 1888 Cooley recorded in his diary that cases brought by the Business Men's Association of Minnesota were "worked up by professional agitators," while an argument on behalf of the Board of Trade of Omaha was presented by two men who were "the instigators of the proceedings and who talked sublime nonsense, really seeming to believe it." On the other hand some witnesses for the railroads did their own cause no good. "No garrulous old woman could have been more voluble or more discursive" than J. C. Stubbs, traffic manager of the Southern Pacific.[32]

The principles upon which Cooley worked, and which molded this far-reaching experiment in regulation, may therefore be briefly summarized. The law must be obeyed. When the wording of a law was imprecise no man should be disadvantaged by loose construction. Discussion and agreement were preferred to conflict and prosecution. Informal proceedings should always be attempted before formal hearings were instituted. If formal proceedings were instituted, no one should be presumed to have broken the law until all the facts were ascertained. When interpreting words such as "unreasonable" or "unjust," it was as well to assume that everyone had acted reasonably and justly according to his lights; unless one party had acted willfully or ignorantly it was the task of the Commission to reconcile two firmly held positions, and the higher concept of justice might be represented by a compromise. It was precisely because the problems were complex that a commission was necessary; if they had been simple an unambiguous law enforced by the courts would have been the easy

---

[32] Diary, Mar. 19 and 20, 1888, Cooley Papers.

solution; but behind these qualifications was the overarching principle that railroads must be regulated in the public interest.

To outsiders the commission looked competent and strong. Apart from Cooley there was Aldace Walker, a very experienced railroad man, Augustus Schoonmaker, a prominent New York lawyer and former state Attorney General, W. L. Bragg, a former member of the Alabama Railroad Commission, and W. R. Morrison, who had seen long service in the House of Representatives as a Democratic leader and been spoken of as a possible candidate for the presidency. The insider's view was very different.[33] Cooley got on well with Walker and trusted his judgment; Schoonmaker he found slow, unimaginative, and, though always critical of others, apt to delay his own opinions which had even then to be drastically revised; Bragg handled correspondence well and was a loyal interpreter of commission policy, but showed no initiative and required much help in difficult cases. Cooley's most frequent and critical private comments were made about Morrison. He liked his good humor and genial company; he was a "comical fellow" with a trained politician's understanding of human behavior; but as acquaintance grew shallows were revealed. Morrison was "lacking in culture, general knowledge, breadth and natural power," and apart from complete honesty was "absolutely without qualifications for the position he holds." It was not only that Morrison failed to understand in detail but that his general approach differed sharply from Cooley. For him there was a simple conflict between right and wrong, between the people and the railroads; he assumed at the outset that every railroad man was "an enemy to the public" and rejected everything proposed from that quarter even if it was for the public good. After two years Cooley concluded that Morrison was "absolutely useless from his utter inability either to comprehend the principles with which we are compelled to deal, or to express any such ideas as he may have and put them down upon paper for use." In addition to railroad men Morrison had "active and vigilant prejudice" against men who were particular about their clothes, commonly wore gloves, or parted their hair down the middle. Cooley retired on grounds of health in September 1891, when he learned that Morrison was to succeed him as chairman. His comments are not recorded.

An important part of the commission's work was to supplement and co-ordinate the work of state commissions. The first circular letter in April 1887 had solicited advice, suggestions, and information, and in December

[33] Diary, Sept. 21, 1887, Mar. 4, 1888, Cooley Papers; letters to Mrs Cooley, Mar. 24, 1889, *ibid.*

1888 a call went out for a convention of railroad commissioners. It met in March 1889 and was attended by forty-two commissioners from twenty-two states, two former commissioners, and three representatives from the railway press. As great importance was attached to uniformity of accounts the convention was also attended by fourteen representatives of the Association of American Railway Accounting Officers (a body with which the Commission developed a close relationship). Cooley gave an opening address in which he said: "It is of the highest importance that there should be harmony in the legislation of control, so that the system can be controlled as nearly as possible . . . harmoniously as a unit."[34] He also emphasized the importance of accurate statistics and uniform freight classification.

The convention continued to meet annually, and committees were set up to study and report upon selected aspects of the railroad question. One by-product was a drive for safety. In responding to the first call one commissioner had expressed the view that the lives of men, "needlessly sacrificed yearly by our railways," were of more importance than rates and discriminations; but it was not until March 1891 that Cooley set up a committee on safety.[35] It reported in November and the details were horrifying. In the twelve months ending June 30, 1889, 1,972 trainmen had been killed and 20,390 injured. The situation was worsening: 300 men had been killed and 6,757 injured in coupling or uncoupling cars during 1888–9, but in 1889 the figures were 369 and 7,842 respectively. With these facts incorporated in the commission's report for 1892 Congress was moved to make continuous brakes and automatic coupling compulsory.[36]

The formal record reveals only a small portion of the commission's work. A very large number of the complaints received were dealt with informally, and there was much correspondence on points of detail. Gabriel Kolko has severely criticized the commission for giving informal opinions to railroad companies but refusing them to individual complainants.[37] This seems to be a misreading of the situation. Companies wanted informal opinions on whether a proposed rate was likely to be reasonable, whether variations in a tariff would be regarded as discriminatory, or what action would follow if they treated a complaint as ill-founded. Informal

[34] *Proceedings of a General Conference of Railroad Commissioners . . . March, 1889*, 1–2.
[35] Hillard Smith to I.C.C., Feb. 28, 1889, General Correspondence, National Archives, Washington D.C.; Cooley to George Crocker, Boston, Mar. 6, 1891, Cooley Papers.
[36] Clipping from the Baltimore *Sun*, Nov. 11, 1891, with I.C.C. Miscellaneous Papers, National Archives, Washington D.C.
[37] Kolko, *Railroads and Regulations*, 55–6.

opinions given to railroads were therefore one way of avoiding more complaints, formal hearings, and lengthy litigation. An individual would want an informal opinion on whether he was likely to succeed; if the answer was that the commission's decision was likely to be favorable he would persevere, if not the commission would be accused of siding with the railroad. If no informal opinion were given the complainant would be faced with three options: dropping his complaint, opening legal proceedings at enormous cost, or leaving the commission to mediate informally on the facts that he provided. The last was the choice preferred by the commission, and in its first report it explained that this procedure was "more useful than any other." Kolko's argument that this allowed the railroads to judge for themselves is puzzling.

A much debated question is whether the commission assumed the power to fix reasonable or maximum rates in these early days. Eighteen years later the then chairman, J. C. Clements, told a House committee that the commission had always decided what was reasonable as well as finding that a complaint was well founded:

It could prohibit the carrier from charging any more upon the apparently good reasoning . . . that any part of the excessive rate above that which is reasonable is just as unlawful as any other part . . . This is what the Commission held from the beginning, when Judge Cooley was its chairman, and it made rates at that time, and continuously thereafter until the Supreme Court said that the power was not conferred upon the Commission by statute.[38]

William P. Hepburn, who had been closely concerned with railroad legislation over a long period, disagreed. When a witness before the same committee (of which he was chairman) credited J. H. Reagan with principal authorship of the 1887 Act Hepburn intervened sharply. The Act, he said, had adopted the principles of the Massachusetts commission, and for that very reason Reagan had opposed it until the last moment.

From my own knowledge I can testify that it was not intended to confer the rate-making power upon the I.C.C. . . . Judge Cooley recognized this; but after his retirement the Commission assumed that it had this power, and exercised it.[39]

In 1897 the commission had written in its report that it had "never claimed the right to prescribe the rate in the first instance," but this left open the possibility of fixing a rate after a hearing and decision if the railroad persisted.[40]

---

[38] House of Representatives, *Hearings before the Committee on Interstate and Foreign Commerce, on the Bill to Amend the Interstate Commerce Act* (1905), 353. Hereafter cited as *Hearings* (1905).   [39] *Ibid.*, 78, 81.   [40] I.C.C., 11th R. (1897), 15.

One solution to this conflict of evidence may be found in the statement to the 1905 committee of Samuel Spencer, president of the Southern Railroad, who had had many years of dealing with the I.C.C. He spoke enthusiastically of the commission's success in eliminating "the very great abuses and irregularities" which had previously existed, but went on to say that the right to fix rates had been specifically disclaimed. In several instances it may have appeared to determine a rate, but the commission was then acting in a way similar to that of a referee in a commercial case. A referee was appointed by a court to investigate the facts and recommend a just solution; his decision did not have the force of law but was invariably accepted by the judges and made the ruling of the court.[41] This seems reasonable. It is unlikely that Cooley, who was imbued with legal caution and had made his reputation by studying constitutional limitations, would have gone a step beyond what was explicitly declared in the act. An official letter from Commissioner Bragg in February 1890 may be conclusive. In it he said explicitly that it "was not the province of the Commission to fix rates for railroads."[42]

Whether the commission should have had this power from the beginning is another matter. In 1897 Commissioner Martin Knapp told a Senate committee: "There can never be any effective regulation of interstate commerce . . . such as the Constitution contemplates and the law intended until you have a tribunal which has the power and authority to determine . . . to the extent of a court of first instance, what the charge shall be when the rate fixed by the carrier is complained of by the shipper."[43] In 1903 Commissioner Charles Prouty told the American Economic Association that the government must "exercise the right to supervise the rate" and must "compel the carriers to impose in the first instance a reasonable charge." The companies should make their own rates, but if unreasonable the government should change them. In 1905 Commissioner Clements gave the strongest possible support to a proposal that maximum rates should be fixed.[44]

By these later years the nature of the problem had changed. The great evil

---

[41] *Hearings* (1905), 94.

[42] Bragg to President of Board of Trade, Waterbury, Connecticut, Feb. 26, 1890, I.C.C. Commissioners' Letterbook, National Archives, Washington D.C.

[43] *Senate Hearings on a bill to amend Section 5 of the Interstate Commerce Act*, Senate Document 39, 55th Congress, 1st session (Apr. 15, 1897), 86.

[44] "National Regulation of Railroads," *Publications of the American Economic Association*, 3rd Series, 4:1 (1903), 76. Prouty would however have preferred a separation between executive and judicial functions. Though the operation of his proposed system is not clear it seemed to require special railroad courts in which the commission would act as prosecutor. For Clements' argument for fixing rates see *Hearings* (1905), 353ff.

was no longer discrimination, secret rebates and unfair competition but concentration of railroad power in a few hands. Extortionate rates imposed by monopolies were now the perceived danger, and to meet it the right to declare what was reasonable and then enforce it was essential. But the weight of testimony and experience suggests that from the first it had been an error not to implant in the act the specific powers to fix maximum, and enforce reasonable, rates. In adopting the Massachusetts model the framers of the act had failed to recognize the difference between a compact state and a sprawling nation.

States which had backed the idea of an advisory commission had good reason to complain when the federal body assumed the power to fix rates, and the Massachusetts commission sounded a note of alarm as early as 1892. In a paper on "Harmony in Railroad Legislation" submitted to the second annual convention of railroad commissioners it asked whether Congress had the right to regulate rates, decide safety requirements, and determine the hours and wages for all railroads directly or indirectly engaged in interstate commerce. Was it true that "the States, by allowing their railroad corporations to take part in interstate commerce . . . thereby parted with all but a shadow of control over the subjects of their creation"?[45] It went on to point out that every inconvenience experienced in interstate commerce, every inconsistency or conflict between state and federal law, every attempt by the companies to evade state regulation, "every cut-throat struggle between competing lines, and, finally, the panacea for most of the foregoing evils, every consolidation," would be used to support the case for extended federal control. Yet if this remedy were adopted, the Massachusetts commission argued, the cure would be worse than the disease. On the one hand Congress was far too overloaded with business to supervise detail; on the other every administrative difficulty would strengthen the case for moving from "absolute regulation" to "absolute ownership."

The advice from Massachusetts to the I.C.C. was to leave to the states the tasks which they could perform effectively, and its advice to the companies was to co-operate with state commissions and especially to work for uniformity in their operational practice. Legislatures should bring their laws into harmony with those of other states, and this should extend not only to police regulations – where their sovereignty was unquestioned – but also to questions on which Congress might act under the commerce power

[45] Commonwealth of Massachusetts, R.R. Commissioners' R., *Public Document No. 14* (1892).

but had not yet done so. It goes without saying that this advice was not uniformly adopted, but there are many examples to show that companies sought to work with state commissions rather than against them, while states brought their laws into harmony to resist the case for extended federal action. Thus federal intervention had effects which were similar to those already observed in other fields. In order to defend their own spheres of interest the states were driven to seek greater efficiency and better co-operation with their neighbors, but their success raised new obstacles to effective federal action. The railroads often preferred accepting the recommendations of state commissions to acting in ways which would invite complaint to the I.C.C. In some states this professed willingness to co-operate may have reflected the belief of the corporations that they had enough political influence to resist unwelcome regulation, but it also developed from the experience that men on the spot understand each other's problems and that conflict did no one any good. Contrary to the views that have been so often expressed, the authority of most state commissions grew during the last decade of the nineteenth century; but this also meant that every state commission had a vested interest in curbing the power of the federal commission.

The purpose of this survey of the early history of the I.C.C. is to identify the links between experience in the states and national regulation, and not to continue that history until the original act was replaced by a stronger measure in 1906. This period was described as a failure by contemporaries; the verdict has been frequently endorsed, and the Supreme Court has usually been blamed. It might be more appropriate to blame the vagueness of the original act and weak direction after 1891. As chairman, Morrison adopted a more aggressive attitude to the railroad corporations, but, as Cooley had foreseen, this generated resistance and the atmosphere of mutual respect which he had fostered was quickly dissipated. The particular order fixing a reasonable rate, which became the issue in 1896 (when the Supreme Court denied this right), was dated June 29, 1891; this was before Cooley's retirement, but he was already sick, unable to make the trip to Washington, and no longer in control of the commission.[46] In a later case the court struck down a commission ruling that imported freight should be carried at the same rate as domestic freight and not given the

---

[46] It may have been with reference to this crucial point that H. C. Adams wrote later that the more Morrison criticized Cooley "the more convinced I am that the policy of the Judge was right" (to his wife, Aug. 4, 1895, H. C. Adams Papers, Bentley Library, University of Michigan; cited hereafter as H. C. Adams Papers).

advantage of special through-rates. The commission was rebuked for considering the interests of merchants in the ports and home-based manufacturers alone, and condoning an artificial increase in the prices of imports.[47]

The long- and short-haul section of the act was virtually nullified when the court ruled that the commission must take into account the effect of competition. The only reason why a carrier lowered a rate on a long haul was to meet competition, and if this was accepted as a valid reason there was no point in challenging a rate charged for a short haul when there was no competition.[48] The power of the commission to fix a maximum rate was finally killed in 1896.[49] Indirectly the Supreme Court rebuked the commission for its tolerant attitude toward pools when it decided that the Trans-Mississippi Freight Association broke the anti-trust law.[50]

On May 27, 1897 Morrison wrote gloomily to H. C. Adams that the Supreme Court had taken from the commission "much of the little power it has long been exercising and believed it possessed."[51] In 1903 Commissioner Prouty said that there was no point in explaining the power of the I.C.C. because there was too little of it "to admit of intelligent discussion."[52]

These unhappy comments should not obscure the magnitude of what had been achieved. A commission existed, and if its powers were too weak they could be enlarged. The form of federal regulation had been determined in a way that would have far-reaching influence. If railroads evaded the law they no longer defied it. Most profound was the change in opinion; forty years before no one had contemplated federal regulation of the nation's largest economic enterprise, but on the eve of the passage of the Hepburn Act the assumption was that existing regulation must be replaced by something stronger. In 1897 Commissioner Martin Knapp told the Senate committee:

There is a growing conviction of national duty in this regard, and the notion that the strong arm of government should hold the balance of power between the carriers and the people has taken a firm hold upon public opinion . . . Transportation is neither a commodity nor a luxury, but a constant and universal necessity . . . The State is bound to see that the terms on which it is supplied are not burdensome or unequal.[53]

[47] 162 U.S. 197 *Texas & Pacific* v. *I.C.C.*
[48] 168 U.S. 144.   [49] 167 U.S. 479.   [50] 166 U.S. 290.
[51] Morrison to Adams, May 27, 1897, H. C. Adams Papers.
[52] Prouty, "National Regulation of Railroads," 76.
[53] Senate Committee on Interstate Commerce, *Hearings on a bill to amend the Interstate Commerce Act* (1897), 102.

The evidence presented in the preceding pages suggests that federal regulation did not flow smoothly from state experience. The attempt to initiate federal responsibility for public health failed in the first instance because it fell foul of the only state board with experience in tackling yellow fever; when the attempt was renewed in the early years of the twentieth century the argument that the state boards were already efficient was a serious obstacle to change. Even more serious difficulties arose out of the proposal to superimpose a federal food and drug law upon an almost fully fledged system of state law. The Federal Bureau of Labor was an important innovation, but the decision to model it upon the Massachusetts bureau meant that it could not play the role expected of it as the voice of labor in national administration. Imitation of the successful Massachusetts Railroad Commission meant that the Interstate Commerce Commission was denied a power which later proved to be essential. There was, of course, no suggestion that the federal government should move into the area occupied by the Boards of State Charities, so here one can go no further than to speculate that the federal government might have been forced to intervene at a much earlier period in the twentieth century had not the most populous and urbanized states already built up agencies to cope with the worst of the social problems. Having said all this, one must repeat the point already made: that federal intervention had to build upon state experience because there was nothing else on which it could build, that without the example of state agencies federal regulation might have taken a very different form, and that experiment in the states had prepared the way for an expansion of public responsibility which would have been inconceivable thirty years before.

The second object of inquiry in this chapter is therefore to understand the contribution of state intervention to the twentieth-century revolution in attitudes toward government responsibility. In seeking answers we necessarily leave the firm ground of evidence drawn from official records and venture upon the speculative task of measuring what cannot be quantified.

Too often the board members, commissioners, secretaries, assistants, clerks, inspectors, engineers, and statisticians are faceless men and women. Occasionally they speak for themselves through their reports, their evidence to congressional committees, and their personal memoirs. A few of the most important, such as Charles Francis Adams Jr, Carroll D. Wright, and Florence Kelley, have been subjects of modern biographies. All too rarely others reveal themselves through collected papers in state libraries. A. G. Byers of Ohio, Frank Flower of Wisconsin, Joseph Jones of Louisiana, and J. H. Reagan of Texas come alive in this way, and there are probably others in this category. For the great army of public servants which grew up in the state agencies, it is possible only to record that they served and to speculate upon the extent to which their influence extended beyond the immediate area in which they made their professional careers. All that can be said with certainty is that they provided a new element in American society. In addition to unpaid board members and salaried officials a great many others had become familiar with the work of the agencies: lawyers handled cases; doctors might be members of local health boards, and were certainly the recipients of much literature sent out by the state boards; clergymen served as chaplains in state institutions and some, influenced by the social gospel, were keenly interested in urban and industrial problems. National dimensions were provided by professional associations, conventions, and journals.

In the short run the influence of any particular agency would depend upon the reputation of the men who manned it. Balthasar H. Meyer concluded from his close study of railroad commissions that far too much time was spent in examining their formal powers and legal limitations. Some that were ostensibly strong achieved very little; others with little authority on paper were diligent and effective: "The efficiency of all control and regulation through commissions must ultimately rest on the men."[54] In the public eye their reputation would often depend upon their success in distancing themselves from the politicians who were their nominal masters. Given the lack of a deeply rooted tradition of public service it is not surprising that some failed this test.

Henry Carter Adams, surveying the scene as an academic economist and as statistician to the Interstate Commerce Commission, was depressed by a visit to the 1897 National Convention of Railroad Commissioners:

If there ever was the necessity of good and conscientious men in public life it is now. This convention has doubtless some good men, but the crowd that makes the most noise is the crowd that drinks the whiskey.[55]

He compared unfavorably "the intelligence of the men whom the railways employ, and the dullness of the men whom the states employ." As an official of the Interstate Commerce Commission Adams had had occasion to seek an opinion on A. K. Teisberg of Minnesota, who was an applicant for a federal post. The Comptroller of the Great Northern Railroad replied that his personal relations with Teisberg had been pleasant, and that

[54] Meyer, *Railway Legislation*, 167.
[55] To his wife, May 11, 1897, H. C. Adams Papers.

though he had not "conceived the highest opinion in the world of Mr Teisberg's ability," he was "above the average secretary of a Railroad Commission."[56]

Recruitment for public service has never been easy, and railroad commissions were more likely than most to be squeezed between popular demands for action and the skillful inertia of the corporations. Yet for many of them weighty reports bear testimony to an enormous amount of hard and accurate work. The reports of all agencies may give too favorable an impression of the men who worked for them. They were often the work of one man, written to inflate the importance of what was being done, and usually designed to present a special case for more money and more power; yet when they have been discounted for these reasons the facts remain that they were usually literate, often solidly based on factual investigations, and seldom strayed into empty rhetoric. On the subordinate staff it is difficult to make a general judgment, but perhaps the most significant evidence is negative. The new breed of agents and inspectors was seldom exposed to criticism, ridicule or abuse. In contemporary caricature they were generally ignored, which suggests that they were not perceived as buffoons, corrupt tools, or agents of paternalism.

An official state agency had ways of influencing opinion possessed by no voluntary body. First and foremost it could present annual or biennial reports, which might be noted in the local press and would certainly be circulated to similar agencies in other states. These reports might incorporate much information collected with the threat of prosecution if refused; in addition they incorporated reports from the agency's own inspectors or field force. An agency was also in a position to convene state conventions, send representatives to national meetings, and disseminate ephemeral publications to educate the public. Official status was a magnet which attracted the interest of other organized groups, so that as time went on an agency could count upon more and more support from groups, associations, and private business. Though legislators were notoriously mean when money had to be spent, individual senators or representatives would find themselves committed to the support or enlargement of any agency; once acquired, the responsibility was difficult to shed.

In many instances the ideas advanced by the original promoters of public action had become institutionalized in a way that made them hard to

---

[56] Apr. 30, 1897, H. C. Adams Papers. Teisberg later withdrew his application because he had "by wire, pen, and personal calls" stirred up his friends to secure his reappointment as secretary of the Minnesota commission (letter to Adams, *ibid.*).

displace. For example, a Board of Public Health, with its central office, professional services, scientific establishment, publications, and network of local boards all sustained by the most active and far-sighted members of the profession, had become a structure capable of resisting all attacks. It was possible to argue over detail and the implementation of policies, but the dismemberment of the whole apparatus was unthinkable. The preceding chapters have noted only two instances of an agency being discontinued – the Ohio Board of State Charities in 1872 and the Georgia Board of Public Health in 1877 – and the first was re-established after a four year interval. In California two weak boards were absorbed into the Board of Horticulture, and there may be similar instances in other states. With these few exceptions all boards, bureaus and commissions established by law were there to stay however weak their powers or inadequate their appropriations.

When institutions have won through to survival they also acquire the capacity to counteract human weakness. Nothing can prevail against a long succession of weak, idle, negligent, or corrupt leaders; but rules, precedents, and customary procedure will carry an institution through a slack period. Once efficiency has become the standard it will take time to replace it by a tradition of inefficiency. The reformers of the twentieth century inherited a flow of administrative activity which, with all the limitations and qualifications that can be made, was directed to the betterment of society.

People working in one agency were likely to look with sympathy upon the work being done in others. While ill-defined responsibilities could lead to overlapping spheres and conflict, the interrelationship of the various agencies could readily be grasped. Penal institutions, poorhouses, pauperism, disease, bad sanitation, impure food and water, unhealthy conditions at work, child labor, low wages, irregular employment, lack of legal protection for employees, and inhumane use of economic power were joined together by obvious links. Persons working to ameliorate life in one respect could count on understanding and support from toilers in other fields.

In his epoch-making *Social Control* E. A. Ross analyzed the nature and growth of informed public opinion in a way that has never been bettered. It was not "an amorphous crowd but an organic combination of people." Public opinion had no power in itself; it was powerful because it was created "by knots of influential men, which . . . constitute the nerve center or ganglia of society." As these groups acquired knowledge, commitments, and defined aims they fed ideas into society, and so wrought subtle but profound changes in attitudes and assumptions. The thesis of *Social Control* was that "from the interaction of individuals and generations, there emerge a kind of collective mind, evincing itself in living ideals, conventions, dogmas, institutions, and religious sentiments which are more or less happily adapted to the task of safeguarding the collective welfare from the ravages of egoism."[57] In retrospect great changes in the "collective mind" took place during the century which began about 1870, and it is impossible to deny to the growth of public responsibility in the states an important place in this transformation.

One of the strongest impressions left by much reading of these early reports is of continuity. Much that was written in the 1880s could have been written in 1910, in 1920, or even in modern times. In the earlier years the reports may be voices crying in the wilderness, in the later preaching to legions of the converted; but the inspiration and the assumptions are the same, and these forgotten and unread documents can be read as prophecies of the society to come. The motions are on the agenda. The problems are defined, and modern failure to solve them may perhaps prompt a charitable judgment upon the first generations to face them.

Continuity between past and present is seen most clearly in the reports of the Boards of State Charities and in some reports of the Bureaus of Labor Statistics, as they place poverty, destitution, bad housing, and shocking sanitation on record; language not precisely the same as would be employed today but recognizably belonging to the same species. Dangerous occupations, precautions against fire, contaminated food, impure water, harmful medicines, and offensive trades were discussed much as they are today, save for changes of vocabulary responding to greater knowledge, increased expectations, and the devastating possibilities unleashed by science. Central to the arguments then as now was the rational, responsible, and humane use of power whether in private or in public hands.

James Bryce had the first word in this book and may be allowed the last.

The sight of preventable evil is painful, and is felt as a reproach. He who preaches patience and reliance upon natural progress is thought callous. The sense of sin may, as theologians tell us, be declining; but the dislike of degrading and brutalizing vice is increasing; there is a warmer recognition of the responsibility of each man for his neighbor, and a more earnest zeal in works of moral reform.[58]

---

[57] Edward A. Ross, *Social Control: a survey of the foundation of order* (New York, 1901; repr. Cleveland, Ohio, 1969), 102–3, 293.
[58] *American Commonwealth*, 3rd ed., II, 539.

Written almost a century ago these words identified one of the moving forces which have changed the world and redeemed the less attractive features of modern times. The identification of "preventable evil" led to investigation, recognition of public responsibility in widening fields, demands for government action, and the formation of an ever-growing number of administrative agencies. The movement has been worldwide but patterns have varied from country to country, ranging from complete centralization under authoritarian control to a conglomeration of institutions with separate functions, and loose control by representative governments. The form and structure in each country depend much upon traditional ideas, early experiments, and the character of the first institutions charged with these responsibilities. It is impossible to separate the modern world from its nineteenth-century foundations. The idea and practice of public responsibility took great leaps forward in the years between the Civil War and the end of the century. The agencies of states which took the first steps and to a large extent determined the shape of what would follow are therefore of critical importance in the history of modern America.

APPENDIX 1

State agencies: some representative samples

The following lists of investigative and regulating agencies in operation in 1900 illustrate the range of activities undertaken in various parts of the country. Note the contrast between the two southern states (typical of the section) and those of the north and west.

Massachusetts

Agriculture, Board of	1852
Arbitration, Board of	1886
Charities, State Board of	1865
Civil Service Commission	1834
Corporations, Bureau of	1870
Dairy Burea	1892
Fisheries and Game, Board of	1886
Gas and Electric Lighting, Commission of	1886
Health, State Board of	1865
Highway Commission	1893
Insurance Commission	1856
Railroad Commission	1870
Sewerage, Metropolitan Board of	1890
Statistics of Labor, Bureau of	1869

New York

Agriculture, Dept of	1893
*Arbitration, Board of	1886
Charities, Board of Public	1867
Civil Service Commission	1883
Dairy Commission (transferred to Dept of Agriculture, 1893)	1885
*Factories, Inspector of	1886
Fisheries, Game and Forests Commission	1868
Health, Board of	1880
Planning, Board of	1883
Railroad Commission	1882
*Statistics of Labor, Bureau of	1883

Pennsylvania

Banking, Superintendent of	1892
Charities, Board of	1869
Dental Council	1898
Factories, Inspector of	1890
Health, Board of	1872
†Industrial Statistics, Bureau of	1872
†Mines, Inspector of	1870
Pharmaceutical Examining Board	1887
†Railways, Bureau of	1872

Ohio

Agriculture, Board of	1846
Charities, Board of	1867
Dairy Commission	1886
Factories, Inspector of	1884
Fish and Game Commission	1875
Health, State Board of	1886
Insurance, Superintendent of	1867
Labor Statistics, Bureau of	1877
Mines, Inspector of	1874
Oils, Inspector of	1878
Railroad and Telegraph Commission	1867

* In 1901 Statistics of Labor, Factories Inspectorate, and Arbitration Board were amalgamated to the Department of Labor.

† Amalgamated 1892 into Department of Internal Affairs.

253

Illinois

Agriculture, Dept of	1884
Arbitration, State Board of	1896
Architects, Board of Examiners of	1897
Canal Commission	1872
Charities, State Board of	1870
Coal Mines, Inspector of	1883
Dental Examiners, Board of	1882
Factories and Workshops, Inspector of	1893
Fish Commission	1885
Food Commission	1899
Health and Medical Examiners, Board of	1878
Insurance, Superintendent of	1893
Labor Statistics, Bureau of	1880
Livestock Commission	1886
Pharmacy, Board of	1882
Railroad and Warehouse Commission	1871

Tennessee

Health, Board of	1877
Labor and Mining Statistics, Bureau of	1891
Railroad Commission	1883

Wisconsin

Agriculture, Board of	1897
Charities, State Board of (from 1890, Board of Control)	1871
Dairy and Food Commission	1890
Dental Examiners	1884
Fisheries Commission	1874
Forestry Commission	1867
Free Library Commission	1895
Health, Board of	1876
Immigration, Board of	1867
Insurance Commission	1870
Labor Statistics, Bureau of	1883
Lands, Commissioner of Public	1850
Oil, Inspector of	1881
Pharmacy, Board of	1881
Railroad Commission	1874
Veterinarian, State	1837

Georgia

Agricultural Department	1874
Entomology, Board of (investigation and control of horticultural pests)	1898
Railroad Commission	1871
State Schools Commission	1870

APPENDIX 2

Checklist of reports issued by boards of state charities, boards of public health, bureaus of labor statistics, and railroad commissions, 1865–1900

Variations in the titles of the agencies are not shown. The date given is that of the first report. If two dates are shown it means that the agency lapsed and was revived at the second date. Reports are annual unless a different interval is indicated (Bi. = biennial).

The states are arranged by region.

State	Charities	Health	Labor Statistics	Railroad
New Hampshire	—	1882 (Bi.1896)	1893	1894*
Maine	—	1885	1870	1858*
Vermont	—	1887 (Bi.1898)	—	1856*
Massachusetts	1865	1870	1869	1870
Connecticut	—	1878	1885	1853*
Rhode Island	—	1882	1887	1865*
New York	1867	1880	1883	1855–8; 1883
New Jersey	—	1877	1878	—
Pennsylvania	1869	1872–3: 1885	1873	(Bureau) 1872
Delaware	—	Bi.1879–80	—	—
Maryland	—	Bi.1874–5 (Ann.1898)	1884	—
Virginia	—	1872	1898	1877
West Virginia	—	1885	Bi.1889–90	1867 (irregular)
North Carolina	—	Bi.1877–8	1887	1891
Kentucky	—	1878	—	1880

* The early railroad commissions in New England were not regulatory or advisory but dealt with routine, fiscal, and legal problems.

State	Charities	Health	Labor Statistics	Railroad
Tennessee	—	Quadrennial 1878	1891	1883
Missouri	—	1886	1879	1875
South Carolina	—	1878	—	1878
Georgia	—	1874–5 (ends 1877)	—	1879
Alabama	—	1883	—	Bi.1881
Florida	—	1884	—	1887
Ohio	1867–72; 1876	1886	1873	1867
Indiana	1889	1881	1879	—
Illinois	Bi.1870–1	1878	Bi.1887–8	1871
Michigan	Bi.1871–2	1873	1883	1872
Iowa	—	Bi.1881–2	Bi.1884–5	1878
Wisconsin	1871 (Bi.1888–)	1876 (Bi.1884–5)	Bi.1883–4	1874 (Bi.1884–5)
Minnesota	Bi.1882–4	—	Bi.1887–8	1872 (Bi.1890)
Kansas	—	1885	1885	1883
Nebraska	—	—	Bi.1887–8	1887
Louisiana	—	1855 (Bi.1884–5)	—	1898
Mississippi	—	1877	—	1886
Arkansas	—	1881 (not continued)	—	—
Texas	—	1888 (Health Officer)	—	1891
North Dakota	—	Bi.1890–1	Bi.1889–90	1889
South Dakota	Bi.1890–1	Bi.1889–90	—	1889
Utah	Bi.1896	Bi.1898	Triennial 1893	—
Montana	Bi.1893	—	1879	—
Wyoming	1891	—	—	—
Colorado	Bi.1891–2	—	Bi.1887–8	1885
California	—	Bi.1870–1	Bi.1883–4	1880 (Bi.1893–4)
Oregon	1891–2 only	—	—	1887 (ends 1893)
Washington	—	1890	Bi.1897–8	—
Nevada	—	Bi.1893	—	—

ESSAY ON SOURCES AND
HISTORIOGRAPHY

The major sources for this study are the reports presented annually or biennially to state legislatures by boards, bureaus, and commissions. A complete list will be found in Appendix 2. The primary purpose of these reports was to inform the legislators about the results of investigations, to record actions taken, and to recommend the passage or amendment of laws; but, as explained in the text, many agencies also recognized the value of publicity and tried to ensure that their reports would be widely read. In addition to stimulating local interest most agencies exchanged reports with counterparts in other states and even sought international notice. Many of the copies of reports in the British Library are inscribed with the compliments of the chairman or secretary. Thus the reports were regularly concerned both with detailed points for consideration by the legislatures and also with the need to awaken public interest by the discussion of broad issues. The wider readership gave a special character to the reports, which served both as organs of a local pressure group and as contributions to a national debate. In the nature of things the agencies had to indulge in a good deal of special pleading; it was, after all, in their own interest to insist that their job was worth doing and that more money was required to do it properly, but they were also well aware that their reputations depended upon their being well informed, putting local issues in a wide context, and studying problems rather than playing politics or attacking personalities. These internal pressures made the reports credible and usually trustworthy. There are exceptions, but the overall impression is that of men engaged in praiseworthy attempts to understand social problems in a time of bewildering change. This is not of course to suspend judgment or to demand uncritical acceptance of all that a report says. One must always make allowance for incompetence, idleness, and error, but it is also a reasonable assumption that the agencies were as efficient, conscientious, and accurate as circumstances allowed until proved to be otherwise.

Though the agencies must have accumulated voluminous unpublished records, few seem to have survived. Some minutes, papers, and correspondence may be stacked away in the recesses of archives in several states, but they do not appear in inventories and a search in selected state archives (Massachusetts, Ohio, Wisconsin, Georgia, and Texas) yielded a very meager harvest. For instance the Massachusetts State Archives retain the Minutes of the Board of Health (and of the Board of Health, Lunacy, and Charities during the period of amalgamation), together with the records of some institutions under supervision of the Board of State Charities,

257

but all the records of the Bureau of Labor Statistics seem to have been reduced to a single folder of miscellaneous papers. No records of nineteenth-century state agencies were found in the very well-organized archives of Ohio and Wisconsin. The official papers of the Georgia and Texas Railroad Commissions seem to have disappeared, though in both states the archives contain other material of considerable interest on the history of these commissions. Perhaps this survey of the work of late nineteenth-century agencies will stimulate further search with rewarding results, and if more can be found there will be opportunities for much further research.

The National Archives in Washington yielded varying results. It was not possible to locate records of the first and short-lived National Board of Health. For transportation the papers of congressional committees proved to be disappointing; it seems likely that the miscellaneous petitions and letters contained in these collections were those on which no action was taken. On the other hand the commissioners' letter books and the large collection of general correspondence of the Interstate Commerce Commission are full of information on every aspect of the railroad problem.

Not much use was made of private papers. The Houghton Library at Harvard contains many collections relating to members of the eastern intellectual establishment. The most important are the Godkin papers and the C. E. Norton papers; but they contain no information about state agencies and very little about the problems considered in this book. The same may be said of the David A. Wells papers in the Library of Congress, and the William G. Kelley papers in the Pennsylvania Historical Society (to name only two of the public men who maintained a close interest in economic and social questions). The Massachusetts Historical Society in Boston holds an enormous collection of Adams papers, and for the present work the diary of Charles Francis Adams Jr was of great value. The society also holds a collection of the papers of Mrs C. H. Dall, who was for many years active in charitable work and a long-serving member of the council of the American Social Science Association; but the many letters to her from F. B. Sanborn nearly all deal with routine matters affecting council meetings and contain few personal observations. At the Ohio Historical Society in Columbus the papers of the Reverend A. G. Byers gave important insights into the work of a long-serving secretary of the Board of State Charities. The papers of Roland Brinkerhoff were also useful for charities and legislative activity; the papers of the Reverend Washington Gladden were peripheral for this study, though of prime importance for the "social gospel" movement. The Western Reserve Historical Society at Cleveland holds some items of interest for railroad history in the Warner Bateman and J. H. Devereux collections.

The very large collection of Lester Ward papers at Brown University, Rhode Island, have attracted less attention from historians than they deserve. As explained in the text, Ward displayed little interest in intervention as actually practiced by the states in his day, but his wide-ranging correspondence and meticulous preservation of clippings, reviews, etc. make the collection a splendid source for the development of modern sociology and for intellectual history generally.

The Bentley Library at the University of Michigan has large and important collections for Thomas M. Cooley and Henry Carter Adams, which were particularly useful for the early history of the Interstate Commerce Commission.

Two libraries specializing in medical history – the Rudolph Matas Library in New Orleans and the Henry Dittrick Library in Cleveland – hold much miscellaneous material on public health. The Matas Library has correspondence, scrapbooks, and ephemeral printed matter relating to the Louisiana Board of Public Health.

The Wisconsin Historical Society manuscript collections include the papers of Frank A. Flower, J. H. Osborn, W. C. Hoad, and Cornelius Harper (of great importance for the early years of – respectively – the Bureau of Labor Statistics, the Railroad Commission, the Dairy Commission, and the Board of Public Health). The Bancroft Library, at the University of California at Berkeley, has a diary of William A. Sawyer which throws light on the work of the State Board of Health at the beginning of the twentieth century.

The papers of John H. Reagan are in the Texas State Archives at Austin, while the Archives of the University of Texas have other collections of importance for the history of railroad regulation, notably of papers of J. S. Hogg, A. W. Terrell, and M. M. Crane. The Georgia State Library and Archives at Atlanta has miscellaneous papers and much rare pamphlet material relating to the state railroad commission.

It may be imagined that a principal criticism of general works covering this period is their neglect of the activities surveyed in this book. Sidney Fine has an excellent chapter on the state agencies in his *Laissez Faire and the General Welfare State*. Morton Keller's wide-ranging and perceptive *Affairs of State* notes the torrent of state legislation but does not give detailed consideration to the work of state agencies. The same may be said of John A. Garraty's *New Commonwealth* and of the two lively interpretative surveys by Samuel P. Hays' *Response to Industrialism* and Robert H. Wiebe's *The Search for Order*. Edward C. Kirkland's *Industry Comes of Age* is a very good economic history of a genre that is now unfashionable – being more concerned with what happened than with econometric reconstruction. There is still much to be learned from volumes in the History of American Life series, now in its second half century. Among them Allen Nevins' *The Emergence of Modern America* and Arthur M. Schlesinger's *The Rise of the City* are of major importance for this period. The political history of the period has been illuminated as historians have moved away from the hothouse atmosphere of Washington to ask what inspired the high level of partisanship and participation in the country. Richard Jensen, in *The Winning of the Midwest*, and Paul Kleppner, in *The Third Electoral System*, emphasize ethno-cultural conflicts but do not contribute much to an understanding of the pressure behind state activities. Ballard Campbell's *Representative Democracy* has much of interest to say about the working of the state political system in Illinois, Iowa, and Wisconsin. There is no comparable work for other parts of the country.

On intellectual history Richard Hofstadter's *Social Darwinism* has probably had more influence than its author expected, to the extent that one now finds too ready acceptance of the thesis that Darwin, Spencer, and other versions of evolutionary materialism dominated American thought. Paul Boller Jr's *American Thought in Transition . . . 1865–1900* analyzes some of the varying strands in intellectual history, and Robert Bannister, in *Social Darwinism: Science and Myth in American Social Thought*, assesses Hofstadter's thesis with some modifications. One feels that waiting off-stage there should be a major intellectual history of the period which will put together what men learned in college, what came to them through the pulpit or semi-popular literature, and what through reaction to social change and scientific novelty. What will emerge is likely to demolish the theory that there once existed nineteenth-century "certainties," which went through a crisis in the 1890s and were broken down by critical attack during the progressive years. Meanwhile interesting work has been done on the emergence of professional social science. The pioneer work in this field was *The Origins of American Sociology* by Luther and Jessie Bernard; and interest in this field has quickened since 1975, when Mary Furner published *Advocacy and Objectivity*, based mainly on the records of the American Social Science Association. This was followed in 1977 by Thomas Haskell's *Emergence of Professional Social Science*, which also studied the American Social Science Association but put it in the wider context of a nineteenth-century crisis of authority. The early development of new authority was studied by Sally Kohlstadt in *The Formation of the American Scientific Community . . . 1848–60*.

Legal history of this period has been dominated since the early years of this century by the argument that the judges attempted to read laissez faire into the Constitution, and that, from at least 1890, a conservative trend was manifest in decisions of the Supreme Court. This attitude influences most of the biographical studies in *The Justice of the Supreme Court*, edited by Leon Friedman and Fred Israel. The roots of this criticism of the judges in the Progressive period are readily apparent, and it was reinforced by the Supreme Court's rough handling of early New Deal measures. In Chapter 3 of the present work reasons are advanced for revising these judgments and taking more seriously the arguments advanced by such defenders of the Court as Charles Warren. Some cogent reasons for continuing investigation on these lines were advanced by John Semonche in *Charting the Future: the Supreme Court Responds to a Changing Society*.

There is a growing body of literature on poverty and its associated problems during the nineteenth century, with Robert J. Bremner's notable *From the Depths* opening a new phase in historiography, while Frank Bruno's *Trends in Social Work* examined changing attitudes on the part of those who had to deal with poverty and deprivation. A stimulating recent addition to the literature is Paul Boyer's *Urban Masses and the Moral Order*, though I would question some of his generalizations which derive from his belief that middle-class Americans normally considered poverty a crime. I hope that my own observations on the work of the state boards of charity may prompt a more sympathetic appraisal of the men and women who sought (in both official and voluntary organizations) to improve the condition of the poor and afflicted.

Anyone who studies the development of public health has reason to be grateful to John Duffy for his study of New York and his edition of the unpublished history of medicine in Louisiana originally prepared by Rudolf Matas. But the student will also be surprised to discover how little else has been done in this important field.

More major histories of public health in the states would be most welcome; or, better still, an overall study of nation-wide developments during this formative period would fill an obvious need.

James Leiby's useful study of Carroll D. Wright stressed the importance of a man who never appears in general histories of the period, but there is an enormous amount of material packed away in reports of the bureas of labor statistics which still awaits the attention of historians. The history of factory and mine inspection is a subject that would repay detailed study. The work of Florence Kelley as Chief Factory Inspector in Illinois is familiar but many other individuals deserve attention. K. Austin Kerr's article on the movement for mine safety in *Ohio History* (1979) shows how much can be gathered from the history of one state.

In contrast to health and labor administration the regulation of railroads has attracted intensive study since contemporary writers first addressed themselves to the problem. The various works of Charles Francis Adams Jr set the pattern for intelligent discussion, but unfortunately Adams knew very little about the western commissions, and his patronizing criticism colored subsequent writings. In the past the demand for railroad regulation in the west was associated with the rise of the Grange, a good deal of attention was devoted to the failure of the California commission to satisfy demand for a firm hand with the Southern Pacific, and it was often implied that other commissions traveled the same road in the last decade of the century. Emphasis began to change with Lee Benson's *Merchants, Farmers, and Railroads* in New York, which argued that the major drive for regulation came from merchants and that the principal grievance was not high rates but rates which discriminated either against the port of New York or against smaller towns upstate. Gabriel Kolko's *Railroads and Regulation* was concerned mainly with federal regulation, and, while accepting Benson's argument about the commercial motives for regulation, he also emphasized that railroads sought regulation to serve their interests – and particularly those of the greater companies – by eliminating wasteful competition. This thesis detracted from some of Kolko's detailed research because all the facts had to be made to fit the model. An important contribution to the subject, which has received insufficient attention, was George H. Miller's *Railroads and the Granger Laws*, in which it was demonstrated that these misnamed laws had very little to do with the Grange and that merchants were always more active in the cause than farmers. The western states emerge from his study with a good deal of credit for rational purpose and constitutional argument. Miller also emphasizes that discriminatory rates rather than excessive rates were always the prime objective for regulation. Many years ago Edward C. Kirkland, in *Men, Cities and Transportation*, demonstrated how closely linked were railroad problems with the attempts of cities – or rather of the merchant groups dominating them – to improve their own prosperity and competitive advantages, and his brief biography of Charles Francis Adams Jr leaves little to be said. Modern writers on railroad questions have paid little attention to regulation to improve safety or to place other aspects of railroad operations under the rule of law.

The bibliography which follows lists the documents and books which I have used and found helpful; it does not aim at providing a comprehensive bibliography for the subjects studied. The next step for any reader who wishes to seek further information will be to turn to the admirable *Harvard Guide to American History* for subject bibliographies for books published prior to 1974, and to hope that the Harvard University Press will make the revision of this *Guide* a decennial event. It is also to be hoped that state libraries and state historical societies – which have done such noble work on records to the period of the Civil War – will turn their attention to the mass of unpublished work and minor publications relating to state or local government and society during the late nineteenth century. There is also much material in the publications of local historical societies that deserves systematic classification.

BIBLIOGRAPHY

The names of the publishers are given for works printed since 1920.

A. OFFICIAL PUBLICATIONS

1. United States Government

a. Congressional documents

Senate. Committee on Education and Labor. *Report and Testimony on Labor and Capital*, 1883.

Senate. Select Committee on Interstate Commerce. *Hearings*, 49th Congress, 1st session, 1884.

Senate. Committee on Interstate and Foreign Commerce. *Hearings on the bill to amend Section 5 of the Interstate Commerce Act of 1887 to allow pooling*, 55th Congress, 1st session, 1897.

House of Representatives. Committee on Interstate and Foreign Commerce. *Hearings on a bill to amend the Interstate Commerce Act*, 58th Congress, 3rd session, 1905.

Senate. Committee on National Health and Quarantine, 61st Congress, 2nd session, 1910–11.

The Industrial Commission. *Report and testimony prepared in accordance with the Act of Congress approved June 18, 1898*, 19 vols. Washington D.C., 1900–2.

b. Departmental documents

Commissioner of Labor, Annual Reports, 1885–

Index of all Reports issued by Bureaus of Labor Statistics in the United States prior to March 1, 1902, prepared under the direction of Carroll D. Wright, Washington D.C., 1902; repr. with introduction by Herbert G. Gutman, New York: Johnson, 1970.

Hanger, G. W. W., "Bureaus of Statistics of Labor in the United States," *Bulletin of the Bureau of Labor Statistics*, 54 (1904), 991–1021.

Interstate Commerce Commission, *Annual Reports*, 1888–

2. State publications

For reports issued by the boards of state or public charities, the boards of public

263

health, the bureaus of labor statistics, and the railroad commissions see Appendix 2. This gives the date on which a report was first issued and whether subsequent reports were annual, biennial, or less frequent. The places of publication were in all cases the state capitals.

In addition to reports most agencies issued pamphlets, bulletins, and other minor publications. The boards of public health issued a vast amount of educational literature and instructions for dealing with sanitary questions, epidemics, and impure food or drink. In most instances there are no available checklists. An exception is:

Ainge, Thomas S., *A Quarter Century of Public Health Literature in Michigan: an index of the principal subjects in the Publications of the Michigan State Board of Health*. Lansing, Mich., 1893.

For an index of reports issued by bureaus of Labor statistics see above (1.b).

Two state boards of health published retrospective histories:

The Louisiana State Board of Health, by "the Secretary of 1904." New Orleans, 1904.

Fiftieth Anniversary of the Founding of the State Board of Health of Massachusetts. Boston, Mass., 1919.

3. National Conference proceedings

This is a list of conferences or conventions on charities, health, labor statistics, and railroads. Not all meetings published proceedings, but the majority did so. Most conferences or conventions met annually; the date given is that of the first volume of proceedings.

Conference of Charities and Correction, 1874 (National Conference, 1882).

National Convention of State Labor Statistical Bureaus, 1883. The title varies: National Convention of Chiefs and Commissioners of State Bureaus of Statistics of Labor, 1883; National Convention of State Labor Statistical Bureaus, 1884; National Convention of Officers of Bureaus of Labor Statistics, 1891. In 1892 the word "officers" was changed to "officials," and in 1909 the title became the International Association of the Officials of Bureaus of Labor Statistics.

Conference of State and Provincial Health Authorities, 1887.

National Convention of Railroad Commissioners, 1890.

4. Court records and reports

United States Supreme Court Reports

The Federal Reporter (circuit and district cases).

Each state published its own reports, but the most important cases were also collected in a series of reports. They were:

The American Reports (all states to 1885)

Thereafter the reports were collected by regions:

Northeastern Reporter (Massachusetts, New York, Ohio, Indiana, Illinois)

Northwestern Reporter (Michigan, Iowa, Wisconsin, Nebraska, Minnesota, North Dakota, South Dakota)

Atlantic Reporter (Maine, New Hampshire, Vermont, Rhode Island, Connecticut, New Jersey, Pennsylvania, Maryland, Delaware)
Southeastern Reporter (Virginia, North Carolina, West Virginia, South Carolina, Georgia)
Southern Reporter (Alabama, Florida, Louisiana, Mississippi)
Southwestern Reporter (Arkansas, Kentucky, Tennessee, Missouri, Texas)
Pacific Reporter (California, Colorado, Idaho, Kansas, Montana, Nevada, Oregon, Washington, Wyoming)

B. UNPUBLISHED WORKS

Benedict, Michael Les, "Class Legislation and the Origins of Laissez Faire Constitutionalism." A paper delivered at the Wilson International Center for Scholars, Mar. 25, 1980.
Elliott, Frank Nelson, "The Causes and Growth of Railroad Regulation in Wisconsin." Unpublished Ph.D. dissertation, University of Wisconsin, 1956.
Porter, Gerald M., "A History of State Organization for Public Health Administration in Texas, 1718–1917." Unpublished M.A. dissertation, University of Chicago, 1942. (Typescript in Texas Historical Society, Austin.)
Spackman, Stephen G. F., "National Authority in the United States: a Study of Concepts and Controversy in Congress, 1870–1875." Unpublished Ph.D. dissertation, University of Cambridge, 1970.

C. BOOKS AND ARTICLES

Adams, Charles Francis Jr, *Autobiography*, ed. W. C. Ford. Boston, Mass., 1916.
The Federation of the Railroad System. Boston, Mass., 1880.
Railroad Legislation. Boston, Mass., 1868.
Railroads: their Origins and Problems. Boston, Mass., 1873.
The Regulation of all Railroads through the State-Ownership of one. Boston, Mass., 1873.
Adams, Henry Carter, *The Relation of State to Industrial Action.* Baltimore, Md, 1887; ed. J. Dorfman, New York: Columbia U.P., 1954 (Original edition also repr. New York: A. M. Melley, 1969).
Addams, Jane, *Twenty Years at Hull House.* New York, 1910.
Anderson, M. B., *Out-door Relief.* Albany, NY, 1875. (Additional Report of the New York State Board of Charities.)
Atkinson, Edward, *Inefficiency of Economic Legislation.* Cambridge, Mass., 1871.
Consumption Limited – Production Unlimited, Columbia, S.C., 1889. (Commencement Address, Univ. of S.C.)
The Railroad and the Farmer. New York, 1882.
Banner, Lois, "Religious Benevolence as Social Control," *Journal of American History*, 60 (1973), 23–41.
Bannister, Robert C., *Social Darwinism: Science and Myth in Anglo-American Social Thought.* Philadelphia, Pa: Temple U.P., 1979.
Barnard, James L., *Factory Legislation in Pennsylvania: its History and Administration.* Philadelphia, Pa, 1907.

Barton, William L., "Wisconsin's First Railroad Commission," *Wisconsin Magazine of History*, 45 (1962).

Beckner, Earl R., *A History of Labor Legislation in Illinois*. Chicago, Ill.: Chicago U.P., 1929.

Benson, Lee, *Merchants, Farmers, and Railroads: Railroad Regulation and New York Politics*. Cambridge, Mass.: Harvard U.P., 1955.

Bernard, Luther Lee, and Bernard, Jessie, *Origins of American Sociology: the Social Science Movement in the United States*. New York: Thomas Y. Crowell Co., 1943.

Blair, Thomas H., *Public Hygiene*, 2 vols. Boston, Mass., 1911.

Blumberg, Dorothy Rose, *Florence Kelley: the Making of a Social Pioneer*. New York: A. M. Kelley, 1966.

Boller, Paul F., Jr, *American Thought in Transition: the Impact of Evolutionary Rationalism, 1865–1900*. Chicago: Chicago U.P., 1969.

Bowen, Francis, *An American Political Economy*. New York, 1873.

Boyer, Paul, *Urban Masses and the Moral Order*. Cambridge, Mass.: Harvard U.P., 1978.

Brace, Charles Loring, *Address on Industrial Schools, Delivered to Teachers of the Schools*. New York, 1968.

   Gesta Christi: a History of Humane Progress under Christianity. New York and London, 1882.

   The Life of Charles Loring Brace, Chiefly Told in his Own Letters, edited by his daughter. New York, 1894.

Bremner, Robert H., *From the Depths: the Discovery of Poverty in the United States*. New York: New York U.P., 1954.

   The Public Good: Philanthropy and Welfare in the Civil War Era. New York: Knopf, 1980.

   (ed.), *Children and Youth in America: a Documentary History*, 2 vols. Cambridge, Mass.: Harvard U.P., 1970.

Bruno, Frank J., *Trends in Social Work 1874–1956: a History Based on the Proceedings of the National Conference of Social Work*. New York: Columbia U.P., 1957.

Bryce, James, *The American Commonwealth*, 2 vols. London, 1883 (and several later editions with revisions and additions).

Cahill, Marion C., *Shorter Hours: a Study of the Movement since the Civil War*. New York, 1932; repr. New York: A.M.S., 1970.

Cahn, Frances T., and Valeska, Barry, *Welfare Activities of Federal State, and Local Governments in California, 1850–1934*. Berkeley: California U.P., 1936.

Campbell, Ballard C., *Representative Democracy: Public Policy and Midwestern Legislature in the Late Nineteenth Century*. Cambridge, Mass.: Harvard U.P., 1980.

Chaillé, Stanford E., *State Medicine and State Medical Societies*, Philadelphia, Pa, 1879.

Clark, Frederick C., "State Railroad Commissions," *Publications of the American Economic Association*, VI:6, 1891.

Commons, J. R., *et al.*, *Documentary History of American Industrial Society*, 10 vols. Cleveland, Ohio, 1910–11.

Cooley, Thomas M., *A Treatise on the Constitutional Limitations which Rest upon the Legislative Power of the States of the American Union*, 7th ed. Boston, Mass., 1903.

Cotner, Robert C., *James Stephen Hogg*. Austin: Texas U.P., 1959.

Crane, M. M., "Recollections of the Establishment of the Texas Railroad Commission," *Southwestern Historical Quarterly*, 50 (1947), 478–86.

Croly, Herbert, *The Promise of American Life*. New York, 1909; ed. Arthur M. Schlesinger Jr, Cambridge, Mass.: Harvard U.P., 1965.

Crunden, Robert M., *Ministers of Reform: the Progressives' Achievement in American Civilization, 1889–1920*. New York: Basic Books, 1982.

Daggett, Stuart, *Chapters on the History of the Southern Pacific*. New York: Ronald Press, 1922.

Daland, Robert T., "Enactment of the Potter Law," *Wisconsin Magazine of History*, 33 (1949).

Davenport, F. Garvin, "John Henry Rauch and Public Health in Illinois, 1877–1901," *Journal of the Illinois State Historical Society*, 50 (1957), 277.

Davis, Allen F., *Spearheads for Reform*. New York: O.U.P., 1967.

Dorfman, Joseph, *The Economic Mind in American Civilization*, 5 vols. New York: Viking Press, 1946–59.

Dorn, Jacob H., *Washington Gladden: Prophet of the Social Gospel*. Columbus: Ohio State U.P., 1966.

Duffy, John, *History of Public Health in New York City*, 2 vols. New York: Russell Sage, 1968.

   The Healers: a History of American Medicine. Urbana: Illinois U.P., 1979.

   (ed.), *The Rudolph Matas History of Medicine in Louisiana*, 2 vols. Baton Rouge: Louisiana State U.P., 1959, 1962.

Edwards, Alba M., *The Labor Legislation of Connecticut*. New York: American Economic Association, 1907.

Fairchild, F. R., *The Factory Legislation of the State of New York*. New York: American Economic Association, 1905.

Fairman, Charles, *Mr Justice Miller and the Supreme Court, 1862–1890*. Cambridge, Mass.: Harvard U.P., 1939.

   "The So-Called Granger Cases," *Stamford Law Review*, 5 (1953), 537–679.

Faulkner, Harold U., *Politics, Reform and Expansion 1890–1900*. New York: Harpers; London: Hamish Hamilton, 1959.

Field, Associate Justice Stephen J., *Address at the Centennial Celebration of the Organization of the Federal Judiciary held in the City of New York*. Washington D.C., 1890.

Fine, Sidney, *Laissez faire and the General Welfare State*. Ann Arbor: Michigan U.P., 1956; paperback ed. 1964.

Fiske, John, *Civil Government in the United States*. Cambridge, Mass. and London, 1890.

Foner, Philip S., *History of the Labor Movement in the United States*, vols 1 and 2. New York: International Publishing Co., 1955.

Friedman, Leon, and Israel, Fred (eds), *The Justices of the Supreme Court 1789–1969*, 5 vols. New York: Bowker, 1969.

Furner, Mary O., *Advocacy and Objectivity: a Crisis in the Professionalization of American Social Science, 1865–1905.* Lexington: Kentucky U.P., 1975.

Garraty, John A., *The New Commonwealth, 1877–1890.* New York: Harpers, 1968.

Gettemy, C., *History of the Massachusetts Bureau of Statistics.* Boston, Mass., 1915.

Gillson, Gordon E., *The Louisiana State Board of Health: the Formative Years.* New Orleans: State Board of Health, 1966.

Godkin, E. L., *Problems of Modern Democracy.* Cambridge, Mass.: Belknap Press. 1966.

Griffin, Clifford S., *Their Brothers' Keepers: Moral Stewardship in the United States, 1800–1865.* New Brunswick, N.J.: Rutgers U.P., 1960.

Gurteen, S. Humphreys, *A Handbook of Charity Organizations.* Buffalo, N.Y., 1882.

Hadley, Arthur T., *Undercurrents in American Politics,* New Haven and London, 1915.

Haferbecker, Gordon M., *Wisconsin Labor Laws.* Madison: Wisconsin U.P., 1958.

Hair, William I., *Bourbonism and Agrarian Protest: Louisiana Politics 1877–1900.* Baton Rouge: Louisiana State U.P., 1969.

Harma, Sandra D., "Florence Kelley in Illinois," *Journal of the Illinois State Historical Society,* 74 (1981), 162–78.

Hart, Alfred Bushnell, *Actual Government.* New York and London, 1903.

Haskell, Thomas L., *The Emergence of Professional Social Science: the American Social Science Association and the Nineteenth Century Crisis of Authority.* Urbana: Illinois U.P., 1977.

Hawes, Joseph M., *Children in Urban Society.* New York: O.U.P., 1971.

Hays, Samuel P., *The Response to Industrialism, 1885–1914.* Chicago: Chicago U.P., 1957.

Hoyt, Charles S., "The Causes of Pauperism," New York State Board of Charities, 10th Annual Report (1877), 197ff.

Jackson, Joy J., *New Orleans in the Gilded Age.* Baton Rouge: Louisiana State U.P., 1969.

Jacobs, Clyde E., *Law Writers and the Courts: the Influence of Thomas M. Cooley, Christopher G. Tiedman and John F. Dillon upon American Constitutional Law.* Berkeley: California U.P., 1954.

Jensen, Richard, *The Winning of the Midwest: Social and Political Conflict, 1888–1896.* Chicago: Chicago U.P., 1971.

Jones, Jesse H., "Henry Kemble Oliver," Massachusetts Bureau of Labor Statistics, 17th Annual Report (1886); also repr. as a separate pamphlet, Boston, Mass., 1886.

Jordon, E. O., Whipple, G. C., and Winslow, C. E. A., *A Pioneer of Public Health: William Thompson Sedgwick.* New Haven, Conn.: Yale U.P., 1924.

Keller, Morton G., *Affairs of State.* Cambridge, Mass.: Harvard U.P., 1977.

Kent, James, *Commentaries on American Law,* 12th ed., ed. O. W. Holmes Jr, 4 vols. Boston, Mass., 1873.

Kerr, K. Austin, "The Movement for Coal Mine Safety in Nineteenth Century Ohio," *Ohio History,* 86 (1979), 3–18.

Kirkland, Edward C., *Charles Francis Adams, Jr: the Patrician at Bay*. Cambridge, Mass.: Harvard U.P., 1965.

Men, Cities and Transportation: a Study in New England History, 1820–1900, 2 vols. Cambridge, Mass.: Harvard U.P., 1948.

Industry Comes of Age: Business, Labor and Public Policy 1860–97, The Economic History of the United States, vol. VIII. New York: Holt Rinehart, 1961.

Kleppner, Paul, *The Third Electoral System, 1853–1892: Parties, Votes, and Political Cultures*. Chapel Hill: North Carolina U.P., 1979.

Kohlstadt, Sally Gregory, *The Formation of the American Scientific Community: the American Association for the Advancement of Science, 1848–60*. Urbana: Illinois U.P., 1976.

Kolko, Gabriel, *Railroads and Regulation, 1877–1916*. Princeton, N.J.: Princeton U.P., 1965.

Larrabee, William, *The Railroad Question*, New York, 1893; repr. Freepost, N.Y.: Books for Libraries Press, 1971.

Leiby, James, *Carroll Wright and Labor Reform: the Origins of Labor Statistics*. Cambridge, Mass.: Harvard U.P., 1960.

Charity and Correction in New Jersey: a History of State Welfare Institution. New Brunswick, N.J.: Rutgers U.P., 1967.

A History of Social Welfare and Social Work in the United States. New York: Columbia U.P., 1978.

Letchworth, William P., *Homes of Homeless Children*. n.p., 1903. (Originally published in the 9th Report of the N.Y. State Board of Charities, 1878.)

Lowell, Josephine Shaw, *Public Relief and Private Charity*. New York, 1884.

Lubove, Roy, *The Professional Altruist: the Emergence of Social Work as a Career*. Cambridge, Mass.: Harvard U.P., 1965.

McCurdy, Charles W., "Justice Field and the Jurisprudence of Government – Business Relations: Some Parameters of Laissez-faire Constitutionalism," *Journal of American History*, 6 (1974–5), 970–1005.

McLaughlin, Andrew G., *A Constitutional History of the United States*. New York and London: Appleton-Century, 1935.

McNeill, George E., *The Labor Movement*. Boston, Mass., 1887.

Mann, Arthur, *Yankee Reformers in the Urban Age*. Cambridge, Mass.: Harvard U.P., 1954.

Mennel, Robert M., *Thorns and Thistles: Juvenile Delinquents in the United States*. Hanover, N.H.: New England U.P., 1973.

Meyer, Balthasar H., "Early General Railroad Legislation 1853–1874," *Transactions of the Wisconsin Academy of Science, Arts and Letters*, 12 (1898).

Railway Legislation in the United States (New York, 1903). (An expanded version of his evidence before the Industrial Commission.)

Miller, George H., *Railroads and the Granger Laws*. Madison: Wisconsin U.P., 1971.

Moffett, Samuel, "The Railroad Commission of California. A Study in Irresponsible Government," *Annals of the American Academy of Political and Social Science*, 6 (1895), 469–77.

Mohr, James C. (ed.), *Radical Republicans in the North*. Baltimore, Md: Johns Hopkins U.P., 1975.

Morgan, H. Wayne, *From Hayes to McKinley*. Syracuse, N.Y.: Syracuse U.P., 1969.

(ed.), *The Gilded Age*, 2nd ed. Syracuse, N.Y.: Syracuse U.P., 1970.

Nash, Gerald D., *State Government and Economic Development: Administrative Policies in California, 1849–1933*. Berkeley: California U.P., 1964.

Nevins, Allan, *The Emergence of Modern America*. New York: Macmillan, 1927.

Newcomb, Simon, "The Let Alone Principle," *North American Review*, 226 (1870), 1ff.

Oleson, Alexandra, and Voss, John (eds), *The Organization of Knowledge in Modern America, 1860–90*. Baltimore, Md: Johns Hopkins U.P., 1979.

Patten, Simon N., "The Decay of State and Local Government," *Annals of the American Academy of Political and Social Science*, 1 (1890), 26–42.

Paul, Arnold M., "Legal Progressivism, the Courts, and the Crisis of the 1890s," *Business History Review*, 82 (1959), 497–509.

Pegrum, D. F., *Rate Theories and the California Railroad Commission*, University of California Publications in Economics, 10. Berkeley: California U.P., 1932.

Pelling, Henry, *American Labor*. Chicago, Ill.: Chicago U.P., 1960.

Peterson, Robert L., "Jay Gould and the Railroad Commission of Texas," *Southwestern Historical Quarterly*, 18 (1955), 423.

Pickett, Robert S., *House of Refuge: Origins of Juvenile Reform in New York*. Syracuse, N.Y.: Syracuse U.P., 1969.

Pidgin, Charles F., *History of the Bureau of Labor Statistics in Massachusetts*. Boston, Mass., 1876.

Pivar, David J., *Purity Crusade: Sexual Morality and Social Control*. Westport, Conn.: Greenwood Press, 1973.

Potts, Charles S., *Railroad Transportation in Texas*. Austin, Tex., 1909.

Proctor, Ben H., *Not without Honor: the life of John H. Reagan*. Austin: Texas U.P., 1962.

Prouty, Charles A., "National Regulation of Railways," *Publications of the American Economic Association*, 3rd Series, 4: 1 (1903), 71–83.

Rader, Benjamin G., *The Academic Mind and Reform: the Influence of Richard T. Ely*. Lexington: Kentucky U.P., 1966.

Randall, C. D., "The Michigan System of Child Saving," *American Journal of Sociology*, 1 (1896), 710–24.

Rawlings, Isaac D., *The Rise and Fall of Disease in Illinois*, 2 vols. Springfield, Ill.: Schepps and Barnes, 1927.

Reed, St Clair Griffin, *A History of Texas Railroads*. Houston, Tex.: St Clair Publishing Co., 1941.

Rodgers, Daniel T., *The Work Ethic in Industrial America 1850–1920*. Chicago, Ill.: Chicago U.P., 1974.

Rosenberg, Carroll Smith, *Religion and the Rise of the American City*. Ithaca, N.Y.: Cornell U.P., 1971.

Ross, Edward A., *Social Control: a Survey of the Foundation of Order*. New York, 1901.

Rothman, David J., "Behavior Modification: Total Institutions: an Historical Overview," *Hastings Center Report*, 5 (1975), 17–24.

Scheider, David M., and Deutsch, Albert, *The History of Public Welfare in New York State, 1867–1940*. Chicago, 1941: repr. Montclair, N.J.: Patterson Smith, 1969.

Schlesinger, Arthur M., *The Rise of the City*. New York: Macmillan, 1932.

Semonche, John E., *Charting the Future: the Supreme Court responds to a Changing Society*. Westport, Conn.: Greenwood Press, 1973.

Shaw, Albert, "The American State and the American Man," *The Contemporary Review*, 51 (1887), 695–711.

Sproat, John G., *"The Best Men"; Liberal Reformers in the Gilded Age*. New York: O.U.P., 1968.

Stewart, William R., *The Philanthropic Work of Josephine Shaw Lowell*. New York, 1911.

Tiedeman, Christopher, *The Unwritten Constitution of the United States: a Philosophical inquiry into the Fundamentals of American Constitutional Law*. New York, 1890.

Trattner, Walter I., *Crusade for the Children: a History of the National Child Labor Committee and Child Labor Reform in America*, 2nd ed. New York: Free Press, 1970.

   From Poor Law to Welfare State: a History of Social Welfare in America, 2nd ed. New York: Free Press, 1979.

Troeltsch, Ernst, *The Social Teaching of the Christian Churches*, trans. Olive Wyon, 2 vols. London and New York: Macmillan, 1931.

Unger, Irwin, *The Greenback Era: a Social and Political History of American Finance, 1865–1879*. Princeton, N.J.: Princeton U.P., 1964.

Vogel, Morris J., *The Invention of the Modern Hospital: Boston 1870–1930*. Chicago, Ill.: Chicago U.P., 1980.

Wade, Louise C., *Graham Taylor: Pioneer for Social Justice*. Chicago, Ill.: Chicago U.P., 1964.

Wadlin, Horace., "Carroll D. Wright," Bureau of Statistics, 4th Annual Report. Washington, 1909.

Ward, Lester F., *Dynamic Sociology or Applied Social Science*, 2 vols. New York, 1883; 2nd ed. New York, 1897.

   "False Notions of Government," *Forum*, 3 (1887), 364–72.

   "What Should the Public Schools Teach?", *Forum*.

Ware, Norman J., *The Labor Movement in the United States: a Study in Democracy 1860–1895*. New York: Random House, 1929.

Warner, Amos G., *American Charities: a Study of Philanthropy and Economics*. New York, 1894.

Warren, Charles, *The Supreme Court in United States History*, rev. ed., 2 vols. Boston, Mass.: Little, Brown, & Co., 1935.

   "The Progressivism of the United States Supreme Court," *Columbia Law Review*, 13 (1915), 294–313.

   "A Bulwark to the Police Power – the United States Supreme Court," *ibid.*, 667–95.

Washburn, Benjamin E., *The First Fifty Years of Organized Public Health in North Carolina.* Raleigh, N.C.: Board of Health, 1966.

Watson, Frank D., *The Charity Organization Movement in the United States.* New York: Macmillan, 1922.

Wells, David A., *Recent Economic Change.* New York, 1889.

Whipple, G. C., *State Sanitation,* 3 vols. Cambridge, Mass., 1917.

Whittlesey, Sarah S., *Massachusetts Labor Legislation: a Historical and Critical Study.* [Supplement to the Annals of the American Academy of Political Science]. Philadelphia, Pa, 1901.

Wiebe, Robert H., *The Search for Order, 1877–1920.* New York: Hill and Wang, 1967.

Wilensky, Harold L., and Lebeaux, Charles N., *Industrial Society and Social Welfare.* New York, 1958; New York: Free Press, 1965.

Wilson, R. Jackson, *In Quest of Community: Social Philosophy in the United States, 1860–1920.* New York: O.U.P., 1968.

Wines, Enoch C., *The State of Prisons and of Child Saving Institutions.* New York, 1880; repr. Montclair, N.J.: Patterson Smith, 1968.

Wines, Fred H., *Punishment and Reformation.* New York, 1895.

Woodard, Calvin, "Reality and Social Reform," *Yale Law Journal,* 72, 286–328.

Woodroofe, Kathleen, *From Charity to Social Work in England and the United States.* London: Routledge and Kegan Paul, 1962.

Woods, Eleanor H., *Robert A. Woods: Champion of Democracy.* Boston, Mass., 1929; repr. New York: Arno, 1970.

Workman, J. Brooke, "Governor William Larrabee and Railroad Reform," *Iowa Journal of History,* 57 (1959).

Wrignt, Carroll D., *The Industrial Evolution of the United States.* London, 1896. *Outline of Practical Sociology.* New York, 1899.

"The Value and Influence of Labor Statistics," *Bulletin of the Bureau of Labor,* 54 (1904).

INDEX

The cases cited are not indexed individually. See the entries for "cases (state courts)" and "Supreme Court (United States)."

273